The Symbols and Magick of Tarot

CW00762920

Rev. Paul V. Beyerl

The Symbols and Magick of Tarot

Seeking the Mysteries

First Edition

by

Rev. Paul V. Beyerl

published by The Hermit's Grove

illustrations from the Rider-Waite Tarot Deck®
courtesy of U.S. Games Systems, Inc.

The Symbols and Magick of Tarot

published by:

The Hermit's Grove
P O Box 0691
Kirkland, Washington 98083-0691

Dedicated to the four pillars of medicine:

Dedication to the Joy of Learning
A Knowledge of the Psychology of Astrology
Skill in Herbal Medicine and Alchemy
Commitment to a Virtuous Life

Front cover illustration of The Hermit card
from the Rider-Waite Tarot Deck©
courtesy of U.S. Games Systems, Inc.

Back cover graphic of the author by Donna Lyon Rhose.

Cover illustration may not be reproduced without permission of the artist.

Library of Congress Control Number - 2005922664
ISBN 0-9655687-4-1

First Edition © 2005 by Rev. Paul V. Beyerl

Second Printing 2007 (Thanks to Kady Douglas for additional proofreading!)

This edition published by The Hermit's Grove

An introduction to

The Symbols and Magick of Tarot

What is the Tarot? We see decks of these colorful cards in many places in today's society. They turn up as props in movie and television productions. Their images are sometimes found in the video images created for contemporary music. The Tarot is clearly part of our society yet it is not well understood. There are popular myths and numerous misconceptions. Some believe it can guide your future - yet I've never heard of anyone winning a lottery or an election due to a Tarot reader's advice. There are those who believe the Tarot is clearly the work of the devil - of the Christian's Satan which was, perhaps, part of the symbolism of the card by that name.

Is the Tarot divination? In the sense that the symbols and archetypes allow one's internal divinity to emerge through the cards the answer is 'yes.' Does the Tarot represent 'fortune telling?' There's a vague negative connotation around that phrase. 'Fortune telling' is often used in a demeaning way to diminish the value of the Tarot. Because my own tendency would be to avoid that phrase when thinking of the Tarot, I looked it up in the dictionary at my desk. And so, what is fortune telling? It is using the Tarot in a precognitive manner: to indicate the likelihood of specific events to happen. In that sense the Tarot may well be used for the telling of one's fortune.

The faces of cards have long fascinated me. I grew up playing cards. Card games (canasta, pinochle, cribbage, even poker) were part of my family experience and were warm memories. In college I played many hours of solitaire and even learned to use it as a subtle type of divination. If I won the majority of several hands of solitaire before an event I would anticipate the outcome to be positive. I knew *of* the Tarot for many years, but it was always one of those odd things. I would see a deck now and then but it was far too foreign to me and I gave it little thought. The Tarot was something I would see now and then in a movie, relegated to the realm of 'fortune-telling.' Although I was a water dowser for many years as a youth, that was familiar territory and it took me many years to realize that I had embarked upon a spiritual journey and that the Tarot was one of the many valuable tools which would become part of my life.

Upon learning that I teach the Tarot, people often volunteer comments about their own experiences and feelings regarding the Tarot and I have encountered many misconceptions about the Tarot. There are those who have tried it once and panicked. There are those who purchase a pretty deck but are unable to make it 'work.' What is the Tarot? There are so many answers found in so many books yet each of us must answer that question personally. When I first encountered the Tarot in the mid-1970s my understanding of it was very different than it is today.

My own spiritual journey took a major step in life when, in the early 1970s and without knowing the Tarot, I stepped off the precipice of my secure life and, like the Fool, plunged myself into an abyss. For the first time in my life I was now in unfamiliar territory. As a child I learned to dowse water and as a teen I yearned for knowledge of the occult. I attempted on my own to experience trance-like states and, as the years passed, learned to understand the precognitive nature of my dreams. My path was circuitous, from the parapsychology interests of the 1960s to the influence of the popular stars of my youth who encouraged us to explore Buddhism, to learn how to transcend life's woes. All of this brought me to my teacher, Judy Durum, a lovely and delightful woman living in suburban St. Paul, Minnesota. My first study of the Tarot was from her for, at the time, I was learning all that I could of herbal medicine as well as the human pursuit for spiritual wisdom. There was so much to learn that I felt like a fledgling, not knowing how to spread my wings as I plummeted off the edge. But, as the Major Arcana shows us, we simply take the journey and today, thirty years later at the age of fifty-nine I have, for some years, enjoyed the fruits of The World card.

Back in those student days of mine, I began taking Mrs. Durum's course in the Tarot which would last several months. I was completely green, knowing almost nothing about these cards. It was a good course and I repeated it two additional times until I had thorough notes. Judy's course had a strong Kabbalistic orientation to which I did not relate well. In the subsequent thirty years I have read much material regarding the Kabbalah (by all of its spellings) and I still choose to not integrate it into the Tarot. Although today I have a strong affinity for the basic paradigm of Kabbalah, I find that, for nearly all students and for every client for whom I have interpreted the cards, the Kabbalah only makes the cards less accessible.

Even today I do not feel that relationship indicated by the correspondences of the Major Arcana to the sephiroth and the paths connecting these archetypes of energy. Yet the underlying structure of the Tree of Life does speak to me and I perceive much of the Tarot embodying the central pillar in that tree which represents a conduit of energy moving simultaneously from the pure divine to the manifest mundane in both directions, balanced on either side by the polarities. For me this is a living mystery I see in the Major cards such as the High Priestess, The Hierophant and Justice and also in a different manner in such Minor cards as the Four of Swords or the Ace of Cups.

My professional work and exploration led me also to astrology. I have taught astrology since the late 1970s, even longer than the Tarot. I find that the correspondences between the Major Arcana with astrology work quite well. Both systems are quite comfortable sharing space in my head.

Over the past eleven years I have been patiently working on a series of columns for a monthly journal, *The Hermit's Lantern*, published for our students and the extended family of our readers. Over the previous decades I had created my own text book of notes from which I had been teaching, often adding phrases during one of my twelve-week courses when the students inspired me and I saw a new mystery shown in the basic symbols of the Waite-Smith tarot (known to most as the Rider-Waite).

My goal as a teacher was not dissimilar to that of my work with astrology: to work to make the subject matter far more accessible. No matter how deep into esoteric lore and trivia the occultist wishes to delve, the students and clients whom I meet as a professional are consistent in their desire. What they want is interpretive material which is uncluttered with the intellectual jargon of an adept. They seek information which is directly relevant to their lives and easy to comprehend. Their lives are already more complex than can always be managed, and the reason they seek information from a professional astrologer or through the Tarot is so that answers and understanding may be given to them in depth and in detail but in terminology relevant to their lives and easily understood. It was through experience that I learned to allow the cards to 'speak' to me through the symbols shown on their faces.

My very first deck was the Egyptian Gypsies deck. I knew nothing of the cards but I had seen Tarot decks in the hands of my metaphysical teachers and I felt that my studies would expand to include the Tarot - and they did! I still recall the newsstand on Hennepin Avenue in downtown Minneapolis where I purchased my first deck. They had a small section of occult books and just a few Tarot decks. Back in those 'olden' days such items were not easy to find. In addition to the scarcity of a store which carried such as a Tarot deck there were internal taboos against delving into anything considered connected with the 'occult.'

Why did I choose that deck? I liked its name: *Grand Etteilla: Egyptian Gypsies Tarot*. When I was a child there were gypsies who made the rounds of the local farms each summer. We were, as children, warned to stay out of the way, to avoid being 'stolen.' I knew little of Gypsies other than a few stereotypes. This was, after all, the very early 1950s in rural Wisconsin. I felt some attraction and remember that I was always disappointed. Traveling with Gypsies - an exotic image in my mind - would have included crystal balls, lively music and ... fortune telling!

There was also an attraction to the use of French, a language I had studied in secondary school and in college. It was the language of many of my ancestors. But the deck proved far too cumbersome. The four suits offered no pictures and the images of the Major Arcana were not easy to interpret. My Tarot lay quiet and it was not until I was in my first course which was taught with the Rider-Waite that I began looking for a deck which would be more user-friendly for my own path.

The Waite-Smith (a.k.a the Rider-Waite) Deck

When my teacher taught Tarot she used the Rider-Waite deck. By 1980 I was also now teaching the Tarot and, as a tool for teaching, there seemed no deck appropriate other than that which we then knew as the "Rider-Waite." I have taught my full course in the Tarot many times and each time, as I refer to the Waite-Smith deck my appreciation for it grows.

How did this deck come into being, and why is the Rider-Waite deck known by some as the Waite-Smith deck? An artist known as Pamela Colman Smith painted the images under the direction of A. E. Waite. Rider was the publisher and, in those days, it was a man's world.

Arthur Edward Waite (1857-1942) wrote his first book on the occult, an anthology of works by Eliphas Lévi, at the age of 29. Waite joined the Hermetic Order of the Golden Dawn in 1891, was an exceptional student and attained one of the highest levels of work - but left in two years. The Golden Dawn was, at that time, undergoing considerable internal political struggle and Waite was part of a group which later established a separate Golden Dawn branch although that fared no better and, in 1914, Waite became one of the founders of the Fellowship of the Rose Cross. John Greer, in *The New Encyclopedia of the Occult,* considers Waite's most notable contribution to be the tarot deck. Influenced by a Sola-Busca deck, one which dated to the fifteenth-century, Waite described the images for Smith.

Pamela Colman Smith's life (1878-1951) leads to an unhappy biography. American by birth, she returned to England where she had spent much time when young. An illustrator of books and theatre posters she came to know the Irish poet William Butler Yeats and, through him, became involved in the Golden Dawn.

The combination of Colman's style (she was well-known for her symbolist style) and Waite's extensive knowledge of the magickal and occult aspects which could be integrated into the Tarot led to their collaborated deck which was published by Rider in 1910. This deck changed the Tarot and the majority of decks in print today are based upon that singular deck.

Colman was paid little and her name alone survived with the deck but, until recent years, the deck continued to be known as the 'Rider-Waite.' Today some of us work to give her belated yet much-deserved recognition. Millions of people globally have literally touched the reproductions of her art as they handle the deck which I like to think of as the 'Waite-Smith' deck as a way of acknowledging the artist.

Every time I teach my basic Tarot course and go through each of the seventy eight cards one by one my admiration for this deck grows.

A Brief History of the Tarot

It is fascinating to hear the many theories regarding the origin of the Tarot. One popular belief is that the Tarot originated in Egypt prior to it being conquered by Alexander the Great. I don't recall ever reading a particular dynasty or time frame, only a vague reference to Egypt. Somehow the thought of someone attempting to shuffle seventy eight pieces of papyrus tickles my fancy; but there is no historical evidence for this theory. In the latter part of the 20th century theories about the 'lost city' of Atlantis were very popular and a number of authors maintained that the Tarot came to us from Atlantis. It would seem that those ancient, mythical people were capable of creating waterproof cards!

I have also read that the Tarot came to us directly from European Gypsies but I had the opportunity to meet a woman who was, by birth, a Hungarian Gypsy when I lived and taught in Minneapolis. The woman was not even yet in her teens when smuggled out of Europe to flee to the United States as World War II was erupting in Europe. The Gypsy peoples were being subjected to extermination just as were the Jews and homosexuals. She told me that her aunt gave her a deck of cards - regular playing cards - and told her that she could always support herself by using them.

When I think of using cards for divination I think often of this woman and how accurate she could be using a regular 52 deck of playing cards. There is not a symbol to be found other than the numbers and the four suits! I learned that, despite the Hollywood view, true Gypsies read fortunes with regular playing cards. Although some of them may enjoy the modern Tarot, it did not emerge from their culture. Where did it come from?

The oldest Tarot cards were created for the Visconti family in Milan, Italy. At that time the deck contained only what we now call the Major Arcana. Reproductions of this deck may still be obtained, both new and used. The archetypes for these cards were derived from life. Reflecting the literature of the time as well, we find figures based upon real life, cards which represent allegories and morals and the like. Rosemary Ellen Guiley, in *Harper's Encyclopedia of Mystical & Paranormal Experience* indicates that an even earlier prototype may have been created by the French painter, Jacquemin Gringonneur in 1392 for King Charles VI.

Despite various theories, we cannot do more than guess what the purpose of these early cards served. Whether they were used to discern the patterns of life through divination or whether there was a card game we do not know but at some point these cards were joined by the four suits of a regular playing deck. By the mid-eighteenth century a deck of cards had emerged as the standard for the modern Tarot.

What about those stories of the Tarot coming to us from Egypt? According to Guiley, we may thank Antoine Court de Gebelin. Born in 1725 (he lived to be only 59 years old), he posited the idea that the cards were derived from the *Book of Thoth*, a mythical, mystical book which supposedly contained the greater magickal wisdom of Ancient Egypt. The Egyptian theory was furthered by a popular tarot reader known as Etteilla (a name you will find associated with some decks even today). Etteilla published a deck in 1789, called *The Book of Thoth*. This deck is still published today and is often known as the *Egyptian Gypsies Tarot.* Yes, it is that same deck I stumbled upon when I began my own Tarot studies. We do know that the symbolism of Egypt was very fascinating to the occultists of Europe, although an interest in things Egyptian is found even among the ancient civilizations of Greece and Italy.

The Rosetta Stone was discovered in 1799 and, although it took some time to be deciphered, it contributed to the desire of people to believe that Egypt was a great source of Magick. It had obvious remnants of great magick found in the pyramids but, unlike the great stone henges of more northern climates, ancient Egypt left behind a rich tapestry of symbols and hieroglyphics. What a wealth of occult trivia this was for a species which has such a desire to validate itself through claiming ancient lineage. Businesses boast about their years of service. Magickal orders and religions take comfort and affirm their validity through claims of direct lineage from ancient peoples. The symbols of Egypt were soon connected with the Tarot.

We have the British to thank for a nineteenth century renaissance of interest in things mystical. Not only were scholars studying what they had learned from the Rosetta Stone but other texts were being brought to European consciousness as well. The impact *The Egyptian Book of the Dead* had upon the late 19th century occult renaissance in England cannot be adequately understood. Dr. E. Wallis Budge of the British Museum acquired a magnificent roll of papyrus from an 18th Dynasty tomb near Luxor. It dated to 1500 B.C. and was a copy of what we know as *The Egyptian Book of the Dead.* The Egyptian influence, combined with the human desire to claim that all new occult material and mystical practices are, in fact, offered intact and handed down from the ancients (all of whom were apparently fluent in the contemporary languages such as 20th century English) is more likely the source for this theory.

Throughout the 20th century into the 21st there is still a fascination with things Egyptian. Whether due to the pyramids or the mysteries found within them, Egypt remains a place of interest but it is not, alas, the source of the modern Tarot.

During the nineteenth century (as well as centuries earlier) various symbols and deities were brought into the rituals of the Freemasons and later into the Golden Dawn as well as other magickal movements. The Tarot was a source of fascination to those who studied the symbols and languages of occult disciplines. One whose place in magickal history remains secure is the man known as Eliphas Lévi (which was his magickal name). It is generally believed that he was the first who gave the Tarot the correspondences with the Kabbalah and Hebrew alphabet. And this was the state of the Tarot when A. E. Waite, using the paintings by Pamela Colman Smith, published his book on the Tarot in 1910.

I have not seen any of Pamela Colman Smith's other work. Her illustrations for Waite's designs are, at times brilliant. They capture the perfect balance which exemplifies an artistic skill which does not sacrifice the importance of the symbolic imagery. If she could but appreciate today how many hundreds of thousands of people, if not millions, have been touched by her art.

The Mountains of the Tarot

The very first card of the deck, The Fool, shows an androgynous youth standing on the edge of a precipice, to the alarm of his faithful companion. In the background we see an array of mountain peaks. The Emperor has seen the view from the mountains depicted in the distance behind his throne. A mountain stands between the two figures on The Lovers, indicating ideological differences. The Charioteer is leaving his urban life behind, perhaps heading out to the mountain pass. The Hermit is shown standing on top of a mountain. Mountains are visible in Strength, Death, Temperance, and there is even a small tor upon which the Tower has been built. A mountain sits at the horizon of The Star, between the towers on The Moon. A range of mountains provides the backdrop for Judgement. More than half of the Major Arcana cards have mountains. These are clearly symbols. There are no visible mountains in the High Priestess but I wager that, were the pomegranate curtain drawn back, a mountain peak would be visible. Mountains are equally prevalent in the Minor Arcana.

What does the mountain represent? It is not so different from what it suggests in real life. Is the view to the horizon more clear from the top of the mountain, or from within the safe, nurturing security of the valley? Can you see further from the mountain top or the valley? The mountain represents that place from which one can see the furthest horizon, peering into the future without being distracted by the present. To attain that view means one has taken an arduous journey. Indeed, taking the first steps and leaving behind the safety of one's home, friends or neighborhood brings cautionary words from family and friends, just as the dog nips at The Fool's heels.

Yet, a steady foot and maturing mind will bring the youth eventually to the perspective depicted in The Hermit. The Hermit has reached the top of the mountain. We can see by his posture that it has not been easy achieving that perspective and wisdom. It has taken him many years.

Our culture places the mountain as a sacred symbol in many cultures. It is interesting that the representations of so many peoples and beliefs are so similar. It is common for the tallest mountain to be the most sacred, from Mount Meru in Tibetan Buddhist cosmology to Mount Ararat. The tallest, most beautiful mountain is where one is able to commune with the Divine. In the mythological beliefs of many cultures, it is the tallest mountain where their gods or pantheon of deities reside.

How amazing is the mountain! It towers above life, always present, even when it has gathered clouds about it. Here in the Puget Sound, people measure the quality of weather by their ability to see Mount Rainier, fifty miles away as it towers, sparkling white and glaciated, three miles into the sky. Those in the northern urban area watch Mount Baker, rising only two miles from the land. Mount Rainier is a symbol of life in the Pacific Northwest, photographed and found on countless calendars, postcards and books, used in corporate logos and displayed in many advertisements. All this is done with full knowledge that, at any time, the gods could bring disaster, blowing the top of the mountain off and releasing thunderous tides of ash and gas, destroying vast reaches. That beautiful mountain could kill many thousands of people.

In all religions it is not an easy task to come face to face with the Divine. Most people are unwilling to face the dangers. They prefer security as does the Fool's companion. But those who have seen the view know more about life. It is that wisdom which the mountain represents. The Ace of Swords is held high and there are no trees to clutter the view. The truth brings challenges and the opportunity to attain those heights. The character in the Three of Wands stands upon a hill and gazes at the ships carrying people and goods. But in the distance is a mountain. There is so much more possible!

And what of the hill? Significant rises in the land are similar to mountains, although on a smaller scale. Hills are where ancient peoples built stone temples and where churches are often found today. But the top of such a hill must be readily accessible to the people, including the very old and the very young. The view from the top of the mountain is a solitary venture although, in these days, one can reach that height with the assistance of trained guides and sherpas, each of whom is a Hermit in his own right.

When studying your cards, watch for the presence of mountains. Are they close? Are they distant? The Knight of Cups must cross a body of water (water is a type of abyss) in order to begin the ascent of the visible mountain. The Fool must step over the edge of the precipice and place herself completely in the hands of the Divine, trusting that she will not be maimed in the descent. Even the Nine of Pentacles, standing calmly in her garden in the midst of the harvest, stands before a fine home in the distance but... on the horizon? Mountains. A careful examination of each card in your deck which contains a mountain (or even a significant hill) will unfold for you a completely new level of understanding of the Mysteries held within the Tarot.

Urban Settings In the Tarot

We are all part of a modern, urban lifestyle. It doesn't matter if you live in the mountains of Idaho or along the freeways of Los Angeles, television and modern electronics make even a rural person part of the modern lifestyle. We are all interconnected and, no matter where you live, you can shop by mail and telephone from retailers throughout the land. The internet has brought us a global urban presence. Because of this, it is easy to pay less attention to the urban landscape, an important symbol in the Tarot.

Sometimes it is obvious. Using the Waite-Smith deck for reference, a city of turrets and towers lies behind The Chariot. The Ten of Pentacles depicts the trading center of a city. In other cards the presence of the urban landscape may be highly subtle. The mortar and stone wall behind the youthful figure riding the horse in The Sun indicates the presence of stonemasons and of construction. The androgynous figure rides to be greeted by many people.

The High Priestess sits calmly in a temple obviously one created by master craftsmen. This must be in an urban center, even though she keeps herself removed from the general public. It is the Magician who works his ritual among the trees as a rural solitaire. An urban temple is also present in The Hierophant, an edifice capable of holding large numbers of people. The religious figure must wear his symbols larger than life so all can observe the rites, even from the distant reaches of the structure.

We find church settings and windows in a number of cards ranging from the Four of Swords to the Five of Pentacles. These do not appear to be country chapels. The presence of civilization in the Seven of Swords depicts a festival, including several figures engaged in a conversation. We would expect the Queens and Kings to be shown in a royal building but their thrones are always presented against a backdrop of nature, perhaps representing their sacred marriage to the land.

What does the presence of buildings represent? Buildings are where people live. The urban settings suggest the various lessons and mysteries which teach us about our interactions with others. Urban centers are places with more people. Our errant ways are more visible when others see us, and may bring us before Justice. Our talents are more likely to bring rewards, as we see in The Sun or in the Three of Pentacles. When buildings or other people are present, their relationship to the main character or symbols of the card is a clue to deeper meanings. In the Two of Wands we are offered a view from a crenelated balcony. The decorative banner at the lower left and the height from which the balcony offers its view of the world offer clues regarding the seeker's status in these circumstances. In the Three of Wands we see no city, but we know that the boats in the distance are carrying goods from one market to another. The figure is not presently involved in trade but the card advises that involvement with others toward a common goal will be successful. Matters of business suggest communal or urban settings.

In two cards we see structures which do not so clearly indicate an urban setting. There are twin towers in Death and in the Moon. Neither card shows other buildings. Between the towers is a path leading to the mountain. What do you imagine this portrays? The towers have obviously been built by people (in the plural) and indicate the presence of civilization but where is the village or city? There is another tower, the well known structure found in The Tower card, itself. Despite the absence of other buildings, this is not a tower one is likely to find in the wilderness. We may assume other buildings are present but the seeker, now tumbling from complacency, is too absorbed in her own chaos to take note of her environment.

When you see signs of urban life, look at the relationship between the main figure and the buildings. Pamela Colman Smith's artwork clearly depicts A. E. Waite's symbolic interpretation of the Tarot. She has done this brilliantly. It is generally true that the closer we look, the more we see. And the more we see in each card, the better our interpretations.

The Magickal Tarot

The last third of the 20th century brought us a quiet revolution in how we, as individuals, manage our spirituality and religion. Today there are many books which guide the reader into working a ritual written by the author or in creating a ritual for one's own use.

Ritual is an intentional process through which one creates a space within which one may draw upon symbols and meaningful items in order to empower the images being held with one's mind.

Over the past decades I have encountered magickal correspondences with the Tarot. My professional work, in addition to Tarot, includes botanical medicine and herbal lore as well as the magickal history of gems and minerals. As I encountered occasional correspondences with the Tarot they quickly stimulated my interest. While much of what I found seemed less relevant, often without any historical perspective, the reality of our modern Tarot being so recent leaves us without a long history of correspondences. As an astrologer I feel strongly about the relevance and value of the standard astrological correspondences and as a Wiccan known for my understanding and creation of ritual forms I can only view the Tarot as a wealth of potential.

Drawing upon the magick, or symbolism, of the Tarot in order to promote change in one's life can be as simple as creating a small altar in one's home. Adding a candle (or several candles), one's favorite herbal oils or perfumes or incense, collecting stones, personal jewelry or photos can all add a sense of personal power to this setting.

Magickal information seems generally focused upon the Major Arcana. Why would this be? Perhaps it is the numerical similarity. There are twenty two Major Arcana cards. When teaching I often refer to the Major Arcana as the 'billboards' in life, appearing when the Universe wants to gain our attention to let us know of something more important and significant than our usual lives. There are ten 'planets' (astrologers use that noun incorrectly, including one star - the Sun - and one satellite - the Earth's Moon) and there are twelve signs of the zodiac giving us another collection of twenty two archetypes.

Those who explore a number of fields quickly discover that the esoteric approach to herbal magick, to the gem and mineral lore and other aspects of folk magick have 'correspondences' which is a way of describing some amount of similarity in energy which allows us to draw upon an expanded point of reference.

If, for example, I wish to bring the quality of the Sun Card into my life to strengthen positive aspects of my personality, to remove some of the shadows of insecurity; if I want my life to move in a direction so that my accomplishment would result in the image of the Sun Card, perhaps adding to my working some of the aspects of the Sun (in astrology), herbs associated with the Sun such as bay or a sunflower, and using a peridot or ruby to bring in aspects of gem lore might all further my progress.

Most who work with ritual find that being able to assemble a collection of items centered around a common image is not unlike some of the best play times we had as children. I so enjoyed foraging in the woods behind our farm, bringing home feathers, being fascinated with the trilliums, finding special stones or an abandoned birds' nest. I've never lost this enjoyment of discovering all manner of wonderful things in the world around me.

When I write of the magickal energy of a card I am writing of qualities which we might find were that card to manifest in ritual. The ritual traditions of most cultures embrace the concept of the polarities of female and male as that which leads to creativity, whether an internal union and balance, or one found with another. The magickal energy also describes the underlying personality and vitality of the card. Living in a world which is perceived by our senses (meaning: sensual), one in which creation manifests through sexual action, the Tarot exemplifies for us how we might exist in that reality. As tantra describes the energy (and sexual energy) of one's spiritual self in a physical body, I will often refer to the *sexual* energy of a card as one might work with the creative polarities within the context of ritual.

Should you wish to change the course of your life's events by using ritual to invoke or manifest the Wheel of Fortune, you might wish to use some of the herbs which are suggested in the text for that card. If you wish to increase your

Strength of character, angelica or sunflower might be plants for your gardens, herbs for bathing or even the foundation for an incense. And how might you create ritual? There are many guidelines and there are no rules. There are countless books, some of which I might think of little value but which you might deem exceptional. Your ritual might be as simple and beautiful as a combination of a candle, a few images and time spent in meditation and visualization. On the other hand it could be as complex as ritual theatre complete with ritual script and costume and mask as one enacts a life-changing scenario at a profound level.

To suggest how you might engage in ritual is far too complex for this book. My goal is to help you better understand the Magick of the Waite Smith and of the modern Tarot.

Onward

Reviewing more than a decade of columns has been a wonderful adventure. As the first months of this year slip past I have spent many hours wearing my editor's hat, reviewing eleven years' work as an author on the Tarot and preparing it for this book.

I am offering you nearly thirty years' experience. You may read the book as a whole or you may use it for reference for individual cards. If you still consider yourself a student, I encourage you to obtain a copy of the Waite-Smith deck (the Rider-Waite). If you are an educator, U.S. Games publishes a large format deck in which it is far easier to see the symbols. I can think of no deck better for learning, no matter which deck you might prefer when you shuffle the cards and lay them out.

Allow the Tarot to change your life. It has for so many.

Paul Beyerl
The Hermit's Grove, 2005 ce

Table of Contents

The Major Arcana

I first looked through the Major Arcana back in 1975. The following year I began an intensive study of the Tarot under a wonderful teacher, Judy Durum, in Minneapolis. I love these cards and, when teaching, begin with the Major Arcana. I like to refer to the Major Arcana as the 'billboards' of life. There are twenty two of these cards which begin with The Fool (numbered 0) through The World (number 21).

There are many ways to see how these cards are interconnected with each other. Some view them as telling a story which begins with The Fool, ultimately passing through the journey of life with its lessons and, ultimately, arriving at The World. There are those who recommend the delightful process of creating a story which describes the journey of the Fool as she travels her path, encountering the other individuals and experiences described by the cards of the Major Arcana.

Others see them interconnected with Kaballah's *Tree of Life*, which is a diagram indicating spiritual evolution and the movement between manifest reality and sublime divinity composed of ten points of intersection (sephiroth) which create twelve connecting lines (paths). No one can provide a genuine answer whether it is simply coincidence that there are twenty-two Major Arcana cards and twenty-two sephiroth and paths. The sephiroth are described as 'emanations' or manifestations of energy. At the very top is *Kether*, the crown, corresponded with the planet Uranus but not always with The Fool (that Major Arcana card which is typically corresponded with Uranus). There are various systems which place the twenty-two cards in different places upon the Tree.

A further coincidence is the ability to correspond the cards and connect them with astrology. Twelve signs of the zodiac plus eight planets (not counting Earth) along with the Sun and Moon is another tidy twenty-two!

The Two Pillars

A recurrent theme found among some of the key cards of the Tarot is that of two pillars. We see this in the formal depiction of the actual pillars which can range from a very ornate style to the simplest of architecture. There are also cards in which the pillars are much less obvious, within which the concept of the pillars may be only a symbolic similarity which some of us choose to perceive.

As we enter the Major Arcana, the first card showing these pillars is the High Priestess. In this card the two pillars are presented in a clearly defined manner, with the left pillar shown black, marked 'B' and the right pillar white, marked with a 'J.' The black and white remind us of the two colors in the T'ai

Chi symbol which depict the active Yang force and the receptive Yin force as archetypes of the primary polarities which engender the Universe.

The historical myth in the Old Testament goes that Solomon spent thirteen years building his house and temple. He cast two pillars of bronze. Each pillar was eighteen cubits and topped by a five cubit tall capital. These are big pillars! They are are adorned with wreaths of chain work and rows of pomegranates. They are set at the vestibule, the one to the south called Joachim and the one to the north called Boaz. Reference to these two pillars is found in two sections of the Old Testament. In my *Revised Standard Edition* they are in II Chronicles 3:17 and I Kings 7:21.

According to many sources, the inner circles of Masons set their temples with two columns to represent these pillars. Although there is little factual information about the two pillars, there are various theories about their mystical significance. One perspective is that the pillar Joachim represents the male principle and Boaz the female; and that together they symbolize the divine source of life. Passing through the pillars becomes a sacred and transformational experience.

The pillars are clearly found in two cards. The High Priestess and the Hierophant each sit between two pillars. Those of the High Priestess echo the above history. From an esoteric perspective we may see this symbolism echoed elsewhere. The Lovers stand, each with their own tree. The two trees are obviously different varieties and could well represent polarities, given that the individuals are male and female.

The Chariot has before it two sphinxes, the left black and the right white, clearly reminiscent of the two pillars. The two large wheels of the chariot continue the theme of the division of the polarities. Justice is seated between two plain pillars.

A very subtle possibility is that of The Hanged Man. What supports the tree from which he is suspended? Very likely two trees or two pillars and, as a counterpoint, is the 'middle pillar.' Are The Star card's two columns of water, one pouring into the pool (representing the astral realm of spirit) and the other spilling its contents down upon the manifest earth hinting at the two pillars? And what of the two towers of The Moon?

Those who understand the deeper meanings of this concept of polarities may even find references within the Minor Arcana in more subtle ways.

Here, then, are the Major Arcana, the 'billboards' of life. When Major Arcana cards appear in your layout, the Tarot wants you to know that these issues are important and how you handle them, whether you learn what the Tarot is attempting to teach you, will determine how well your life progresses.

0 - The Fool

Uranus

THE FOOL.

The Fool ranks high among people's favorite cards.

The energy represented by this first of major cards touches people in their need to "lighten up" about life. But there is nothing 'foolish' within the first card of the Major Arcana. This card does not indicate the manifestation of good news, it only heralds the potential of wondrous changes and shows you that the path to success is as far removed from the safe, well-trod paths as possible.

The main character is The Fool and, although frequently referred to as masculine, he represents the process through which one's spirit moves through initiation into rebirth, bringing a new 'spirit' to one's life and coming into a renewed incarnation. Always remind yourself that The Fool can just as easily be a feminine character.

We see The Fool on a journey. She carries all her worldly possessions of importance tied to the end of her staff. Whether she is at the beginning or near the end of her journey is unknown, but we see the magnitude of what lies before her. Standing perilously at the edge of the cliff, we wonder if she will heed her dog's advice and step back, returning to the security of the known path, or if she will take the plunge into the great unknown.

Obviously, this chasm is a most important symbol. There is no easy descent into the gorge. It reminds me of the sensations experienced when standing at the edge of the rim overlooking the vastness of the Grand Canyon. The Fool stands at the very edge of the abyss, a metaphysical concept found in the symbology of numerous cultures. An abyss is, by definition, bottomless, or deeper than one is able to comprehend. You might think of the abyss as the Cauldron of the Universe, filled with pure, raw magick.

The Fool represents the creative originality of youth in balance as a polarity to the untold ages it took Mother Nature to carve the abyss. What we do not see are the visions of The Fool, gazing up into the cosmos or the visions generated by that wisdom evolving throughout countless ages.

3

The Fool is not unaware. He knows that things could be happening, that something is there, waiting to be embraced yet it remains unknown. This card contains essential lessons about learning to trust life and to trust one's self.

When this card appears in a reading, it is the interpreter's role to encourage the seeker to embrace certain qualities, to do one's best to don the ritual robes of The Fool and adopt aspects of that spiritual persona into the seeker's own life. The Fool lives his personality. Because he has such faith in the Universe and in himself, he is able to step off into the abyss, and fall into his new reality in perfect safety. Sometimes I like to tease my students that, upon falling into the abyss, the bandanna tied to the staff can be opened and becomes The Fool's parachute. Being pure of spirit, filled with the radiance of Perfect Trust, The Fool is able to move into the unknown with the protection associated with children. We see this symbolized within the white flower held in The Fool's hand. He has the ability to land on his feet, entering a new vision of reality.

This is a quality similar to that found within children. Indeed, even Christ speaks of this childlike quality as essential for entry into that place of pure spirit Christians call heaven. This is the childlike quality which can make things happen. It is born of innocence (the absence of a negative outlook on life). It contains naivete (the opposite of believing you can always 'know' what will happen). Indeed, cynicism within The Fool's path makes failure a certainty.

Becoming pure of spirit may not always seem easy. From a practical standpoint, this becomes a matter of understanding your motivation in the quest for change. When The Fool appears in a reading, the seeker should be advised to take some time and examine the motivations surrounding this situation. Being pure of heart does not require one to be a saint, merely to be approaching the abyss with an open mind and no ulterior motives.

And how should The Fool approach the abyss? In a similar manner that a child is able to jump off the end of the pier and, through trust, swim for the first time. The Fool knows that she must be willing to let go, to avoid dragging her emotional and physical past with her during this time of magnificent opportunity. Should The Fool try to hang on, she will end up like the character 'Sarge' in the Beetle Bailey cartoon strip, inevitably hanging on to a small branch, ready to fall into the canyon below. The Fool is prepared to let go, prepared to enter a new reality.

"He who hesitates is lost." When The Fool appears in a reading, take advantage of the situation. Put yourself in motion. If you stop to worry about the details, to wonder if you need to return home and repack your bandanna, the opportunity will be lost. You must take initiative to make this card manifest its potential in your life, to make your dreams become reality.

The Fool knows that one can take such a journey only with great freedom, unencumbered by possessions. This card embodies the saying, "you can't take it with you." She has approached the magnitude of change by bringing only the barest of essentials, knowing that excess possessions will only weigh down her spirit. A safe landing requires being light of spirit matched with a freedom from bondage to one's material possessions. This card encourages you to set yourself free and try something new, just for the fun of it. The Fool knows how to try something just for the elation of pure joy.

Pay attention to the dog, attempting to warn the fool. The dog is a symbol of those who mean well and who sincerely hold care and affection for The Fool. Yet they do not share the vision and can only express distrust. We are familiar with the type of questions The Fool will hear. "Do you have enough money?" "Are you sure you'll be able to reach the other side?" When The Fool appears in a reading it indicates that the seeker needs to listen politely but to be wary of these negative images. They could be planted in The Fool's psyche and lead to an erosion of the Perfect Trust so essential in this situation. People love to give cautionary advice but this card advises you to set aside worry and move forward into the unknown. If you stop to worry, you'll topple off the edge and do serious damage to your future.

This card teaches many principles regarding initiation. Initiation is a rite of passage in many religions and cultures which takes the novice through death and rebirth. When The Fool lands, one will be 'reborn' into a new level of existence. This card indicates that there is a great potential for change, but change may only be found by letting go. For those seekers who walk paths of spiritual development, this card foretells great expectations. The pure spirit within The Fool is the seed which will bloom into wondrous manifestation if the journey is taken.

Will the journey be easy? Nothing is easy if we seek profound, spiritual growth. Transformation does not come easy. Look carefully at the card. Simplicity is respected as a virtue. There are no signs of urbanization in the images on this card, no structures, no social trappings. The Fool is drawing upon the natural forces, filling herself with strength and natural magick. And, breathing deeply, her dreams are made vibrant and she keeps her enthusiasm bright and shiny.

Historically, The Fool is reminiscent of the court jester, whose role it is to bring levity to an otherwise serious situation. Spontaneity will help you break free of the mold. There is no safe stairway descending into the gorge. This card asks you to create a sense of fun and of adventure. It is time to leave behind the familiar, beaten path.

The Universe, with Her awesome sense of humour is tempting you to find delight while transforming yourself into a new, improved spiritual being. She wishes to divert you from your well-trod path which is leading to boredom, and She is not tempting you with anything negative nor dangerous. While you may be called a 'fool' by those who will warn you against taking this adventure, you will be 'foolish' if you do not accept this offer from the Universe.

The Reversed Fool

But if this card appears reversed in a reading, you may well be following a 'foolish' course of action. It may be true that, 'on a clear day you can see forever,' but the reversed Fool cannot see across the chasm. You may think you can, but the vision is clouded. When this card appears reversed, it is warning you that you do not have foresight. It is time to stop and take a solid, pragmatic examination of the earth beneath your feet.

Plunging forward if The Fool is reversed is, indeed, perilous. Your naivety is about to get you in trouble. What you perceive as youthful freedom is immaturity and there is a need, now, for a mature view of reality. The polarities of your natural energy are not functioning in harmony and this lack of balance may cause you to topple right off the precipice. The reversed Fool is warning you that you are foolish, that what you are doing needs a careful and honest self-examination.

The Magickal Fool

In looking at this card, we see The Fool as the connection between the Divine Father, symbolized by the Sun, and the Earth Mother, upon which The Fool is standing. The staff, a symbol of magick which indicates that this path being taken is one upon which others will subsequently follow, is found as a ritual tool in many religions. It is similar to, but not quite the same as, a wand. The Fool is absorbing the energy of the Sun and will carry it within as she embraces the Mother after stepping off into the abyss. This union of polarities will lead to The Fool's death, rebirth and represents a form of initiation.

It is not necessary, for the magickal person, to wait for this card to appear in a reading. It is possible to invoke the Fool Card. You must believe that you have what it takes, that you truly can manifest your dream and that you have the ability to cross the abyss.

The natural energy described within The Fool is somewhat androgynous. This is the magick of sexual energy which is not yet fully developed. It could also represent one's 'leap' into sexuality but without preconceptions which would weigh it down.

Achieving the poise between the masculine and feminine within will set free the sparks of delight emanating from the Universe. When The Fool is used as a role model for exploring sexual magick, there should be no guilt. Innocence and wonder are called for.

Herbes which could be used are aspen, elecampagne, mandrake, peppermint and star anise. Stones include the adamant, opal or the topaz. The planet Uranus provides access to the unexpected, to deviation from the path to boredom which provides The Fool with inspiration.

For ritual work, The Fool approaches the Circle with only the minimum of magickal possessions. The Circle can be worked as a metaphor for the abyss or one could even set up one's temple to represent this divine chasm. Ritual should be manifested with simplicity, with the recreation of innocence. The Fool is your opportunity to enter the realm of the pure, the sacred. Structured magick is inappropriate; spontaneity is the ideal. One might, as but one example, take a complete ritual bath, cleansing as much of the past (and even the present) and stripping away preconceived ideas as possible, then enter the Circle and draw upon the youthful purity of divine inspiration.

The magick available to you is drawn from trusting the unknown, from leaving behind the familiar. And yet, it should be noted that The Fool wears a robe embroidered with magickal designs, with symbols of the cosmology. He is not one who has had no training. This is it. This is the moment to seize, to set aside the known and move with joy into the Cauldron of Rebirth.

I - The Magician

Mercury

THE MAGICIAN.

The Magician is a striking figure, holding a memorable pose with one hand reaching with his wand toward the Universe and the other hand pointing toward the Earth.

He represents "The Hermetic Principle," named for Hermes, who is able to move into either realm: that of manifest or physical reality, and that of the underworld, or of inner-spiritual being. The Magician is equally comfortable in either realm of energy. The Hermetic Principle is commonly reduced to the simple phrase "as above, so below" but should also be thought of as "as within, so without."

This card of the Major Arcana contains lessons teaching us about the manifestation of ideas. If you wish to make an idea manifest 'out there' within the 'real world,' you must be adept as seeing that image as a reality 'within here' cherished by your imagination and by your soul.

The Magician stands before you capable and disciplined, able to exemplify an adept. Representing mastery, The Magician embodies intelligence which is filled with the energy of divinity and is always in control. He knows that the most appropriate method of bringing an idea into manifestation is without wasting any energy, whether mental or emotional, that of time or labour. Despite the span of his arms, he holds a most peaceful posture and wastes no gesture. Trust me, The Magician is as calm internally as he appears to be externally.

I find a humourous dichotomy between The Magician and The High Priestess. For some reason, a great number of the Wiccans I know claim The High Priestess as one of their own. Yet, while she sits in the midst of a highly ceremonial temple, it is The Magician who works at an altar in the midst of nature. There are no sources of energy present other than what are found within and those which arise out of Mother Nature, Herself.

We see a table standing before The Magician which is, actually, an altar. Upon it sit four tools which represent the four suits of the Tarot. These tools indicate both the level of mastery and also our lessons regarding the path toward being adept at bringing ideas into manifestation. These four tools are resting upon the altar to exemplify The Magician's balance within himself and his ability to move through life without losing this balance and his control over himself. These four tools are symbols. Whether The Magician chooses to have them embodied as an actual sword, wand, chalice or pentacle, this character represents a person who has the skills these four represent within himself at all times. At any point in time should an idea emerge - whether an artistic vision or a scientific breakthrough - The Magician has these four tools readily at hand.

The sword is a tool associated with communication. We see that The Magician thinks things through carefully. He values his ability to be truthful and honest with himself even should it be painful. He also values integrity when dealing with others, living as a man honest of word and of deed and expecting the same of others when he chooses to set aside his solitary work. He never speaks loosely nor moves into action without first thinking things through and weighing the consequences. It takes physical strength to wield a sword but it takes strength of character to confront honesty at all times with nothing held back. The Magician is skilled at both and is mentally focused upon his goal at all times during his work.

On the near side of the table we see the staff. This tool symbolizes will and one's ability to continue moving forward. Whereas the sword represents self-discipline of thought and speech, the staff represents self-discipline applied to action. This is the key which keeps him motivated until his goal is achieved. The staff provides The Magician with strength of character and enables him to move through life in control of his own actions rather than being bounced about by reactionary behavior in response to others. The Magician is, as a result, able to maintain his focus and uses his self-control and will to avoid distractions which would make it impossible to achieve his goals. The staff provides The Magician with a focus for his will.

In the Tarot, a chalice (or the suit of cups) represents the emotional issues in one's life. With this tall, golden chalice sitting firmly upon the altar, we know that The Magician has control over his emotions. In his wisdom, The Magician understands the connection between his emotions and his imagination. When his imagination begins to play with reality, it can quickly affect his emotions. He has learned to trust his imagination and use it as a positive force in his life, working for him rather than against him. The Magician is not someone who will waste energy through inappropriate emotions nor through allowing his imagination to create illusions destructive to his goals. His chalice sits steadily upon the altar so as not to waste emotional energy. It is a tool for emotional focus.

The fourth tool, the pentacle (sometimes called a 'coin' by authors) represents The Magician's knowledge in handling resources. He knows that one must have the resources it takes in order to bring ideas into manifestation. The pentacle is, in one sense, The Magician's work ethic. He knows that he must have the necessary resources at hand or that he must work to acquire them. The pentacle brings The Magician a practical outlook on life. He must keep his feet on the ground at all times. This tool represents careful planning so that he will have the means necessary to achieve his goal and the ability to remain grounded and conservation minded until he has achieved success. The pentacle represents his focus upon the end result. Within the pentacle (the five-pointed star shows that all five elements are kept in balance) does The Magician keep focused the image of success.

What is the fifth element? This is 'spirit,' whether tapping into the Divine Spirit of the Universe or keeping his 'spirit' alive and vital, and The Magician is truly wise, knowing that this element is as essential as the four elements more commonly recognized. We see the presence of spirit represented by the symbol of infinity which is elevated above his head. This element shows us that The Magician has the ability to transcend the human condition. We find another aspect of the fifth element depicted by the cord worn about The Magician's waist. Often referred to by authors as the Ouroboros, the serpent of wisdom which holds its tail in its mouth, the Ouroboros is another symbol of infinity in which the end is also the beginning. Having his tools always ready at a moment's notice allows The Magician to draw upon the fifth element and, when the spirit moves him, to utilize one of his lessons: just do it. Don't worry about it, just do it.

There is one additional tool which is significant in this picture. In his hand, held high, The Magician is holding a small wand. Reaching toward the heavens, this wand represents The Magician's ability to attract, channel and harness the spiritual forces of nature and of the Universe. Each end of this wand has a small, shaped knob.

The two ends of The Magician's wand represent his ability to maintain a balance of polarities within himself. He holds it high, almost as one might set a lightning rod up toward the sky, ready for the spark of inspiration. When The Magician is struck by an idea worth bringing into manifestation, he channels this Divine energy down, filling himself with it. One end of the wand represents his ability to be receptive to the Universe, a vessel waiting for the energy to strike. The other end is pointed at the Earth, just like The Magician's finger. He is ready to channel this energy and use it to manifest the images within his mind. His tools are at hand, ready for the ritual form he will embody as he achieves his goal. The Magician represents the Divine spirit brought down into human manifestation, a goal which can be attained by any one of us through self control and discipline.

If this character seems unattainable, know that The Magician will not appear in your reading unless the Universe believes that the seeker assuredly has these abilities - whether you recognize them or not. It is important to trust this card when it appears. Remind the seeker (or yourself) that The Magician is filled with self-confidence. This major card is telling you that you have what it takes, that it is time to initiate action following the lessons within this card and the role model of The Magician.

The Reversed Magician

If The Magician appears in a reading reversed, you can be assured that his head has been turned in the wrong direction. All of the 'tools' are still present, but either your motivation or your reasons are misdirected. It is possible that your source for energy in these circumstances is not based upon honesty with yourself. The reversed Magician may well indicate someone who has all the power of The Magician but who is misusing this power, whose ego and desire to avoid self-honesty and discipline have gotten in the way. There are times the Tarot will use the reversed Magician to alert the seeker to dishonest practices which need immediate attention.

Counsel the seeker not to waste time. A careful and honest self evaluation must take place. Avoiding the sometimes painful process of facing the music will definitely lead to life taking a definite turn for the worse. Already it is likely that things are not going smoothly, but the reversal of The Magician usually indicates that the seeker has not yet been ready to admit his own complicity in these negative events. Things are very much out of balance. It is time for the seeker to take all four elements in hand and make immediate changes. Without these changes, the seeker may face a continued downturn that could have serious ramifications with significant damage to his life or to his health.

The Magickal Magician

Standing there, before his altar, it is apparent that The Magician is prepared for a ritual working. He is calm, embodying a masculinity which is gentle without any sacrifice of strength. Depicted as a man, The Magician can easily represent maturity of the inner self within a person of either gender. As a solitary worker, he is able to work the Great Rite (the ritual merging of the Divine Feminine with the Divine Masculine) even though no other person is present.

The Magician is someone who is trained in sexual magick, who understands and has studied the spiritual aspects of sexual energy and is able to work with it, keeping his ego and the base desires of his flesh under control at all times. The Magician is able to invoke the Yang energy of the Divine Masculine through the wand, only because he is able to open the Yin receptive processes within himself.

Herbes which might be selected to enhance the practitioner's desire to invoke the positive qualities of this card include cedar, elfwort (elecampagne), honeysuckle, horehound or vervain. Excellent stones are chalcedony or opal and metals include either gold or quicksilver. Astrologically, one would work with the pure, magickal intelligence of the mercurial personality.

The symbols engraved in the edges of the altar are not easily discerned, but they indicate that The Magician has knowledge of traditional symbols, that he is connected to a tradition of training and initiation. He draws upon an established cosmology as a means of yoking himself to the Universe. His cincture can easily be thought of as a ritual item connected with one who has been initiated into a Priesthood and has access to a wealth of knowledge. Yet, despite what would have likely been a formal system of training, he chooses to work beneath the flowered trees, working with the most natural of forces.

The Magician has chosen his ritual tools carefully. It is significant that he works with the sword and staff rather than the more personal forms, the athame and the wand. These show that he is a trained teacher, a role model for those who seek to follow his path. The Magician has not only been initiated, but he has the ability to initiate those among his followers who learn to exemplify the lessons of this card. One of those lessons which would open to the seeker great Mysteries is that of using one's corporeal being to create a tabernacle. In order to fill himself with spirit, he must set aside masculine ego and allow himself to receive magick from the Universe. Whether this process is achieved prior to the first movement of his ritual or whether The Magician works his ritual to achieve this process depends upon his particular path: neither is better.

The Magician will be drawing upon natural energies. He works with the forces of nature and is not so arrogant as to see himself as the source of magick.

Thus does he use his resources wisely and replenish them as he moves forward. His rituals would be carefully thought out, choreographed and structured, moving logically from beginning to conclusion. All his ritual tools have been carefully cleaned and polished and he sees himself as one who walks many paths and pursues many studies. The deeper, more spiritual levels of alchemy are the type of interest which stimulate The Magician's mind, for they show him how to take the idea from within and give it life and manifestation.

II - The High Priestess

The Moon

THE HIGH PRIESTESS

Seated upon her throne as the image of the quintessential cool, calm and collected adept, **The High Priestess** is a card people tend to like immensely, responding with an emotional feeling which arises out of the seeker's very soul.

The High Priestess may be the most wise of all feminine characters in the entire Tarot, representing perfection of the Divine Feminine as it exists within incarnate human form. This card is laden with subtle symbolism and deserves careful attention.

We see The High Priestess seated between the two pillars; the white pillar is Joachim and the black is Boaz, representing the necessity of balance between the polarities of mercy and severity in her judgements and counsel. She knows that she must be both gentle and strong beyond the normal human capacity. These pillars are drawn from the Kaballah, both in knowledge of the Tree of Life and in Kaballistic magick. Seated between these pillars, she opens herself to the Universe, and creates a flow of energy from her feet upon the earth to the Universe overhead, moving simultaneously in both directions.

She is wearing the headdress of a Priestess, the equal-armed cross of a religious figure. This pendant represents her ability to keep all four elements in perfect balance. The center of the cross is directly over the heart chakra, indicating her ability to manifest Divine love directly into the world. She is in complete control of her life.

Cradled in her arm is a sacred scroll, often depicted as a torah. The torah, more than a Hebrew symbol, represents a Book of Knowledge, providing her with access to all the wisdom of the Universe. It represents the rich heritage of all sacred and oral traditions and has been passed down through the ages, even as The High Priestess will continue the custom.

At her feet we see the crescent Moon which has been loved by the peoples of many cultures as a symbol of the maiden aspect of the Divine Goddess. She sits before a screen or curtain upon which we see what are often described as pomegranates, representing her access to the Mysteries. It is significant that there are seven pomegranates positioned about her - this is a number associated with the Divine Goddess.

The High Priestess' position in the world of the Major Arcana is that of an adept. She embodies a type of majesty: her power is obvious. She is able to bring people into the Mysteries through initiation; she has the skills necessary to serve her people as an oracle, providing advice and intuition; she offers counsel within a secluded, sacred space. When this card appears in a reading, the seeker is being shown that she does have the skills to emulate The High Priestess and needs to accept the mantel of this role. While this rarely encompasses initiation as an actual rite, it may well indicate initiation in some symbolic sense or as a metaphor. Usually it will refer to the qualities of The High Priestess which function when providing a sacred space within which she is able to offer her wisdom. It is not uncommon for this card to appear in a reading to alert the seeker of the need to seek out The High Priestess. It is your role as interpreter of the Tarot to draw upon the meaning of cards adjacent The High Priestess to determine whether she represents the seeker or a person the seeker needs to consult.

The High Priestess represents the manifestation of spiritual love. Many see her as a symbol of the Maiden aspect of the Goddess, but she is that aspect of the Maiden who has full awareness of her path. Her future is that of becoming the Divine Mother. She represents a path to perfection, holding superb control over manifest reality and also over the spiritual world. This balance enables her to be aware of both worlds at all times.

The High Priestess is frequently described as virginal. There is a coolness about her, just as the Moon itself is beyond our reach. Her control is maintained through detachment. With the numbers of people who depend upon her, she must be conservative with her energy. She is involved in both worlds but is not emotionally attached. This is the primary quality which is perceived as 'virginal' but I do not believe it likely she would have reached that level of wisdom without having thorough experience in both worlds.

When this card appears, it is important that the work be done internally rather than externally. She is able to draw upon her wisdom by remaining physically calm. Her very posture represents stillness and serenity. In some ways she might be considered a counterpart to The Magician. While his is the active role, she is able to work with manifestation through the passive role, in which activity is internal and imperceptible to the world around her. This card is speaking of the need to calm the self and to begin manifesting one's Highest Ideals and deepest desires. It alerts the seeker to the presence of pure creativity.

The Reversed High Priestess

When The High Priestess appears reversed in a reading, the seeker is strongly cautioned by the Tarot to pay heed. The reversed High Priestess indicates that the seeker is removed from the good qualities of this card. It is essential that one undertake some major internal changes to embrace the ethics of The High Priestess. Depending upon the other cards of the reading and of the situation, the reversed High Priestess may be indicating negative attitudes brought about by having set aside one's spiritual ideals.

Sometimes the reversed High Priestess attempts to tell a seeker that one is portraying the self in this role when it is inappropriate. This leads to one's ego projecting illusion and setting one's self up as being better than others. One's access to intuitive wisdom has been skewed to suit an internal agenda which is unfair to others.

The serenity which The High Priestess cherishes is, when reversed, turning to inner turmoil. The wisdom which we associate with this card is not present, lost either through ignorance or through perverting her talents toward selfish aims.

It is also possible for this card to reverse itself in a reading to alert the seeker to a need to attain to the High Priestess's separation from sexual activity in order to restore the seeker's spiritual values. The reversed High Priestess can be restored through careful, diligent work. Without restoration of the positive values, the situation will sink the seeker deeper into a negative quagmire, one which is caused by the seeker's own attitudes. Indeed, the interpreter must counsel the client to work careful to remedy both self and situation.

The Magickal High Priestess

For the duration of the situation covered by this card, energy which might otherwise be expended sexually should be directed toward opening one's inner self as a lotus. Physical activity is stilled in counterpoint to the opening of one's spiritual insight. Although The High Priestess need not be considered a virgin by lifestyle, her approach to sexual activity removes her from the mundane world. Her options include chastity or sexual abstinence in order to direct her primal energies toward her Highest Ideals. She is skilled in invoking the Divine Feminine as the maiden or virginal aspect of the Goddess. The High Priestess represents one who would also be skilled in working with sexual energy, but not in a manner directed toward orgasm nor procreation. She would obviously have knowledge of the Great Rite but uses that knowledge to move the magick through her being in solitary fashion.

The High Priestess might make use of a number of herbes: almond, camphor, ginger, jasmine, juniper, orris root, pennyroyal, peony, pomegranate or poppy are her favourites. Astrologically, she corresponds with the power of the Moon, ever-present in our lives yet removed and coolly distant. She works magickally with a number of gemstones, including the amethyst, aventurine, emerald, ivory, moonstone and the pearl.

The scrolls upon her lap represent her ability to tap into unlimited information and wisdom and contain everything you would ever want to know about magick. She represents a tradition which is passed down from generation to generation. Thus did she receive her knowledge and thus will she pass it on in the appropriate time and method: she is skilled at conducting a formal initiation.

Seated between the two pillars, she works with the 'middle pillar' merging the energy of the polarities within herself and using it to create a force field from the earth beneath her feet to the Universe above. In this manner is she open as a receptacle to the wisdom of the ancients and knowledge of the future.

Years of disciplined training have given her access to the innermost temples. She works with ritual forms more akin to those of the ceremonial practitioner: she is wearing a formal headdress and seated upon a throne within a formal temple. She understands the role of hierarchy within an initiatory system and accepts the throne upon which she is seated. A throne, symbol of royalty or of religious hierarchy, shows that she has accepted her role among people as one who holds serious responsibility. The primary ritual symbols depicted in this card are her headdress and the two pillars. Her ritual work is done prior to her taking this position upon the 'throne' and opening herself to Divine wisdom.

The High Priestess has created her Circle, established the entire temple, and then placed herself at the center. It is from the Circle's centre that she works, allowing the elemental and spiritual energies to move through her before she speaks her first word. Although she holds the keys to her written tradition, she is not reading from the book. It is her foundation but in her role as an oracle, she speaks from her soul.

If one seeks to emulate The High Priestess, it is important to recognize the need and importance of experience, of having been trained by skilled teachers and of the commitment to an initiatory path. It is through this path that she has attained her throne and it is for this reason that people will seek her out at those times they need the voice of an oracle.

III - The Empress

THE EMPRESS.

Venus

How beautiful is **The Empress** sitting upon her throne. I am particularly fond of the decks which show her visibly pregnant, for The Empress is fertility incarnate. She is the womb of birth and rebirth. When this card appears, the seeker knows that things have been done right and now one must prepare for an expected harvest.

The Empress is the full, conceptive aspect of the Mother Goddess. Hers is the Mystery which knows how to manifest creativity. The power of her staff represents her power within the temporal world and her throne an indication that she is a role model for many.

Resting against her throne is a heart-shaped shield upon which we see engraved the symbol of the planet Venus, indicating that The Empress knows the wisdom of the paths of love. Sexuality is, for The Empress, a spiritual discipline and an act of joy. She has knowledge of the Mysteries and knows that a woman's womb is as sacred as the Cauldron of Cerridwen, the womb of the Divine Universe. The shield is her protection and her defense. It shows us that the manifestation of pure love is strong and keeps all which is destructive and impure far removed from her domain.

The Empress wishes to teach us that the harvest is a gift to those who have been generous. Her own harvest, the life within her womb, is a gift unto her realm. The child represents far more than carrying on the family name. The new life is of royalty and is a 'gift' to her people. The fruit of her womb will be human, will be of royalty, and will also be divine. This is truly an act of love and she knows that accepting her role as a leader of her people has also been a path of initiation. She is a symbol of creativity within the manifest world. The Empress shows us that we must learn to take pleasure in worldly things so long as we balance these pleasures with spiritual wisdom.

Upon her head is a crown of twelve stars, frequently interpreted as the twelve constellations which create a necklace of magick, the zodiac which continually circles our beloved Earth. She knows well these twelve aspects of human personality but also knows how they are always part of the Divine. The stream which emerges out of the woodland spills into the pool of her dreams. She knows the wisdom of the High Priestess but her path is more social. The Empress lives within the mundane world yet is never unaware of her spiritual training.

Her head in the stars, her feet upon the ground, she encourages us to take time to stop and smell the roses. Her crown may also be seen as a symbol of the successful achievement of her goals. The appearance of The Empress card in a reading indicates that the seeker has the ability to have her life's desires brought into fruition and that she will be deeply moved by this process. The manifestation of this success will be life changing and will bring into creation that which will be a 'child,' present in the seeker's life to be nurtured into maturity for many years to come.

The Empress is wife and companion to The Emperor and will soon share with him the Mysteries of parenthood. This card represents a role in which one will work in harmony with another, usually represented by her consort, The Emperor. Together they bring forth life. The Emperor sows the seed and she brings it into birth. If The Empress is the Divine Mother, then The Emperor plays the King Stag when their union brings blessings and fertility to their peoples. With her partner she extends warmth and devotion and brings him happiness. She is the ideal feminine partner, able to bring pleasure and comfort to others.

Despite her maternal nature, do not underestimate her power. Should the Emperor be off defending their realm, she is more than capable of running the empire without him. The people of her land are devoted to her for she emulates charity and gives freely and willingly to those who live within her realm. She is never removed from her people, but lives an active and creative life. When this card appears in a reading, prepare yourself. Know that the seeker has done well, but also know this card speaks of that fruitfulness which is borne of giving in love to others, of setting aside all selfish motive and of working to manifest one's Highest Ideals.

The Reversed Empress

Should The Empress appear reversed in a reading, note that her head is turned away from the heavens. Rather than reaching to the Divine, the seeker is caught in the mundane. Energy which might be directed to success both spiritually and within the world is, instead, misdirected and will lead to sorrows.

The reversed Empress indicates that, during this time in her life, the seeker is likely facing a barren period of time. The seeker's creativity has become dysfunctional and the available resources are being wasted. What may be thought of as spiritually-based pleasure is actually self indulgence. The spiritual insight which is much needed is being ignored in order to pander to one's more base desires. It would be wise to stop and consider the training as a High Priestess which enables The Empress to hold her position in the world. Unless one brings serious and positive spiritual work and perspective into the worldly life, failure will be certain.

The Magickal Empress

The Empress knows the deepest mysteries of sexual magick. She has been trained to emulate the womb of rebirth. She can guide you along the path to fulfillment, not only spiritually but within the joys of life. A manifestation of the wisdom of Venus, she knows that a solid foundation in spiritual wisdom is essential if one is to attain the Divine through earthly pleasure.

Her wand represents a very strong will, discipline borne of a love for the spiritual which will keep her from straying and from being lost in the pleasure aspect of sensual delights.

The Empress might choose to wear emerald, coral or amber as the beads of her ritual necklace. She works with many herbes, among them bergamot, columbine, elder, heather, moonwort, myrtle, patchouli and sandalwood. Her preferred scent is musk, worn to elevate her self into ecstatic union, representing the Mother Goddess when she celebrates the Great Rite with The Emperor as the Father God. They work their ritual together, removed from the people, bringing their complementary energies and personalities together to create a whole which transcends the two lives they represent. Only they know whether the Great Rite is shared within the ritual or later, when they have left their private temple and turned into their bed.

Her magick is warm, flowing freely like the spring which pools near her feet. Her rituals are less formal than those of the High Priestess; she embraces her natural setting. The question one must ask when working with The Empress magickally is a question of timing. Does the magick lead to fruition or is the magick born of fruition? Does the magick lead to conception or does it lead to birth? If you wish to invoke the magick of The Empress, you should carefully consider the most appropriate timing for your work. Remember that the Divine energy you will call upon is that of procreative forces. You must be willing to embody The Empress at her very best and be prepared to joyfully serve those in need of your service.

IV - The Emperor

Aries

The Emperor is the partner to The Empress. Together they are the perfect couple. As she represents the perfect feminine counterpart, The Emperor embodies the ideal male partner. He holds a scepter, showing that he is more than capable of being the leader of his people. The scepter may be seen as associated with different cultures, but its design, the long shaft topped by the circle, reminds you that his strength is tempered, his masculine prowess balanced by compassion and a willingness to show his peoples his gentle side. This particular scepter is of a style reflecting spiritual symbolism yet it also reflects his ability to have control over the world and people around him. The masculine symbol of his scepter is matched by the feminine symbol of the orb in his left hand. It is through this balance that he avoids impulsive decisions and actions by maintaining objectivity with an awareness of his own intuitive abilities.

His throne may be larger and have not the pillowed comfort of his wife's but, then, The Emperor is not the one to bear their child. Frequently depicted as older and grey of beard, perhaps he has a bad back from his many years of labor, from riding his horse into battle and bearing the weight of his armor. Neither Emperor nor Empress is more powerful than the other, but it is The Emperor's role to ride off to battle when it comes time to defend the realm. The Empress provides protection for the people spiritually through the manifestation of love and the bearing of the future head of state.

The Emperor carries her protection into battle and knows that she will rule wisely and lovingly, but it is he who must face the wages of war when their land is beset by the enemy. No matter that he is wearing his robe with the eagle, symbol of his mastery embroidered upon the shoulder. Even when at rest do we see his armor clad feet. The quality of his armor and robe reflect his success within the manifest world. He has a mature ability to provide for all the needs of his family and, as well, to be generous to others.

As the father of their child-to-be, The Emperor represents the Divine masculine archetype. The Emperor knows well the mysteries of mental discipline, of keeping his ego from taking control of his life. It is only through maintaining a keen sense of focus, of using his scepter as a tool to hold his emotions under control, that he has come to represent wisdom as the fulfillment of masculine ideals. He does not sow wild oats but, rather, knows how to plant the seed which will bring forth the ideals of the future. No matter where his work takes him, he is ever-mindful of the child growing within The Empress's womb.

He has the ability to originate, to start something new. He is filled with energy, with initiative; but his ability to create requires the presence of The Empress. We see behind his rams-headed throne majestic mountains, indicating the heights which The Emperor can reach, the unlimited creative masculine force which lives within him. He has the physical strength and stamina to reach the top of the mountain, there to view all possibilities before making any decision.

The royal tools which he holds in his hands are complemented by the crown upon his head and all hold spiritual significance. It is through this balance that he can attain such heights. The Emperor's spiritual development is not overtly visible but its presence is as vital to him as is his armor. His discipline is essential to his success but it means that there is balance in their rulership: The Empress is more accessible to the people.

Although he is lord of his realm, we do not see a castle nor city behind him. He and The Empress both know the value of working with the natural forces. The mountains of his card are a counterpart to the gentle woodland shown with The Empress. Depicted as a full embodiment of masculine energy, The Emperor knows well what qualities bring greatness. Without the disciplines which bring him patience, he could be off chasing battles just to satisfy his ego. In order for him to bring forth the Divine seed and share the magick of Creation with The Empress, his role is to use his power to maintain a stable and normal life.

The Mysteries of fatherhood bring The Emperor the ability to transform the impulsiveness of the Aries' ram into that of being a catalyst for change. He maintains control over his energy and does not charge forward. His strong and forceful personality manifests itself through the virtue of patience. He does not act until he knows, logically and intuitively, that the time is right.

This is a man with a keen intellect. He prefers victories which are won by his mental skills to those which require strength and force alone. He is inventive, brilliant of mind and finds great pleasure in being able to explore life's Mysteries. Not only does he pursue the deepest facets of his mind, he knows intimately the furthest recesses of those mountains and is frequently the first to scale the heights, capable of gazing far into the horizon and far into the future.

The Reversed Emperor

When The Emperor appears reversed, this alerts the seeker to recognize that self-discipline and self-control have been lost. The reasons that life is not moving forward have been created by the seeker and no other person is responsible.

It is time to evaluate one's ego and sense of self. More maturity is needed in handling this time in one's life. Look more deeply within the self. The seeker will need to be very honest in this soul-searching. Errors in judgement have been made based upon misconceptions regarding the self's capabilities. It is time to stop deluding the self and rectify the situation.

The Magickal Emperor

The Emperor represents a very strong, active male sexuality. His is a magick which arises out of generating fertility to bless the seed of his community, to ensure the fertility of the land. He represents the Planter and Father aspects of the God.

When he joins with The Empress in the Great Rite, it is a true marriage to the land consummated by both as a working partnership. They work together in their larger-than-life roles, engendering the procreative powers of the Universe. He balances her receptive role with his knowledge of action as his path to fulfillment.

The ritual workings of the Emperor may be more formal than those of The Empress, although when they work together in their Circle they share the same ritual forms. His magick is as warm and loving as is his partner's.

The Emperor corresponds to Aries, the spring-time energy which aids the seeds in thrusting new life through the fertile soil. He would wear amber, rock crystal or ruby set in his ritual jewelry and chooses, among his herbes, blessed thistle, dragon's blood reeds and patchouli. He grows the tiger lily in his garden and finds the scent of musk arousing both to his body and to his soul.

The ritual tools in his hands, the orb and wand, symbolize his religious training. During the time of his coming to prominence, his education would have included priests and priestesses among his mentors. He uses his training to embody the paternal aspect of the God incarnate, manifested within the human form. He brings control and benevolence to The Empress's birth, yet does not participate in this greatest of rites. Work with the magick of The Emperor in care and wisdom.

V - The Hierophant

Taurus

The Hierophant is one of the more misunderstood and misconstrued cards in the Tarot. In a few of the older decks this card has sometimes been represented as the pope which is very misleading for contemporary Tarot work.

With a strong, modern movement away from highly organized religion, there has been a common tendency to assume this card portrays negative aspects within traditional religion, such as hypocrisy and inappropriate control over people. Let me assure you that this is not the case with this card. The Hierophant should not be allowed to stimulate the interpreter's personal stereotypes.

THE HIEROPHANT

The Hierophant appears rich with symbolism. He is seated upon a throne positioned between two pillars much as is The High Priestess. His throne and the pillars, however, are larger and more ornate. The headdress he wears is one which signifies the high office he holds spiritually and socially.

While The High Priestess functions within what might almost be a cloister, The Hierophant has accepted a highly visible role and must do his work in public. The ornamentation on the pillars shows us that this is a very urban temple. The city temple is usually far more substantial and ornate than is the rural temple. This reflects the need of people for a religious edifice which will 'inspire' them when they live in a more 'civilized' environment, removed from the wondrous inspiration of nature, herself.

He wears heavy robes, embroidered and adorned with symbols of his office. Upon his feet are the slippers of an ordained clergy, one whose role it is to teach teachers, to initiate priestesses and priests, and to better serve the people through the ordination of clergy. His is the power which, during an initiation, brings The Hierophant the ability to transfer wisdom and power into a newly ordained priest or priestess through non-verbal transference. The Hierophant could accomplish this magickal feat through the laying on of his hands.

Indeed, just beneath his feet we see the 'keys' which open the doors to the Mysteries. The Hierophant knows how to use these keys and he also knows when it is appropriate. The doors unto the greater Mysteries are not to be opened in public ceremonies, but in private. This aspect of The Hierophant is depicted in some decks by his wearing of gloves.

In his left hand he holds a scepter, a staff giving recognition to his role as spiritual shepherd. Its height represents his ability to bring unity between the earth and the heavens, his ability to bring together the polarities of the moon-lit night and the sun-bright daytime, of the deepest, occult mysteries and the outer, mundane world. He is an adept not only within the spiritual but also within the management of the mundane. Is it coincidental that the ornament at the top of the scepter is composed of seven rays, that same number associated with the Goddess? There are many interpretations available in the 'seven' at the top of the staff. The associations with this number, however, usually denote spiritual mastery at some level.

Do not confuse The Hierophant with the oppressive practices of many patriarchal bureaucracies of politics or religion. His right hand is raised in a position which echoes the posture of The Magician. The Hierophant raises two fingers and a thumb toward the Mysteries of the Universe with two fingers folded down pointing toward earthly manifestation. He is constantly aware of the balance between the extremes of polarity but he is a benevolent figure. The Hierophant is one who will guide the seeker away from becoming too caught up by the attractions of the manifest world.

The throne of The Hierophant is a seat of power, but this role is not taken in order to serve himself. He is a willing servant of the people. Before him we see two male characters, each wearing the robes of a religious order, their heads shaved to indicate that they live a religious lifestyle. The Hierophant has ascended the ranks within a religious hierarchy because of his wisdom. People will trust him, even if seeking him for the first time. When this card appears in a reading, adjacent cards will help the interpreter determine whether this means the seeker should be emulating The Hierophant during this time or if the seeker needs to seek counsel from another who has attained that role.

The Hierophant has learned one of the more difficult spiritual Mysteries. He knows that one of the functions of his religious office is to emulate the Mysteries, to present them to large numbers of people on a scale which can be seen by all present. He must be able to move among royalty. He must be able to lobby government officials. He will be present at important public ceremonies and it is he who may well place the crown upon the king. Without demonstrating his power in a wise manner, his religious tradition might be unable to survive changes in the political climate. The Hierophant must do his work carefully so that even if the monarch is deposed, his church can survive for future generations. His knowledge and training must embrace both the spiritual and the social. His presence brings grace to any social function and when he raises his hand to bestow a blessing, as he is doing in this card, it is more than a symbolic gesture. His very presence stirs religious awareness in all present.

The path of The Hierophant is not an easy path. It is not one a person can assume nor seek out. The true path of this wisdom is one which is bestowed upon a person. It is a mantel placed upon one's shoulders only after they have attained more than enough wisdom, when they have shown they are able to walk securely in both worlds. He must, at all times, emulate a balance between both pillars. He must have direct knowledge of many of the Mysteries of which he shares insight with The High Priestess. He represents another perspective of the Hermetic Principle: his hand points to the 'above,' his feet rest upon the 'below' and he sees himself as a bridge by which those who have not placed themselves upon a serious spiritual path may ascend toward the Universe.

The Hierophant is well-trained in the use of symbols. His own sense of self must willingly be sacrificed or sublimated at the appropriate times in order that he can project what is needed by his peoples. There may be many days he would prefer to work his rituals on a smaller scale at home in his private temple; but he must function in public and must both appear and move as a symbol, himself. At the risk of appearing pompous, The Hierophant knows that he must present himself as a symbol which appears larger-than-life. This allows him to serve his people and, as such, he may be thought of as a 'father' to his people. He enjoys this paternal role, for it enables him to manifest benevolence and blessings.

People turn to The Hierophant in times of strife or for the most important rites of passage in their lives: he represents stability. He attempts to show people how to manifest this stability through the slow and patient evolution of a religious tradition which is able to outlast many generations of people. His throne is one which has been well-earned and will be there for whomever next holds this religious position. The very size and weight of this throne could withstand a change in political power or even an earthquake!

With his feet planted solidly upon the temple floor, he represents a conservative, economical use of his energies and skills. The Hierophant is strong-willed but exhibits this quality in subtle ways. He does not have to impose his will upon others. Patience is his virtue and he knows that if he quietly waits, others will recognize what he had already perceived. It is not that it is 'his' way but that it is the best way. He does not attach his ego to his wisdom.

In some decks there is an aspect of The Hierophant which may seem inconsistent with his religious life. In these decks the appearance of this card may sometimes indicate the possibility of a relationship appearing in the seeker's life. An objective view of this character's position and of the totality of knowledge he would represent indicates that The Hierophant would not have arrived at this station in his life by having always been solitary. In some decks the romantic aspect of this card is interpreted as being the recipient of blessings bestowed by the Universe or in having an evolved, spiritual masculine figure as a partner who seems like a blessing.

His Taurean nature has a great love of nature and, when he needs to retreat from the splendor of his temple, seeks solace in gardens, among trees and with the gentle breath of Mother Nature. The Hierophant knows the spiritual joy found in the appreciation of the manifest world's beauty. He appreciates the aesthetic qualities found in life; it is one of the blessings he counts. He also takes pleasure in fine things. His staff, the headdress, all his ritual tools are of superb quality. His craft is his lifestyle and he chooses to live his life in harmony with beauty.

He might be thought of by some as too concerned with the material, but he knows that these items belong to his office and will be used by those who will next hold his position. The sacred tools of his religion must be capable of reflecting the significance of the ceremonies he conducts. The initiations within his temple are more than life-changing for the initiate: they will frequently alter the course of events for the social fabric of the realm. He also knows that one good chalice will last many lifetimes. He is a good person.

The Reversed Hierophant

When The Hierophant appears reversed in a reading, then the interpreter ought suspect that the seeker may be caught up by the trappings of spiritual or temporal power and may be a pretender to that throne without the wisdom and skills which are necessary. Hypocrisy may well be present.

Using the powers of the world or presenting yourself as being powerful when there is inadequate substance behind the facade represent a negative practice which The Hierophant would abhor. Should The Hierophant represent another individual in a reading, beware of that person's weaknesses and avoid taking any advice from a reversed Hierophant seriously. It is not to be trusted.

There are occasions when this card might appear reversed to indicate that someone has broken the rules of social convention, that someone has disregarded tradition. Other cards in the reading will help the interpreter determine whether that behavior may have been wise.

Generally speaking, should The Hierophant appear reversed in a layout, the seeker is advised to take seclusion and work with diligence to get in touch with the inner spirit. It is time to experience anew one's initiation or entry into this station in life, to reclaim the serenity and balance found when seated between the two pillars. Beware the temptations of ego which lead to prejudice, to believing that The Hierophant is better than others. If one wishes to follow the true path of The Hierophant, honesty and humility must be present at all times.

The Magickal Hierophant

The Hierophant is well-trained in working with sexual energy. Indeed, many believe that his correspondence with Taurus is an esoteric indication that he is a sensual, romantic character. He knows, however, that sexual energy is inappropriate under the circumstances indicated by this card. These are public, social events and not the appropriate setting for the Mysteries of sexual magick. The creative spark of The Hierophant leads that life which will keep his religious tradition alive for many ages.

His is a magick that evolves organically. Nothing is rushed and every move is deliberate and choreographed with great care. He knows that it will take generations to bring a religious truth into solid manifestation. The Hierophant does not frolic at Beltane, although he surely did as a lad. The Hierophant must explore the sexual mysteries and work with them removed from view. His station in life has been accepted. At the most sensual of Sabbats his attention is fully placed within his responsibilities, in making certain that others may share the joys which bless the crops. The seeds The Hierophant plants are not for this growing season, but are those which will sprout following death.

He has a great love of herbes. His favorites include borage, cumin, lovage, mallows, periwinkle and storax; but he will often choose to work with 'liturgical mixtures,' herbal preparations crafted by skilled priestesses and monks, pungent and able to carry scent to the furthest reaches of a cathedral. The gemstones which represent his magick are the jasper and topaz.

The Hierophant is capable of conducting an initiation but his larger role is that of ordination. It is from his role as one who conducts rites of passage, who opens the doors into the Mysteries of the Universe, that much of his magick is drawn. It is this role which increases his patience. He is someone whom other religious leaders seek in order to gain insight into their own roles. Although they may be esteemed spiritual leaders doing their work within social order, his view is yet larger. He is more likely found within a religious university or mystery school than a coven. The path which has led to his throne took many years as a student and would have been marked by his voracious appetite for religious history and occult sciences. He is undaunted by the more challenging studies and has spent considerable time learning such studies as Kaballah and alchemy to a greater depth than many who profess themselves to be teachers.

The Hierophant knows the Mysteries of religious evolution, of the place religion holds within the development of humanity and within the rise and fall of civilizations. He holds a larger view of religion than most are capable of holding within their grasp. Despite the grandeur of his office, he never loses sight of humility.

In many ways, walking a magickal path with The Hierophant is more challenging than are many of the other paths. Ritual must be worked slowly and painstakingly when the ramifications extend far beyond one's lifetime. All students walking a magickal path who dream of their work or influence moving them into the roles of teachers and socially-recognized adepts ought study this card at a profound level.

VI - The Lovers

Gemini

In common use, **The Lovers** is often misinterpreted as a card portending the appearance of a romantic interest. The Lovers card should be understood as facing the necessity of choice. There are many other cards in the Tarot which deal with romantic issues far more directly than this so the reader must be careful and avoid automatic assumptions that this card is relationship-oriented.

Look carefully at this card. The two human figures are presented as separate from each other. Although there seems to be the semblance of attraction and desire, neither is able to act upon this but, rather, hesitates and wonders "should I?" In the background appears, for the first time, a singular high-reaching mountain and, in the foreground, by each character stands a tree. Overhead is an angelic figure who is brightened by the full sun.

Sometimes interpreted as Raphael, [one of the four Archangels in Western religious and magickal traditions], this angelic figure represents the potential for having access to Divine energy. Although the angel has its hands outstretched, we may likely expect to find the sword which represents truth girdled about his waist as a reminder that a high degree of honesty with the self is essential. This angel holds further significance for the seeker: The need to trust your intuition is very important. The woman is looking upward, seeking a higher level of wisdom than will be found within her own logic, for her reasoning is mixed with emotional responses, desires and needs regarding this situation. The angel is present in this card to remind us that we must rise above what lies before us in order to have a clear view far down the road and, if we seek the angel, Raphael can provide healing for the couple.

Most frequently, this card appears in a layout when the seeker is caught between two choices. Rarely is the situation a solitary period in life, but one or more other people are typically involved in the situation. Just as the mountain appears in the distance positioned between the two human figures, the seeker must choose between two directions, having encountered a fork in the road of life which has far-reaching implications for the seeker's future. Which choice is the best? Although there may be differences, each divergent path adds up to a very appealing choice and there is not enough difference between the value of each for a clear decision to emerge. The seeker, instead, appeals to the angelic figure.

When this card deals with relationship issues, (for it does in some readings), there are a number of circumstances which the seeker may be facing. Johanna Gargiulo-Sherman (in The Sacred Rose Tarot Deck) does a wonderful job of presenting us with a view of this dilemma: the man is shown unable to choose between the religious archetypes of Eve and Lillith. It is possible that the seeker must choose between two different relationships. It is also possible that the seeker faces anxiety, unable to move forward and embrace the future or to retreat from the relationship. Another possible interpretation of the figures is to indicate that this situation is not a solitary venture: other people are involved and interaction with others must be evaluated in arriving at a decision.

Will the Tarot present the seeker with an easy solution and a clear answer? The cards and the layout are more likely to present an honest evaluation of the complexities and, hopefully, assist the seeker in finding a better level of self-understanding. Whatever the details of the decision at hand, the card contains symbolism to help the interpreter gain a deeper understanding of the seeker's situation. Both figures are shown unclothed, reminiscent of Adam and Eve. This may represent an internal conflict between spiritual goals and sensual desires. Both figures are hesitating and are fraught with indecision. The seeker is feeling tension, for the desire to move forward juggles itself with the desire to stay where it is 'safe;' but the Universe compels the seeker to make a decision and to act upon it. Prior to encountering this 'crossroads,' the seeker was able to live with a sense of innocence. This innocence is depicted by the nakedness and, as told in the Adam and Eve myth, will never be recaptured. The path to the future is not, however, so much the loss of innocence as of naivete. The Lovers card is a path to growth and increased wisdom regarding life's processes.

Each human figure is shown standing by a tree. The man's tree bears flowers and the woman's tree bears fruit. There is much fertility and abundance available if they move forward and join forces. The serpent coiled around the woman's tree is a symbol of temptation. The seeker is tempted by and attracted to both forks in the road. Each tree represents a path toward wisdom, a path which has both positive and negative aspects of attraction. The seeker feels a deep, almost magnetic pull to move into whichever path he may be thinking most of at the time. This desire to take both paths when the reality only allows the seeker to take one fork is a major source of tension for the seeker.

The Lovers indicates the presence of tension due to anxieties and a need for a decision to create resolution. The right answer could further the seeker spiritually, opening up the path to the heights of the mountain. The wrong decision could be negative in its implications. There are some striking similarities between The Lovers card and The Devil. Compare the imagery of both. There are lessons to be found in this process. What is the wrong decision? It is choosing one path and then, rather than moving forward in joy, dissipating your energy by wondering if the other path might have been better. Oftentimes neither choice may be wrong, but the seeker's inability to accept resolution can create harm for the path taken.

There are other sources for the tension indicated by this card. The seeker feels attractions to both choices. The inability to choose, to see clearly, creates anxieties. The interplay between this card and The Devil suggests that one might be playing too much the 'devil's advocate' in sorting out the choices which lie before the self. For those who know astrology, it is easy to see why this card is associated with the Gemini qualities of personality. The seeker is usually too focused upon the present, upon what the decision means to the wants of her ego. It is difficult to see far into the future, to take the view from the top of that mountain.

The Lovers contains lessons and advice for the seeker which is helpful for anyone faced with the making of a serious and life-changing decision. The similarity of the scenario between this card and The Devil shows the seeker that, once a decision is made, a commitment to it must be made as well. Looking back can get you in trouble. The snake of temptation is just waiting to conjure up all manner of emotional turmoil. The counsel offered the seeker when approaching the decision is this: if a person can let go of the emotional 'need' of having the answer, the chances of a clear, correct answer emerging are increased.

It is helpful to remind the seeker that behind the angel's head the Sun appears, almost like a halo. An abundance of joy is possible and the situation should not be perceived as troubling. By seeking the answer from the spiritual, the better choice (and the confidence to embrace it) may be found.

The Reversed Lovers

When this card appears reversed, time should not be wasted. There is more than enough disharmony in the seeker's life and this energy is manifesting in a number of ways, all of which can lead down a path to ill health and the serious loss of goals. Disagreements are likely getting out of hand, and the emotional investment of all concerned will make healing difficult.

This is a time to seek experienced skill, to obtain guidance from someone with training. This is often the time when the interpreter of a Tarot reading must recognize that she may not adequately be trained in counselling nor adept in knowing the psychological or emotional functions of human nature. The client may well need someone with more skill than a Tarot reader to assist them through this change. Proper advice can increase your client's confidence in you.

Without the proper help, the relationships involved in the situation could become damaged to the degree that a permanent dissolution occurs. Pay attention when The Lovers appears reversed. It contains an important message.

The Magickal Lovers

The magick of The Lovers is found within the working of polarities or in the concept of a single unit dividing to become two. This latter idea may be seen in Kabbalah as the Creative Divinity moving into the polarities in order to begin creation in the manifest world. This may also apply in the creative force of an idea, or of energies, bringing it into a polarized separation so that unity can again take place but now between two separate forces.

Herbes associated with this card include cinnamon, dragon's blood, elfwort, orchis or wormwood. The astrological correspondence of Gemini is found in the balance between the two separate entities which want to become independent and at the same time long for union. The gemstone for this card might be the garnet or it might be the tourmaline.

The approach to ritual when invoking The Lovers would ideally be through working with the polarity manifest in a ritual partner. It is important, in studying this card, to remember that each person is a 'tree' unto the self. Each partner will be drawing upon that self, developing the flow of energy called 'The Middle Pillar,' for this tree represents the Tree of Life of Kaballah. Each whole entity represents either the yin or the yang energy.

The movement of both partners should frequently emulate that found in pairs figure skating, in which the movements mirror each other, in which each moves at the outer edge of the Circle in balance with the partner moving at the opposite side. These two will then be brought together during the context of the ritual working. The goal of this magickal work would be fruitfulness. One of the trees bears flowers and the other bears fruit. The serpent is representative both of the human condition through which spiritual energy can be diverted toward the pleasures of the flesh; but it can also represent the energy of the Kundalini.

The natural magick of The Lovers is drawn from the energy created out of indecision. In its positive aspects, there is almost a delicious quality in knowing that change will be forthcoming but tantalizing by not yet having it settled. The Lovers card can be used to create excellent energy within which to pursue divination or the invoking of an oracle.

VII - The Chariot

Cancer

The Chariot card contains more symbols than readily meet the eye. The driver's clothing, the chariot itself, and the juxtaposition of the city behind him, across the river together create a composite archetype of the balance between emotions and action.

Who is the charioteer? Someone who desires to move forward, who must take control over the dichotomies of the yin, black sphinx and its opposing yang, white partner. The Chariot driver is well-protected, sheltered by the chariot, itself, dressed with layers of fine clothing and handsome armour, all marked with extensive symbolism. The staff in his hand balances the star upon his crown. Although he desires to put the chariot in motion, the sphinxes are, at the time this card appears, at rest. They represent the dichotomy within the available energy of the situation which the charioteer must harness in order to begin moving toward his goal.

We cannot be certain if he is leaving the city to set out toward the mountain which appears in so many of the cards, or if his goal lies within urban civilization. Only the charioteer (or the seeker) can answer this question. The river must be crossed and this represents great emotional change before the goals can be achieved. Of course, we might also believe that it has already been crossed. Such a change requires self-control while moving through the emotional experience. There is no bridge available allowing one to pass over the situation without becoming dampened.

Standing tall and proud, the charioteer is depicted as a man but can easily represent a seeker of either gender. Upon his head we see a wreath of laurel and a stunning star upon the crown. He has already experienced some success, but has not yet reached his ultimate goal. This is not the time to stop and feel triumph. The star shows that he has access to spiritual wisdom, that he is highly intuitive. His shoulders bear two crescent moons. One appears to be smiling and one reflects anxieties, an even different aspect of archetypal polarities implicit within the sphinxes. The presence of so many emotional feelings requires that the character is well-protected. We see rich clothing and pieces of armour to protect his vulnerability. The seeker should acknowledge these feelings of vulnerability, for those feelings can be transcended only through self-knowledge. The panels of the armour's skirting are marked with numerous symbols. The girdle about his waist appears to have astrological symbols upon it and over his heart chakra is a radiant square as if a protective talisman. Even his wrists are protected.

What an amazing chariot we see in this card. The canopy is brightened with many stars showering spiritual energy and bestowing divine protection upon the passenger. This canopy enables the charioteer to see the world but shelters him against all weather. The front of the chariot bears a winged shield, a symbol representing his ability to handle the active forces present in this situation. The wheels of the chariot are sturdy, old fashioned chariot wheels. The charioteer will certainly feel the bumps in the road but will never be delayed with a flat tire! The wheels represent a subtle symbolism for the interpreter: they may be seen as reminiscent of the two pillars already discussed. Both the shield and the wheels indicate that the situation is filled with very strong energy, with highly active magickal forces.

The sphinxes are filled with kinetic energy. Although they are at rest, their cat-like bodies are able to spring into motion at the slightest indication from their Master. They can be yoked and their energy harnessed, but not through physical means. The charioteer must bring their power into use through his mind and through his spirit.

Rather than allowing the sphinxes to go their separate ways, The Chariot card reminds the seeker that she has the ability to affect the outcome. Unlike The Lovers, in which the union of the differences did not seem an option, it is essential for The Chariot to work the polarities.

The staff is held firmly in the charioteer's hand and she is prepared for success in battles both within day-to-day life and within the spiritual realm of existence. Even though 'battle' may not appear in the seeker's life, preparation is very important. The seeker is extolled to be strong of will, prepared to take charge of the situation, to move forward and go where she thinks necessary. This is no time to allow your insecurities to hold you back.

Success will be had, but only if no passengers are allowed to board the vehicle. There is only room for one, and The Chariot holds the seeker. Waiting for others or trying to help people unwilling to help themselves will cause the chariot to lose its momentum. Failure to follow the advice of The Chariot can lead to stagnation. The seeker is advised to be alert, on guard, and prepared physically, mentally and spiritually. Only then can he move the self forward with creativity, as if riding a magick carpet into the future.

This card may sometimes appear when there are domestic tensions or dissention between two family members with the seeker caught in the middle. One may feel a desire to find some vehicle and ride off into the sunset to avoid further confrontation, but this card encourages you to move forward, avoid taking sides, and steer your own course. The Chariot is a very positive card and should be reassuring to the seeker when it is turned up in a layout. Self-confidence is a very important key and the seeker should be mindful of the staff which lends poise to the charioteer. Stand flexible and you will not fall down when The Chariot is put in motion.

The Reversed Chariot

When The Chariot is reversed in a reading, the direction you are moving needs to be reconsidered, as well as the energy which has been moving you in that direction. Perhaps you have not adequately consulted what might be thought of as your spiritual map? You are not acting upon your feelings but are holding back due to emotions regarding one of the key players in this situation. Rather than using the chariot as a vehicle toward success, the seeker has taken refuge in it and it has become a protective shell with which to avoid confronting reality.

The reversal of this card cautions the seeker that he is not strong of will, that the emotions of fear are interfering in reaching a successful outcome. Unless changes are made, the consequences could be serious. Some decks, in fact, suggest that the reversed Chariot might foreshadow litigation or the need for roles of decision-making being handed over to another. If you cannot handle the reins of your chariot, another may step in and take over. Self-discipline is lacking, but these reversals can be remedied by careful action on the seeker's part. A thorough interpretation of the other cards in the layout is very important.

The Magickal Chariot

The magickal energy of the charioteer is masculine and caring, wanting to extend benevolence and nurturing to many people. The Chariot represents the vehicle through which energy and blessings are bestowed. Such action must be done without any thought of reward. The sole purpose must be the moving forward to reach the Highest Ideals of the seeker's spiritual self.

The Chariot is associated with the zodiacal sign of Cancer. Internal tension arises out of fears and emotional hurts, but the external realities must be faced and transcended. Herbes which would promote magickal use of this card include anise, balm, camphor, hyssops, lotus and watercress. Some might choose wormwood. The desirable gemstones would be lapis or amber and anything made of shells would promote good energies.

For the magickal student, the symbolism of The Chariot's shield requires meditative study. It represents the bringing together of the polarities. The active rod has been inserted through the receptive, circular form. This leads to the spreading of the astral wings. However, just as the yin and yang of the sphinxes are kept separate, so too does the charioteer remain removed from sexual activity during the ritual. Perhaps the charioteer's partner is waiting at the desired destination but this is, at present, a solitary journey.

The magick of this card is derived from anticipation, from the process of building the energy, of creating tension which seeks release, but not until the proper moment. The magickal staff is present throughout the ritual and The Chariot is a card which leads one upon a profound path.

VIII - Justice

Libra

Justice was, prior to Waite, numbered VIII. Waite changed this card to XI. Today, some decks maintain this card as VIII but more follow the numbering system of the Rider deck. Whether she is the eighth card or the eleventh, as Judy, my Tarot teacher, once said, "Justice is not always fair but it is always just."

I personally work with a deck (The Sacred Rose) which maintains the original numeric sequence within the Major Arcana. I have an affinity for the arcana when Justice is found in this order, growing out of The Lovers and The Chariot. The symbolism within Justice should be studied as a balance with The High Priestess and The Hierophant. It also pleases my Virgo nature to see these three steps in their own context along the path of the Major Arcana. And now, with the issue of Justice's number out of the way...

Justice, along with The High Priestess and The Hierophant, is presented in a similar manner. Each figure is seated upon a throne between two pillars. Each is clothed in robes befitting their station. Each holds symbols of their profession. In addition, both Justice and The High Priestess sit before a curtain or veil, indicating that they alone can move into the unseen. All three have considerable power and all three demonstrate great wisdom. As does The Hierophant, Justice must do her work within the public realm. No matter how extensive her spiritual training, her role is to maintain order within society.

Justice wears a crown, for her realm extends into the upper reaches of government and her decisions are to be treated with respect. The gems set in her crown and at the clasp of her gown represent her stature in both social and spiritual circles. The curtain behind her is a visible reminder that the seeker must turn to Justice for she alone knows what the future may hold. In some decks she is depicted with a blindfold to represent the same principle. Seated between the two pillars, Justice holds both her scales and her sword. These pillars remind us that she is in a temple of sorts, even though her decisions extend into the practical, manifest world.

The sword reaches upward, following the vertical thrust of the left pillar as it extends its energy from the earth to the heavens. There are two sides to this sword and there are two edges. Both sides of the situation are easily reflected and the seeker is reminded to carefully consider both perspectives. Becoming overly emotional or involving too many aspects of ego will cause the seeker to feel the sharpness of the honed edges of this sword, a tool of honesty, fairness and truthfulness. Justice is as prepared to make a decision as was Solomon. Truth can cut both ways. In a fair decision, both sides may need to compromise to some degree.

It takes strength to wield such a mighty sword. Compared to Justice's stature, it is a large sword and would have considerable weight. Her posture in extending her arm to hold her sword in a position similar to the Ace of Swords requires strength of arm and strength of character. Although the sword in the Ace leads to the birth of a new situation, in Justice the sword indicates that the decision could be (at the least) life-changing. Her face is stoic, for among her Mysteries is the knowledge that one who seeks Justice but does not accept the verdict is on a path which will lead to the painful severing of something in the seeker's life. The sword of Justice may have been consecrated in an initiation, but its role within society is more likely to confer knighthood for the seeker who accepts Justice in her life and successfully embraces honesty and growth.

The scales of Justice remind us that she is associated with the zodiacal personality of Libra. She holds the scales, weighing all possibilities before any motion toward a decision is made. When Justice appears in a reading, the seeker is asked to embrace a period of evaluation, of weighing and balancing any decision or outcome of the situation. The scales represent her ability to see both sides of the situation and are symbolic of her professional training as mediator, or one able to find the middle ground.

Justice offers many facets of wisdom for the seeker. She is a path unto Mysteries which provide a person with maturity and wisdom. Justice offers us a sense of balance and appears in a reading when we should cease activity, evaluate what has been taking place and open ourselves to honesty and to adjustments within the directions we have been going. This is a time to stop acting, to stop one's emotions from affecting activity, and to stop meddling and interfering (even psychically) in the outcome of the situation. Now one ought step back and take space and time before making any further decisions. Study how Justice sits upon her throne. She is a role model for the seeker.

Emotional involvement will cause the scales to tip unfairly yet this is a time when all aspects, when *everything* must be placed upon the pans of the scales and weighed to see the merit of each aspect. With one foot emerging from her robe, we know that Justice is prepared to move toward resolution, to the handing down of her decision. The seeker is advised to accept the appearance of Justice and to adopt all mature attitudes (honesty, openness) which are necessary for a fair verdict. No matter what you may have done in the past, you are being tried by the Universe. The ordeals and lessons in life which may accompany the events heralded by this card are part of that trial. Trust in the Universe is important. The seeker will be held accountable and the outcome will be just. Fighting the decisions of Justice will lead to the severity of her sword. Accepting her role will lead to the correct decision and a future made more positive.

The appearance of Justice in a reading requires acceptance by the seeker. One cannot avoid facing the music when Justice has called for a fair evaluation. Whether we've done well or whether we have committed actions which require the hand of Justice to intervene and provide correction, an acceptance of both the sword and the scales must be embraced. Avoiding her will place the seeker upon a path with serious ramifications.

Reversed Justice

When Justice appears reversed in a reading this is, in many ways, the antithesis of the very nature of what is fair and just. The card may be warning the seeker of narrow-mindedness, of a disregard for a fair, ethical approach to the situation. One's ego has gotten in the way. It is also possible for this card to appear when one is confronted with a situation or with another person who represents the reversal of Justice.

Depending upon the other cards of the reading, it may be possible that the situation needs careful attention. Without Justice, an abuse of one's power is possible. Frustrations and fears arising out of such events can lead to bitterness or lawlessness. The complications from such actions may be the result of bigotry or an unfair bias toward others. Someone is attempting to sway the hand of Justice, to tip the scales in their favor without regard to fairness. It is important to note that, should this be describing the seeker, the situation can be corrected. If it applies to someone else it will be most important for the seeker to emulate, as much as possible, the qualities of Justice in her upright position, to seek balance and weigh all action with great and judicious care.

Magickal Justice

Justice can be a most magickal card. Seated between the ritual pillars, she represents the feminine principle of the Universe. Hers is not a passionate, sexual approach to life. When she emulates this path, sexuality is not an issue. Abstinence would be appropriate if one chooses to work with Justice ritually or to invoke it for magickal purposes. Her robe represents a removal of the emotional, sexual self in order to be impartial as she enacts her role.

Herbes which would further one's work with this card include aloe, hyacinth and verbena. The Libra aspect of her nature requires preparations to have one's life in balance. There are three gems which could assist one in this magickal work: amber, emerald or jasper.

If we study this card, the presence of the pillars and of Justice's ritual sword indicate that she has the ability to conduct Initiations. Although that function is not part of her role in this card, it is part of the path which led to her throne. Within many Wiccan traditions, the sword is an amplification of the ritual knife and imparts the ability to speak for the community, raising one above solitary status.

Seated between the pillars, Justice has the ability to work keenly with her intuition. Working to open her chakras and move the natural and divine energies so that she, herself, is a flow of magick between the manifest and the Universe, she becomes the Middle Pillar and would represent the training necessary to function as an Oracle for her community.

How would Justice approach her ritual disciplines? She would develop detachment. Her ritual form would be very controlled, exhibiting well developed skill. She might create the temple or cast the Circle within which to divine an answer. It is also possible that the ritual work might have taken place prior to her moving between the pillars and addressing the community. She is careful to remove herself from ego, to disconnect herself from the intricacies and attachment which ego has to one's perceptions. Her forms of divination are more likely to be an established 'system' and she works carefully to open her intuitive powers to the Universe. The presence of Justice is as commanding as that of the Goddess. She may lay the sword of truth upon the seeker's shoulder and require an acceptance of Perfect Truth and a willingness to act upon the Oracle accordingly.

IX - The Hermit

Virgo

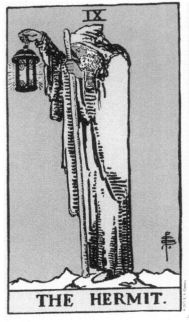

THE HERMIT.

The Hermit holds, within his lamp, the light of the Universe. He has learned the Mysteries of the Universe as well as how to best communicate them to others. The Hermit does not speak of himself, he speaks first through his lantern. This is the first card of the Major Arcana in which the personality of the character is not dominant, the first card in which the personage has chosen to be removed, to place the seeker's focus upon something other than the image of the figure. Our attention is drawn to the lantern and its light.

There are many methods of teaching the Major Arcana which describe The Fool setting out upon a journey during which he meets the other characters of the major cards and experiences the lessons of death, judgement, and so forth. One version of this tale has The Fool returning from the first segment of his journey as The Hermit, wizened, his face and posture reflecting the trials, lessons, and the distance which he has covered in his Quest. We see him, here, having successfully garnered the meaning of life, his lantern filled with the light of Divine Truth.

The Hermit does not wish to attract attention to himself. Other than his lantern, only a staff accompanies the robed figure of this humble Hermit. These two tools stand out against the quiet, grey tones of the illustration. The simplicity of symbolism within The Hermit may mislead the seeker. He does not sit, enthroned, between the pillars but chooses to interact only with those who perceive, correctly, that his staff can lead you to the enlightenment contained within his lantern. His lamp is bright and he knows that only those who seek the light merit the support of his staff.

The Hermit is a living representative of the Mysteries. He is symbolic as a religious figure and also symbolic due to his unique place within society. The Hermit may not live within the ebb and flow of society but he should not be thought of as isolated, either. There are many who know the path to his door, from The High Priestess to the gardener. Holding his lantern high, The Hermit knows that its light will be visible to those who wish to find it. The Hermit knows that he can make the Mysteries available to the seeker, but only if he can be found, if the light of his lantern is visible in the dusky grey of the card.

The staff represents both his leadership and his independent, solitary nature. He has not been leaning upon another person but he has learned that a student of the Mysteries can only depend upon the self for strength and motivation. No matter whether the path has been well-trod by other students and teachers, even a well-established path to the light requires a student to emulate The Hermit.

The Hermit is the primary card for spiritual teachers. It frequently is the significator card for those who guide others to wisdom. The Hermit teaches the keepers of the light the true path of spiritual leadership. It is not the ego of the teacher which is elevated, it is the light. The Hermit would rather teach his students the Mysteries than be a leader. His love of the wisdom of the Universe radiates outward and he has learned through his journey that he does not favor social situations which keep him from his teaching.

When The Hermit appears in a reading, it advises the seeker that it may well be time to withdraw from the activities of life and contemplate its deeper meaning. Study, however, the Four of Swords which has a far more direct message. The Hermit has already completed most of this journey. It is more likely that his message reflects his role in life, having already journeyed far removed from the whirlwinds of life, meditating upon the Mysteries of the Universe. He has already spent time emulating the Four of Swords. Other cards in the layout and the events of the seeker's life are important keys in fully determining what role The Hermit is asking of the seeker.

The seeker may be advised to adopt the demeanor of The Hermit. When approached by students, he remains a hooded figure. When providing answers or knowing which question to ask the student, The Hermit's mind remains focused inward, journeying toward union with the Universe. He is conservative with words, wishing the Mysteries to speak for themselves. He would rather open his student's spirit like the lotus than embroider his wisdom with flowery speech to further his own ego. The Hermit walks a quiet path. He does not announce himself to the world as a teacher. He is not shown orating to a crowd. If you wish his wisdom, you must seek the light of his lantern. He requires effort of his students.

And when a student has trod the path to The Hermit and asked of this teacher the first question, even then this Mentor may not provide the answer. He understands what it means to be a guardian of the Mysteries and will not accept a student, will not agree to guide a student to the depths of the Universe until he is certain that the student is worthy, that the student lives and breathes life as a quest for wisdom. His sacred lamp represents a search for truth. He has the ability to initiate a student but his is not the path to ordination. The Hermit's lantern represents a key which opens the door to the wonders of the Universe. The seeker will not be overwhelmed, will not be blinded by the light. This teacher is not visibly a priest but he is priestly in the manner he lives his life. The Hermit's manner of instruction is to guide a student along a path of independent study, of self-motivation.

When The Hermit appears in a reading, it may sometimes advise the seeker to emulate this path but at other times may be recommending that she seek out that person who represents The Hermit in her own life. The situation calls for a time to retreat and contemplate what one has learned, a time to harvest one's knowledge. The Hermit's journey has taken him through many harvests. He is able to see into the future because his path is one based upon sound experience of the past. He has learned from his mistakes and profited from his learning.

We can look at this card and see a virtuous man. He is cautious in his approach to life, careful of his step and prudent in the paths he chooses to walk. No matter how brightly shines his lantern, he will never stop being a student and knows that true wisdom arises from experience rather than from the intellectual gathering of words. If The Hermit is the path indicated for the seeker, it cannot be avoided but must be embraced.

The appearance of this card in a reading may indicate that this is the time to turn to The Hermit for strength, for wisdom, to seek the light of his lamp and the strength of his staff. The Hermit will not treat the student as one would a close friend, for his path of humility and removal from the mainstream of society creates a sacred space around him which begets an humble demeanor. But The Hermit is warm and friendly, inviting the student into his retreat where he will allow the seeker to peer into the light of the lantern. And then, before the student departs, The Hermit will kindle the flame of the Mysteries, a lesser light, in the student's own lamp.

The Reversed Hermit

The reversed Hermit is a most unflattering card to have in a reading, but there is no getting around the truths it communicates. Rather than emulating the virtues of this wise teacher, the seeker must look into the mirror. There he will find reflected errant behavior which needs correction. This could be manifested as stubbornness rather than a receptive attitude to new lessons. It may have arisen from having created an illusion of knowing more than one truly does. This is the time to withdraw, for it will be easier to face the truth in private.

In his upright position, The Hermit reflects maturity and wisdom which accompanies age. Reversed, he projects immaturity and false humility. In one sense, the reversed properties of this card are some of the lessons the Hermit had to overcome in order to become the ideals of this card. The reversed Hermit indicates that you may be talking when you should be listening, promoting yourself when you should be facing your responsibility in the way you carry the light.

The seeker is advised to study what has been taking place in communication. Rather than the light, it may be the ego which has been expressing itself. In other situations the seeker may be advised that he has been shielding the light from the lantern and needs to open its shutters so that others may benefit from learned wisdom. Study the reading as a whole to know which may be the moral of the reversed Hermit.

The Magickal Hermit

The magick of The Hermit is, in many ways, a path which has taken him to know, intimately, the Crone. His journey has taken him both through Western sexual magick and the tantric disciplines of the East. At this point in his life, his path appears to be solitary and his sexual adventures are relegated to his cherished memories. Upon occasion, the path of The Hermit may be in conjunction with a partner but only if they reside within the same hermitage.

The herbes grown in his garden for magickal purposes include lavender (lots of lavender - perhaps even a hedge lining either side of the path to his door), maidenhair ferns and the narcissus. He draws upon the Highest Ideals of his Virgo nature to become the best teacher he may and chooses to wear jacinth, a stone of the zircon family, peridot and jade (his favourite).

Although The Hermit is not depicted in a formal ritual setting, nor even an informal temple, he has full knowledge of ritual and, only within the privacy of his temple, will reveal himself as an adept. The Hermit prefers to leave the public displays of skill to those trained in the performance of ritual as public pageant, such as The Hierophant. The Hermit's is not an ego which propels him into the limelight. He is far more comfortable hanging his lantern in his quiet temple and letting the joy of the Universe permeate his ritual workings. Many of the more public figures of the Major Arcana learned their skills within The Hermit's tutelage. His ritual staff may be subtle, but it shows his position as spiritual leader.

The magick of this card is drawn from the journey. It is the magick of pathworking, the magick of the Quest. It combines the illumination of

Universal wisdom with solid experience, patience with commitment. The cowl of his robe demonstrates his skill at providing the Mysteries with an absence of ego. The magickal workings of The Hermit are the product of hard work and his wisdom endures far beyond this incarnation.

X - The Wheel of Fortune

Jupiter

The Wheel of Fortune is a truly amazing card. It appears when life moves through a period of great activity, as if you are on a quickly moving carousel trying to snatch the brass ring of opportunity. Just as it would seem from that carousel, life is spinning past and appears to be fast paced. This is a card of life's ups and downs.

WHEEL of FORTUNE.

The Wheel of Fortune is a card advising the seeker that this view of life, "As The Wheel Turns," will seem far clearer if one moves away from the outside edge of the carousel to the very center. The correct perspective, one of calm, one from the very hub or center, will be the one which best leads to stability and success. This is similar to the principle learned by a dancer - that of focusing upon a stationary spot when turning in a pirouette. If one's eyes attempt to focus upon all of the detail which is whirling past, the seeker will become too disoriented to recognize opportunity when the brass ring is easily within reach. This is not, however, a matter of luck. It is not the fortunes of luck which will bring the ring into your grasp. The seeker must grow spiritually and expand the very foundation of her wisdom before having a secure grip upon opportunity. And how can one achieve this? The Wheel of Fortune contains an array of symbolism which is a guide to the seeker.

The symbolism within this card is the most complex of any Major Arcana card thus far. At the center we have the wheel itself. Upon it we see a variety of characters. The outer rim alternates Roman with Hebrew letters. The Hebrew are Yod Heh Vav Heh, representing the most powerful name of the Hebrew god, known as the Tetragrammaton. The remaining four letters may be read beginning with the "T" and ending with the same letter "T" which then spell 'Tarot.' If, on the other hand, you wish to begin with the letter at the nadir, you have 'rota,' which also means wheel. Within the inner circle of the wheel we find symbols drawn from alchemy positioned upon eight spokes which represent the changing and flux of the seasonal tides. What this wheel represents is the presence of very active forces. The seeker is being touched by the flux of the Universe and it seems like change is present everywhere. It is not by coincidence that the Wheel is set against the sky. To the seeker it seems like the events of life are certainly ordained by the heavens.

The center wheel is surrounded by three figures. At the very top we find a blue sphinx. The sphinx guards mysteries and, interestingly, holds a sword to show us that it is a keeper of truth. Even though the wheel is turning, the sphinx is able to sit comfortably without being thrown off. This reminds the seeker that, in the midst of what may seem like chaos, the calm, mysterious center will open one to a deeper understanding of the Universal Truths which permeate change.

The yellow serpent moving down the left side can be interpreted in many different ways. Some see the snake as something to be feared, something which represents the temptation of the flesh. It is the reaction of one's ego when the seeker begins moving forward upon the path toward wisdom and seeks to assert itself. In the process, the ego separates itself from union with the Divine. There is both attraction and repulsion within this symbol. With care, it is also a path toward wisdom. The seeker is advised to avoid making choices based purely upon attraction and upon what appeals to the ego.

The red figure is Anubis, a jackal-headed man. Anubis is a guide for souls, helping them move safely into the afterlife following the death of the body. This figure is often linked with destruction, but not in a negative sense. Moving forward to embrace the future requires some destruction of one's past. The combination of all three figures teach us much about change. There are various aspects of polarity present. There is much activity which requires stepping back rather than being swept away in the whirlwind. There are some aspects of death (e.g. 'letting go') which will be important in moving through this vortex of energy with the brass ring of success firmly in one's hand. Indeed, this card (the eleventh if we count The Fool as the first) completes the first half of the Major Arcana. The World (the twenty first) completes the second half and the two may favourably be compared. Should one learn the wisdom being offered by The Wheel of Fortune, one may gain great insight into the mysteries of The World.

Both The World and The Wheel of Fortune have the four elements depicted in the four corners of the card. They are shown in The Wheel of Fortune each holding a book. The High Priestess also holds a 'book' which contains all of the wisdom in each of these four (plus more). Yet, each elemental creature's book contains all of the wisdom necessary to understand and manifest the existence of that element. Each elemental text contains all knowledge needed for that element to exist in harmony with the other three. Each of these four books holds all knowledge of the relationship of that element to the pure spirit of the Universe. Each elemental being holds that book which embraces the entire magickal lore for the realm of its element.

In the upper left, we see seated a winged human figure for Aquarius. This figure, comfortably up, above the Wheel, represents the element of air. To her right is a winged eagle, representing the height of perfection of Scorpio, which signifies the purity of water. At the bottom left, we see resting a winged bull. This Taurean figure symbolizes the patience of earth. The winged lion at the lower right shows us Leo, representing the element of fire. If the seeker is able to expand the learning process, gaining knowledge of life within each of the four elements, great progress can be made. These wings show us that the elemental forces are certainly active within the astral, and that much spiritual wisdom is available if one but stops to contemplate the meaning of life rather than rushing off to tilt at windmills or getting loss in the glitter of gold. The wings further symbolize that the wisdom of these four elemental creatures is illusive. The knowledge in these books will not easily be perceived by our physical eyes.

But what does this mean from a practical perspective? Air represents the intellectual knowledge. A solid mental understanding will be needed. Water represents the emotional aspects of the self. No matter what is taking place during this time, the seeker needs to learn how to keep his emotions from interfering in a calm decision, learning to use the deeper emotional self to aspire to embrace change and growth as a means of moving forward toward spiritual evolution. Earth is teaching the seeker the importance of patience, the value of avoiding rash behavior. The bull is reading the value of stepping back and viewing the changes of life from a perspective of one's entire existence, rather than seeking immediate gratification. Fire represents passion and enthusiasm, the sustenance of one's will. This energy is not designed to stoke one's ego but to achieve one's Highest Ideals. If the seeker is able to embrace the lessons offered by The Wheel of Fortune, his life will be in balance and centered despite the flux of change. The spiritual energy which is available from the very core of the Universe will expand and manifest within reality aided by these metaphorical four elements.

When The Wheel of Fortune appears in a reading, the seeker is alerted to this time being a period not only of change but of the appearance of opportunities. The reality is that there is not just one 'brass ring,' but that there may seem to be many manifestations of opportunity taking place. Things in life may seem to be manifesting quite rapidly, or appearing out of nowhere. One of the hidden Mysteries of this card is that we need to keep strong our sense of humour during these ups and downs of life. There is little the seeker can do to change the course of events, although she can do much to develop the knowledge and wisdom necessary to snatch the brass rings of choice. Stay humble and maintain good humour. Letting one's ego rear out of control is a sure way to tempt destiny. The gods have placed the Wheel in motion. You cannot stop it. Arrogance will surely encourage them to speed up the Wheel or bring it to a crashing halt. Relax. Enjoy your ride. You may not be able to change the Wheel, but you have within your control your ability to affect the results.

The seeker must pay attention to all four elements. Any one of them could be holding the key to the best opportunities. This is a time to pay attention to the maturity of one's thought processes, to the manner in which one's emotions manifest. Pay heed to your deepest desires, to what creates fears and to that which impels you to move forward. There is a great amount of good luck and opportunity available but one of the lessons is that you must be careful in choosing your goals. As the saying goes, 'be careful of what you wish for ... or you might get it.' In other words, stepping back to give yourself time for contemplation regarding the meaning of life means rethinking your goals and thinking far into the future about any change in your path. The forces of what we call karma are very active when this card appears.

Remind the seeker that it will 'seem' as if life is moving too fast. This is inherent in The Wheel of Fortune. Because this flow of energy arises out of the Universe, we have no control over it. The seeker will not be able to stop it. What is important is not the turning of the Wheel. What matters is the manner in which the seeker handles herself during this period of time. Good fortune will be plentiful yet may seem to constantly slip back out of one's grasp. Golden opportunities may seem to be appearing over the horizon only to disappear. Keep yourself in good spiritual health, live with positive ethical values, grow and learn as the Wheel has taught us and your awareness of life's potential will greatly expand. Do not count on luck or upon the goodness of others to bring you successfully through this period of time. Rely upon yourself. Willingly embrace any trials or lessons the Universe offers you. Stay adaptable. Making changes within the self is often the key which allows the seeker to find that destiny which will be bringing one to a golden horizon, the brass ring firmly in hand.

The Reversed Wheel of Fortune

When this card is reversed, take a calm, deep breath and remind yourself that it is not The Tower card. Reality and the wisdom of the Universe are attempting to confront you with your own folly, to show you where your wisdom is lacking. This may often seem like a 'reality check,' an event or series of events which bring you back down to earth. The brass ring you thought you were holding may have slipped away, never to be recovered. But don't falter and become lost in feeling sorry for yourself.

With a healthy attitude and a willingness to learn, the reversed Wheel of Fortune need only represent a minor setback. Avoid the temptation of retreating into delusions, of placing responsibility for the setback upon others or upon life. The truth is that you were poorly prepared. Your work was insufficient and you are reaping your own karma. Do your best to learn quickly and get on with life.

It is important to note that the interpretation of this reversed card may vary from deck to deck. In some decks the reversed Wheel indicates an even greater hazard, cautioning that the lessons being taught the seeker will be very hard, indeed.

The Magickal Wheel of Fortune

This card represents a pure flow of energy. Although nonsexual, it is a highly active magick and can move into manifestations either as dreams or nightmares. You are dealing with pure, instant karma and must function as an adept.

Herbes to promote the wisdom of this card would include agrimony, horehound, magnolia, myrrh, oak or saffron. Jupiter is the planet associated with this card and offers the student of Tarot magick valuable insight. If one is going to work with The Wheel of Fortune to improve one's lot in life, to bring about more opportunities, it would best be done in order to improve one's ability to bring benevolence to others. Working the magick of this card to serve one's own needs is not the wisest approach. It tempts the Universe to teach us lessons we may not wish to learn at this time. Stones which can further the magick of this card are amethyst, diamond and malachite. Copper is also associated with the good fortune of this card. Think of the lore surrounding the finding of a penny and that penny representing good luck.

From the ritual perspective, other than the sphinx's sword, there are no ritual tools present. however the four elements are present in a very active state. This might be perceived as the process of invoking the Four Watchtowers. The concept of the 'Four Watchtowers' refers to the elemental energy which has been brought into a ritual space. Although we do not see a human figure who appears to be trained in ritual, the magick of this card is very much like the Cone of Power, that swirling vortex of active energy which arises out of the center of a well-worked ritual. The magick itself is neither good nor bad. The very cauldron of the Universe is amoral.

The open books of the four elements advise the student that learning is an important key to success. It might be wise to expand one's skills, to further one's knowledge before taking any active step to create this energy in one's life. The ritual student and adept have some advantages in working the magick of The Wheel of Fortune: the ritual circle is not unlike a metaphysical gyroscope which provides stability during the chaos, a chaos which can spin off the vortex of energy. The difficult issue for the magickal Wheel of Fortune is in letting go of 'timing.' Only the Universe will be able to determine the 'when' of manifestation. That timing will be closely related to your growth and progress toward your Highest Ideals. Asking the Universe to bring this magick into your life also asks for any trials and lessons which are necessary to mature you and shake you free of that which is holding you back. It remains for the magickal student to work this card as chaos leading to harmony, a work which requires astute caution.

XI - Strength

Leo

Strength, as mentioned earlier, is the eighth card in the majority of modern decks but here is eighth. She appears as a vision of simplicity with her faithful companion, the mighty lion. In the distance behind her we see the mountain, showing us that this card offers us a path toward perfection and enlightenment. Strength wears a plain white robe, unadorned with the embroidered symbols of those figures representing worldly power. Her power is found within the spiritual values of life. The symbol of infinity above her head, which we also saw in The Magician, reminds the interpreter of her wisdom and virtue. Although she does not appear as an initiated Priestess, she has unrestrained knowledge of the Mysteries.

She wears garlands of flowers and leaves in her hair and about her waist. They drape her figure with symbols of fertility, of a knowledge of the ways of natural magick, of nature and of growing things within the earth, all of which lead to an assurance of fruitfulness in the seeker's life. Strength embodies the virtue of the demure, gentle feminine principle in life. She is as gentle as the lion is masculine, for the beast represents the presence of passionate, primal energies.

Look carefully and observe the interaction between the lion and Strength, between the physical and the spiritual. They represent the interaction of the polarities, of the masculine, yang energy and the feminine, yin energy. They have been brought together and the manner in which this occurred has led to happiness and pleasure. The lion is so content that his tail is relaxed and his tongue extended, sensually licking her hand. Strength, on the other hand, is caressing the creature. They are free in their exchange of physical contact. Neither exhibits any of the negative possibilities of life. They are joined in mutual enjoyment of their affection, respect and ability to work together.

Strength often appears in a reading when the seeker is to experience a test, when a situation challenges the seeker to make progress in bringing together the spiritual and the physical forces within her own life. When facing a divine test of this nature, the wisdom offered us through this card will change our lives. If we handle these lessons well, the path which leads to the very summit of the mountain will unfold before us. No matter what demands life places upon us, a patient and loving equilibrium will surely be ours. The solution to the trial lies through better integrating our spiritual beliefs and practices into our daily lives.

It is also possible that this challenge is to impel the seeker to accomplish a similar balance between the conscious mind and the subconscious mind, perhaps learning to become more sensitive, opening one's personality and behavior so that intuition may become integrated into one's life. The conscious mind and the subconscious mind are much like the partnership between the woman and the lion. One's ego can be as dominant as the lion, wanting its 'roar' to be heard throughout the land. When you hear a person verify the accuracy of their intuition through failure to observe it ("I *knew* I should have trusted it...") it is the ego which had been unable to trust.

There are virtues to be learned through this card. The lion represents strength. Although this card recommends that the seeker allow the gentle side to tame the beast, this does not decrease the lion's strength at all. Among the Mysteries of this card is the wisdom that balancing the dominant, aggressive side of one's being with the gentle, receptive side allows the lion-like ego to become far stronger. This function of the ego leads to an increase in will power and is the force which will carry them to the mountain's top. When both parts of our nature work together, there is not only a peacefulness born of this balance but there is inner joy, reflected in this card as the affection between the two.

Strength does not see the dominant aspects of ego as wrong. These desires arise out of the incarnate condition of human nature. They are the animal counterpart to the anima, or soul. The king of the jungle will truly be lord of the realm when attention is given to the spiritual side, when these two functions of personality have been reconciled and both given their role in life. Appearing in a layout, this card indicates the importance of maintaining a strength of character, of being true to one's Highest Ideals. The seeker's ego is not being dominated by another human being and there are occasions when this card turns up to admonish a seeker to maintain a strong sense of self, to avoid being dominated by another. The seeker is admonished to follow the path through Strength in order to successfully pass through these ordeals.

What are the virtues of the woman? She has been very patient, in counterpart to the lion's tendency to be impatient. This is a further aspect of the infinity symbol she wears almost as a crown. The path to success through Strength requires the passage of time (but don't expect the Universe to tell you just how much). Through her persistence the lion has learned that he can trust her. The timeless quality of one's spiritual essence tames the savage nature of the ego's beast. Strength has been willing to demonstrate both her courage and her compassion. Upon occasion this card arises in a reading when the situation is like the beast and the seeker must embody the virtues of Strength. In those situations, no matter how much one's ego wants to take strong action, the path to victory will be through internal patience matched with a gentle attitude. Remind yourself, this approach did not harm the lion, it brought him affection. No matter how much the seeker's ego may want to roar, even to attack through wounded pride, in this card it is not the animal strength but the strength of the woman's character which has dominated.

The animal side of the self is represented as the masculine, yang side of the self. This is primal energy, not always willing to listen to reason, often preferring to react by projecting its ego louder than anyone else's. Through the gentle touch of Strength, this primal magick can be transformed into a most sublime type of energy, one which provides impetus to the achievement of one's most difficult dreams. Great strength can be derived from the feminine, yin side of the self. When these two are integrated and balanced, the end result is much like alchemy: the final product is larger and more perfect than the sum of both parts.

And what of the lion? There is a quality of sacrifice being taught the seeker by the lion. In setting aside the ego's desire to dominate the seeker's life (and, perhaps, the lives of others as well) courage is called for. The lion comes to terms with the inner, emotional self and becomes aware of his responsibility for all actions, no longer placing that responsibility upon others. By an attunement to the inner, spiritual self, self-awareness is expanded and becomes far more acute. The tendency toward the animal side is sacrificed in order to achieve unity within the self. It is not that the lion is dominated nor is the lion, itself, sacrificed. The element of sacrifice exists only in as much as is needed to achieve perfect balance. The sacrifice of the dominant ego is matched by the sacrifice of time offered by the gentle, spiritual self. In exchange, the primal aspect will emerge in sublime ways and, ultimately, the pride one's ego will feel will be justified and of an enduring quality.

The path to the top of the mountain is not an easy one. It represents the lessons involved in setting aside self-gratification, self-grandeur, and pursuing goals for one's Highest Ideals. Although difficult, it leads to great pleasure in life. Strength - true strength - can only survive into the far distant future when it is resilient, made flexible by spiritual values.

Reversed Strength

This card will often appear reversed if the seeker has been unsuccessful in completing a test of his spiritual beliefs. Rather than having found a healthy balance, the easier path was taken, falling prey to the desires of the physical world or sacrificing one's spiritual beliefs in order to appease the ego. What may have seemed like a victory at the time leaves the seeker unfulfilled because his spirit is left wanting.

It is time to give pause and provide nourishment for the spiritual self and time to tame the beast. If the seeker is feeling pride, it needs a gentle and loving self-evaluation. If the truth be known, what occurred is not something to be proud of. Consider what the ego has wrought from the perspective of your Highest Ideals, but do not do so in a condemnatory, judgmental manner. Your conscience should be garbed in the simple robes of Strength, knowing that it takes time to bring a loving, domestic quality to the beast. This is, truly, an opportunity to live the maxim "to err is human, to forgive divine," and apply it to yourself. The lion cannot be conquered through domination nor through castigation. It will only, at a later time to the dismay of your inner self, rebel and go off on a rampage.

Reversed Strength indicates that there is a thorn in your metaphorical paw. Something has gotten in the way of your ego, rendering it unable to feel the sense of joy and pride it so desires. It may feel mistreated by others or it may be mistreating your own spiritual needs and desires. When Strength appears reversed, it is important that the seeker restore balance before the lack of internal stability leads to a loss of health. No matter how strong the seeker may feel about herself, there is a thorn waiting. Reversed Strength indicates that the path will lead to unhappy, humbling circumstances unless balanced, self-control is restored.

Magickal Strength

The magick of Strength is drawn from the sublime quality of pure, primal energy. The natural energies of this card might be thought of as gentle passion, or a passionate gentility. It is born out of allowing one's primal side to have great freedom because one is responsible both with actions and with one's emotions as well.

The magickal approach to this card could include angelica, bay, rue or sunflower, herbes associated with Leo. As one might expect, the feline aspect of Leo's lion also enjoys working with catnip. Sage is another herbe with which to enhance the magick of this card. The wise practitioner would choose either peridot or ruby as preferred stones. Then again, the cat's eye might be what is needed. Scott Cunningham considers the garnet appropriate.

Strength provides the occult student with a bridge to both worlds. So many who approach spiritual development falsely believe it requires rejection of sensual pleasure. Strength teaches us that magick is a blend of the animal and of the Divine. Within the arms of the Universe, neither is better. This card offers a path to transcendence, when sexuality is matched with spirituality and both are uninhibited and both are consistent with one's Highest Ideals.

Whether or not this card is emulated within the context of ritual depends upon the student's path. There are no visible ritual tools. The tools are internal. Patience and passion are the polarities brought together whether they are found within ritual partners or merged within the self.

When the practitioner works with sexual magick, the energies to invoke would be sensual and warm, as if to make one's soul purr like the gentle side of the lion. One might pause prior to orgasm in order to enjoy the sensuality of what is taking place, bringing the gentleness of time and patience to balance the physical drive and hunger for release. The divine nature of the Universe is blended with the animal nature of manifest, tangible reality. One's approach should be loving and accepting of both aspects of the self, taking time to enjoy the pleasure of the moment and to seek the deeper spiritual reality within. A genuinely balanced approach to this magick will lead to a greater understanding of some of the deepest Mysteries of the Universe.

XII - The Hanged Man

Neptune

People frequently misinterpret The Hanged Man when their logic trips over the name of the card and ignores the beauty of its image. The figure in the card has placed the mundane activities of his life in suspension so that he may contemplate the meaning of his life as he hangs inverted from the living tree which represents the structure of his spiritual belief system.

The Hanged Man has placed himself into a yogic position in order to observe and contemplate what is taking place within himself before he returns to the outer world of activity. He has intentionally made it impossible for himself to be distracted by the world and its activities.

There is little to distract us when we gaze at this image. The Hanged Man, his head to the ground and the living tree which suspends him, are the sole images. Once again, as with the previous card, we see the mystery of time. An important lesson inherent in this card is the patience required, for one must embrace the time spent waiting as we contemplate the inner workings of life. Only when the answer has arrived may we return back to the world of action.

During the time spent in contemplation, the day-to-day activities of the Hanged Man have been suspended. He has reordered his priorities. The Hanged Man placed those daily demands of his life on hold. He cannot 'do' anything. He knows that he cannot change the situation at hand but he is able to take control over the manner in which he handles it. He is not communicating with others. He is not going to work nor carrying on other life activities, for he is placing all of his attention into the internal movement of energy as he contemplates the process of letting go. This period of silence and quiet is important, for the ideas he

THE HANGED MAN.

finds within himself have not yet finished gestating and are not yet ready to be manifested. We see through this the correspondence with Neptune, for the wheel of life must continue to turn as the Hanged Man continues to learn the process through which dreams are made manifest. This is an essential understanding before the work of creating within the world of reality is undertaken.

The manner in which the Hanged Man's hands are placed behind his back is reminiscent of a position used in some traditions of initiation. Seeking to become one with the Universe, the Hanged Man is to become a vessel of wisdom, a vehicle through which enlightenment may manifest and, in the process, he will be transformed. To accomplish this elevated goal he knows that he, himself, must become changed, transformed through the principle of sacrifice. Willing to make sacrifices in order to have this sacred time, freedom and control have been set aside in order for the seeker to become a passive vessel, dependent solely upon one's own spiritual beliefs.

When this card appears in a layout it is not uncommon for the seeker to claim that she hasn't the time to set aside life's demands. She may feel that her responsibilities are more important than her inner growth. Always take the Hanged Man seriously. When this card is turned up, the time must be taken. One's ego must make this sacrifice for the survival of one's dreams.

The Reversed Hanged Man

The image of the reversed Hanged Man shows that the ego and its desires have been placed above himself on the tree of wisdom. The seeker has placed himself above his spiritual ideals. Typically, the card in this position is a warning that the person is ignoring her spiritual beliefs.

A strong and direct omen has appeared in the reading. The seeker is in violation of his own ethical beliefs and will be moving toward certain failure. In its balanced (upright) position, one is held securely by the strong support of a solid belief system, pondering the present and the future. But in the reversed position, we see that the security of those beliefs has been removed and any visions one might encounter are not to be trusted.

This card can be restored to its upright position if the seeker is willing to do the necessary work. We must encourage an immediate change, a willingness to embrace the wisdom and lessons embodied by the Hanged Man. A failure to make these corrections will inevitably lead one toward the pain of failure.

The Magickal Hanged Man

In the image of The Hanged Man we clearly see a figure who is moving great forces of energy within herself. Not overtly sexual, this is more the energy which is that of tantric studies. Sexual activity is but one of many activities set aside, sacrificed until a future time. And yet within the chakras of the body the energy is activated, the polarities brought together in order to work with the kundalini.

Were the Hanged Man to burn incense, it might well be composed of fern or lotus. Corresponded with the planet Neptune, the gemstone associated with this card is turquoise. Gems and herbes would be used to better understand the principles and ethics involved in learning to bring one's dreams into manifestation.

There are no ritual tools visible other than that which is the greatest: the mind. The traditional 'pillars' are implied and we might well imagine that the Hanged Man is working with the ritual form of the Middle Pillar, that wonderful disciplined exercise of visualization and sound. His is a quest, the seeking of a vision. His is a work which may be considered not too dissimilar from the vision quest of a shaman.

The Hanged Man's mind has been opened to allow her to sort out the mundane. All thoughts of her job, of her 'things,' of other earthly matters have been allowed to tumble down to the mundane level of reality. Her entire being, body and soul, is fully open to the spiritual processes at hand.

If there is to be any ritual work, it has taken place prior to this activity. This is the time of meditation, of moving into the astral. The Hanged Man is seeking the answer from within, opening his dreams, seeking the information from his dreams. This is a passive, gentle process. He is able to draw upon the energy of the Universe which is to be utilized for other than physical activity. He is not drawing substance from the earth. It is to be assumed that he is fasting. It is, however, possible that the ritual has been worked to create sacred space and he is now within that sacred Circle. In its simplest form, this card might represent sleeping within the boundaries of your Circle as you pursue information in a dream quest.

When it is time for you to take the path of the Hanged Man, remember that most of the work to be done lies in all the preparation beforehand. The Hanged Man has made many arrangements so that she is not distracted by those activities now suspended as she herself is also suspended from her personal Tree of Life.

XIII - Death

Scorpio

The **Death** card card is certain to send tingles traveling the spines of those who only see this card by its name. Those with a discerning eye pay more attention to the two towers which frame the rising sun. The towers appear later in The Moon, reminiscent of the symbolism of the two pillars. There are beautiful mountain spires representing the attainment of goals and dreams for those who remember to turn toward the light.

The figure of Death dominates the scene, an oftentimes frightening image for those who are not versed in the Mysteries. Riding a beautiful, white horse, Death is garbed in fine armor, bearing a large staff from which flies a banner with a white flower symbolizing purity. Embrace even a metaphorical death when pure of heart and you will fully know the joys of rebirth.

Death is passing through and this stage in one's life which has felt like death is now ending. Death's horse is restless and will be moving on. This card indicates that the person is undergoing a transition, evolving from one state of awareness to another. Death is a dramatic card as well it should be. The changes in one's life patterns or lifestyle from these transitions should be significant. At the least there should be a major level of transformation in one's world view. It is not possible to be visited by this card in a reading and have one's life remain unaffected.

This period in the seeker's life requires letting go. There must be some death of the personality, of the conscious mind, so that the inner self might rise with the radiant sun. Death is here to announce that the past must be left behind. Death's banner announces the new rising.

The human figures in the card are so involved in the emotional reaction to this symbolic death that they are unaware of the ship sailing down the river. They represent the sense of loss that has rendered the seeker dysfunctional. Those who have not adequately matured are stricken with grief over the situation. Similarly, the immediate friends and family of the seeker may also be grieving over the seeker's loss of vitality, the perceived loss of interest in the joys of life. The religious figure stands in clerical robes, hands gloved to protect the secrecy of the Mysteries, offering consolation more to the living while seeking the spiritual evolution within the spirit of the seeker, represented by the figure laying upon the ground. This is not a burial. Although the prone figure may seem to be dead, no grave has been dug, the body has not been embalmed nor placed into a coffin. No matter how desirable the reality of death might seem, this is not the ending time of one's incarnation.

Even as the ship is sailing, life has continued to move forward. The rivers of the spiritual life force are waiting to be crossed. Atop the escarpment a path appears to lead to the sunrise. Soon the entire landscape will be filled with the glowing sunlight. As the sun rises, the new dawn will emerge which represents a new era in one's life. In order for the new day to replace the night, one must have descended into that darkness. That descent is much of which this card speaks. The seeker is dealing with deep, internal forces and has spent time moving into the inner self, so deep as to transcend the nature of this incarnation in order to now be ready to reclaim a sense of innocence which will be embraced at the rebirthing. Despite Death moving across the landscape, the growing sunlight heralds the arrival of the rebirth. And the seeker, having spent time internally, may now return to the work of activity. She has the opportunity to affect the outcome.

To bring the greatest spiritual growth into your life when this card manifests, the process of 'letting go' must be embraced. You are being offered a choice and may either remain in the foreground, caught up by your grieving and sadness, or you may climb upon the horse and allow Death to transport you across the abyss to embrace the light. There is much joy to be found in this card - but only when one remembers the Mysteries. Shed your fears, remain mindful of the light and embrace the unknown. This is a time to be calm and trusting, for you are being transported by the loving hand of the Universe. By allowing aspects of your old self to die, you may now experience a greater sense of unity with the Divine than ever before.

Reversed Death

When the Death card appears reversed, you are likely to be feeling much of what accompanies this card in its usual position, but are holding yourself back from being able to perceive the rising sun. In this position Death indicates such qualities as lethargy, stagnation, inertia and boredom, a boredom so strong that it feels like death. The seeker is suffering from a sense of failure and is likely to be sinking into a depression caused by the lack of momentum in his life. Change is essential and must be initiated. Bringing this card back into its upright position will bring one face to face with the joys of that rising sun.

Magickal Death

How would one describe the natural magick of this card? At first glance it would seem that there is an absence of sexual energy until one remembers that a white horse is frequently a symbol of a vibrant, sexual strength. When Death is indicative of a difficult situation in one's mundane life the woes may well depress one's sexual interests. But when one actively embraces this card in order to bring about the images of death and of rebirth, sexuality is not necessarily removed. Do not allow yourself to believe that the Crone is past sexual joy. Death is often perceived as solitary and yet, within the ancient myths of our ancestors we learn otherwise. Those legends tell of the rebirth of the life forces in the spring. Mother Nature descends into the Underworld at Hallows and, during the dark, wintery months, embraces the Mysteries with Death and makes love with Death, ensuring continuity in the endless circles of life.

What correspondences might we explore for so potent a card? The herbe of choice would be basil, an herbe used to empower those seeking death and rebirth, whether through Initiation or at the hand of the Universe. The other herbe strongly associated with this card is belladonna, an herbe best used without allowing its constituents access to your body. Whereas basil may safely be ingested, belladonna's magick can be accessed through growing the plant, placing its shiny dark fruit upon your altar as an offering, or working with images of the plant in order to commune with its deva (its plant spirit).

Drawing upon the depths of the Mysteries, there can be no doubt that Scorpio is the astrological correspondence. Gemstones associated with the Death card include jet, lapis lazuli and sardonyx. Malachite and tiger's eye have also been connected with this card.

The Mysteries of this card are, I believe, more easily embraced when one intentionally moves into the Magick of Death. When caught up by the mundane lessons of life when this card is turned up, we may feel that death is preferable to the stagnation of one's life. A seeker may be unable to see her way past the inertia of the figure lying upon the ground. But to embrace change, to see the death of the past and be reborn of the light? When adepts speak of bliss and ecstasy, these are the Mysteries which have touched their souls.

And how has Death prepared for this ritual? In this image Death carries the ritual staff, that tool which functions much as the ritual wand but is carried by those who guide others toward increased wisdom and knowledge. The staff bears a banner upon which is the five-petalled flower of purity. Some artists depict death carrying a ritual blade, usually a scythe with its lunar sliver of sharpness in place of the banner.

Any ritual working should be somewhat stark and devoid of trappings. Certainly an invocation of the Crone (which can be of either gender) is essential. One must also have a willingness to move through death as metaphor and mystery. If the ritual work is to embrace sexual power as well, know that the pursuit of sexual energy creates death of some other areas of life. All work being done in this sacred space and sacred time leads to a recreation of death and rebirth for this is a card of transition: strong and fertile.

What might you choose to work with? In the grand scale one might enact a symbolic burial or entombment. You must remove yourself from the mundane in order to develop the ritual, to plan and prepare for it. You must set aside time. Remove yourself from light, from the Sun and embrace the darkness of the night. While we do not recommend burying yourself in soil, taking one's self into solitude is essential. Spending time among the trees in a tent is but one way to provide this.

The ritual duration should be substantial, at the least a matter of days. Fasting and any other processes which further the sense of change are important. Choose your sense of timing. One might recreate the process of death with the actual ritual incorporating the rising sunlight and the rebirth beginning as one steps into the Circle. Work with the Mysteries of Death with great care for they are potent and should be undertaken only by those who wish to bring about a profound change of life.

XIV - Temperance

Sagittarius

In this image, the figure of **Temperance** stands both upon the fertile land where grow iris and in the watery abyss. We see, emerging from those mystical waters, a path which leads to the distant mountains of wisdom and experience. Unlike the path as it appears in many other cards, this is a direct and easy journey toward those sacred elevations. Upon those faraway peaks one may have an encounter with the Divine. Indeed, the shape of the sun, itself, suggests that we are viewing events during an eclipse. Tempting though it may be to pursue the thrill of the journey, the seeker is shown that the path of this card is to work with the divine within one's self. The Temperance card represents that spiritual awareness found through the maturing of one's own life.

Temperance stands in both worlds, one foot resting upon the shore, the other dipping into the mystical waters. Her figure offers us a lesson, reminding us that our lives unfold in both worlds and that we must nourish both as well. Our realities are created not only from the sticks and mortar of the physical, manifest world, but from the fluid realms of our dreams and desires as well. Temperance draws from the fertility of the land, represented by the spring flowers of the iris yet what supports her are the waters of the astral. Looking at her image in the card you can readily see upon which foot rests her weight.

Temperance's entire being is depicted as symbolic of the spiritual realm from her foot in the water to the energy radiating from her head. She wears a ritual robe, one unadorned with the finery of society required by the work of the High Priestess, and she is winged, for her journeys are of the spirit.

Her weight rests primarily upon that foot which is in the water as the waters of life are poured from one chalice to the other, moving in both directions at the same time. This is the passage of time and of dreams. This is the flow of one's reality. Only the chalices of one's dreams are present: Temperance has no need for the Magician's altar nor the High Priestess's throne. With Temperance, magick will be worked through restraint for, so long as one is patient and takes joy in the passage of time, the changes needed in your life will manifest.

The nature of the virtue temperance is that of moderation and restraint. The garland around Temperance's hair, gathering at the solar symbol, combines with the energy radiating from her head. Clearly indicated by Pamela Colman Smith's illustration is that this magnificent, winged being is one of purity and divinity.

As the water pours from one chalice to the other it is being purified by the very presence of Temperance. She alone is enough to bring harmony and balance to her environment. The chalices, Tarot symbols of emotion, are held in perfect balance and, along with her posture, indicate that she is in control not only of her thoughts and emotions, but also of her self and her environment. Perhaps the beautiful, outstretched wings are the source of such poise!

The wisdom reflected by Temperance is that borne of patience, of observation and learning. Temperance has learned to transcend the youthful desire to rush forward. Whereas the unenlightened would hasten toward the eclipse, seeking divinity from an external force, Temperance is fully aware of all aspects of the Divine, and she manifests it through her very being.

Rather than the gratifications of immediate action, Temperance views reality in cycles larger than even her own incarnation. As a consequence, she is able to adapt to the ebb and flow of life, making changes as needed so as to work with (rather than against) the will of the Universe. As Temperance continues to sustain mental focus and concentration, the activity is of the internal energy, the manifestation of one's dreams.

Temperance represents the virtues of cooperation and understanding, knowing that the path to success is that found by working in partnership with the Universe. When this card appears in a layout, Temperance counsels the seeker that the work to be done is internal, is within the spiritual self. Action within the physical world is to remain on hold until one has manifested the virtues of this card.

Reversed Temperance

The reversed Temperance card is indicative of a situation in which the goal of spiritual balance may have been supplanted by the desires of the ego for immediate gratification.

The emotional behavior of the ego and its desires for the physical self are in discord with the wisdom of one's spiritual instinct. This leads to disharmony in one's life. The waters no longer flow back and forth and the individual is filled with increasing frustration. As the seeker continues to avoid paying heed to the inner, spiritual self, the ego attempts to force the outcome of the issue. This creates an image for the Universe of a person who believes her desires to be of a greater value than the wisdom of the Divine. Such foolhardy behavior will ensure that the Universe will teach the seeker some lessons.

Poor management of one's life will lead to sorry times. When this card appears in the reverse position, the seeker is warned that it is essential to make change within one's self, without delay. Temperance is to be one's role model. We ought not place ourselves in positions of power which are not merited.

Magickal Temperance

The natural energy of this card is, for the present, removed from the pleasures of life. The wings imply nonsexual activity although certainly, sensuality may very well be present. The spirit of the polarities of masculine (yang) and feminine (yin) must be controlled and directed through a trained, inner spiritual self.

Herbes and botanicals which may be used in conjunction with this card include dill, flag, iris, parsley and sage. A gemologist might choose among azurite, lapis, garnet or turquoise.

Although the astrological correspondence of Sagittarius is not noted for its patience and moderation, that lesson is at the heart of the magick of Temperance. The wise Sagittarian who learns this virtue can manifest her greatest dreams. Her life knows no boundaries.

In bringing the mysteries of this card to your ritual work, note that the chalices are the only ritual tools. The posture of this figure shows us that the work to be done is that from the astral and, if we note the breastplate upon her ritual robe, it would seem appropriate that this be a Hermetic type of ritual or perhaps one drawing upon the arts of the Asian systems, working within to balance Yin and Yang. Upon the square representing the balance of the four elements of air, fire, water and earth we see the triangle, representing the manifestation of the Divine, of dreams being brought into reality.

Although the magick is to manifest in both worlds, the ritual is best worked from within the cast Circle, where the polarities have met within the self and are conjoined. The role model presented for us is one in which we learn to balance the mundane with the spiritual, working within both worlds simultaneously. All ritual gestures and choreography should be worked with patience, performed with care. Deliberate actions require poise and balance. Nothing, not a word, not a breath, should be rushed.

XV - The Devil

Capricorn

If there is any card in the Tarot which convinces fundamentalists that the Tarot is the work of the devil, this is the card in which they see Satan. The Devil is a very misunderstood card yet the word 'devil' is used commonly in the very situations which can apply in this scenario. Sometimes life can be 'devilish.' There are many who bedevil themselves and bedevil others.

The couple we see in this may well have been the Lovers, a card which represents the nature of choice. In The Devil we can see that the choices made have become shackles. Although both the man and woman could easily represent fertility (note the crescent horns, the grapes on the woman's 'tail' and the fire on that of the man), they are now chained to a pedestal upon which is the symbol of their greed.

THE DEVIL .

The hand positions of this demonic figure echo what we saw earlier in The Magician. However, Waite and Smith show us a wonderful bit of symbolism. Whereas the Magician held his wand aloft, here the wand is lowered, the flames upon its end a reflection of the flame at the male figure's tail. What does this represent? Perhaps this is the burning passion of compulsion or of obsession. The Devil card represents all aspects of temptation. By having placed themselves willingly into their own bondage, the humans can no longer resist. They have lost control over their desires.

Should this card be turned up in your reading, the Devil card represents many of your own inner demons. Lurking within the caverns of the dark regions, the bat wings seem appropriate. Here is the 'devil' created from the internal darkness of a soul which set aside its higher ideals in favor of materialism, greed or the demands of one's carnal ego. How much easier it is for people to place the blame for our self-imposed miseries upon some external lost deity such as the Christian devil! But the Tarot speaks to our need to take responsibility for our own actions.

This card represents those who can not resist temptation. These individuals are compelled to continue upon this path, even though it takes them toward their own unhappiness. Few will be able to correct the course without outside help, such as that from a professional. The figures are in such bondage to their carnal desires that what was once a dream or fantasy has become an ever-present nightmare.

What is a throne for spiritual and religious persons and icons in the other cards is, in The Devil, an altar to one's greed. For many, the pursuit of money or the cravings of lust become a divinity. The Tarot warns them that setting aside wisdom and balance risks ending up in shackles.

The Devil is not a fatalistic card. Should it appear in a reading it is a strong warning. Yet no matter how strong one may believe those chains to be, the seeker is still held in bondage to his desires only because he is unwilling to let go. Continuing on this path brings destructive forces into one's life and the sense of burden will only increase. The seeker has willingly placed herself here. She will be dragged through hell unless the pedestal is replaced with the altar of one's Highest Ideals.

Some authors view the devilish figure as a representation of the animalistic desires which have transcended the spiritual needs of the seeker. In the Christian perception this may be seen as the fallen angel who chose to fall. This 'devil' may genuinely believe that the pursuit of the dark side will ultimately lead to the evolution of one's self. While not philosophically impossible, for the general public The Devil of the Tarot speaks to those who suffer the shackles of their self-indulgent material passions. The average person draws security from the chains and clings to her unhappy ways, unwilling to take responsibility and embrace change. The reality of this image is that the chains could easily be removed if one was but willing to take the first step. They could be lifted right over one's head should a person choose to set himself free. The first step requires recreating the internal images of that which we worship, of replacing the self-destructive with that which leads to spiritual health and growth.

The Reversed Devil

The Devil is not an easy card to read in its reversed position. According to many, the meaning is not so different as before. In many decks the reversed position indicates that, despite the presence of the shackles, they have not been riveted shut. The potential for restoring emotional, mental and spiritual health and wellness is considered greater than if The Devil were in the upright position.

The majority view is that the reversed position is not as severe. This indicates that the potential for breaking free of one's own devil is more possible, despite one's preference for the dark, negative side. There is also the view that the reversed card may indicate that some test will be forthcoming, that events may prove to be the catalyst enabling the seeker to turn her life around. It is advisable to check the book or booklet which describes the specific deck you use. The reversed Devil does not have a consistent interpretation among all decks.

The Magickal Devil

Despite the common beliefs regarding the mundane aspects of this card, it represents a body of knowledge which contains very powerful Mysteries. Although certainly not for everyone, those Mysteries are not a path toward evil and are not self-destructive. Now we speak of a very occult path, one which has existed within most religions, but one which is for the very few, for this is a path which is very seductive and can entice the practitioner to become entranced with the pleasures, forgetting that it is only a path which leads to spiritual evolution.

The sexual nature of this card is powerful. Those who might work with this card as a conjunct to sexual magick must be wary. Should one forget to maintain concentration and hold tight to spiritual wisdom, the sexual energy can become overwhelming, the pleasurable aspects so enticing that one can forget that this energy is merely a tool. The pleasure aspects of this sexual magick should never be elevated to the position of the ideal.

It is through this path that one might learn the realities of true "Sex Magick." One of the paths embodied by The Devil in the magickal sense is that of pure, primal lust. The key word is 'pure,' for without this primal purity, the man can become shackled by his gonads, forgetting that this card of sexual magick which yokes the manifest physical to the astral is also a card of caution. This path is alluring. It is also greatly misunderstood and to those of the 'outside' world who do not grasp the potential of these deep Mysteries, this seems surely a quick route to hell.

And yet, this is the card corresponded with Capricorn. It is an arduous path requiring commitment and responsibility. The goals will only be achieved after hard work which must endure far longer than nearly any other path. For those who might choose such a path, an herbe would be asafoetida. Gems include diamond, onyx, lapis lazuli and jet.

From the ritual perspective we see interesting symbols. Although the inverted pentagram was appropriated, in relatively recent times, as a symbol of the Christian Satan, it has long held magickal significance and is not, in and of itself, representative of evil. The inverted pentagram remains an important symbol today in many ritual paths. That pentagram represents a level of work during which one must break free of the shackles of one's own desires, accomplished through placing one's self in bondage to one's highest spiritual ideals. One example of this approach is the level of commitment some take during the vows of their priest/esshood, a contract at the level of one's soul which must transcend even death. For these the ritual wand is able to sustain the flame of creativity and of rebirth.

From a ritual perspective, this card represents the principle of breaking free of one's shackles to the mundane in order to enter the ritual circle. This card may be worked ''as is' but requires extensive training. For the seeker of wisdom through occult mysteries, The Devil may represent working with lust in order to achieve the sublime. The seeker must embrace pure, primal, unbridled animal lust without losing control of the spiritual. One must always remember that lust for lust's sake, brought into a Circle, likely brings destruction.

It becomes essential to transcend the shackled nature of the card. The spiritual work of this card embodies the need to break free of the mundane in order to do ritual. I recommend that you work within a cast Circle. Although you may bring forth the lust, you must ultimately move through it and beyond it. This is a highly active magick. It can be procreative. It can induce change. It can bring forth manifestation.

XVI - The Tower

Mars

The image of The Tower often reminds me of the bell tower of the Episcopal Cathedral in Minneapolis which was struck by lightning. At the time I lived just a few blocks up Oak Grove Avenue and a photograph of the tower with its damaged corner of the beautiful tower in my daily paper would have made a perfect Tarot card!

The symbols of this card are prominent against the dark of night, the same dark background we saw in The Devil. This darkness represents the depths within the seeker's soul, neither positive nor negative forces. And yet it is the constraints of our ego which shackled the seeker to her own devil and it is the folly of the ego which has built a tower to the false god of itself, constructed upon a mountain top. A sense of security exists within this refuge, but it is false security. The crown, toppled by the bolt of lightning, may represent feelings of self satisfaction. The ego believed it had done better than others and was now exempt from hard lessons.

When The Tower appears in a reading the seeker must accept reality. There is nothing which can be done to stop these tower-like events from happening. But we may make changes in how we respond to these unexpected events. What seems like a catastrophe may actually be an opportunity. The brilliant flash of lightning illuminates the sky. The tongues of flame (often interpreted as being variations of the Hebrew letter Yod) represent the presence of a fertile, divine spirit. It is lightning which charges the soil with life-giving energy, which can burn away weeds and brush so that new tree seedlings may take root. When The Tower arrives in one's life, it may sometimes seem like an 'act of God.' Although the Tarot is capable of great divination, not even this card nor those arriving with it in the layout will prepare the seeker for the actual event. Just as a flash of lightning appears out of the sky, startling those beneath, The Tower brings with it a guaranteed element of surprise.

In divinatory work, The Tower often portends unexpected catastrophes. Frequently it is a singular event, one of destruction and reconstruction. Less often it may be a series of events, a pattern of 'lesser Towers' which accomplish the same task. And what is this task? The Tower, in its pre lightning phase, represents the reality of living confined in a tower of one's own construction. The seeker has created an edifice, feeling she has achieved some degree of being above things. It is, in fact, to be expected that the seeker has achieved success or status which is akin to being atop the mountain, upon which this tower stands.

But this monument to one's past has become a place without growth. In the context of the Major Arcana, The Tower follows The Devil with continuity. The seeker is now trapped by the old ways of one's ego. Although one has success, his ego has created an inflexible ivory (or ivy) tower which, over the passage of time, has lost its ability to change. The Universe, in Her wisdom, knows that this bolt out of the blue is essential to break you free.

When The Tower appears in a reading the seeker is likely to react by believing a terrible event will arrive. The figures in this card appear to be falling, but that plunge to the earth is an illusion. You will only 'feel' that you are falling. Your ego and your emotions are likely to respond to the perceived disasters of a lost job or ended relationship. There is more to life than this passing loss. It is important to counsel the seeker that The Tower will only seem terrible until you have stopped and reflected upon the changes with hindsight. Those who are spiritually adept will watch for The Tower and, during the brilliant flash of illumination, look to see all the mountains silhouetted against the horizon. During this divine moment many paths to success are visible. I like to advise people that if they are spiritually balanced and alert, they can land on their 'cat feet' when the tower's collapse seems imminent. But does it collapse? No, only its crown comes tumbling.

The events of The Tower card should be life-changing, a release of old values no longer of use. This is a transformation by fire. The average person may experience panic, not knowing what the future will bring. She will feel out of balance now that the security of her tower has been lost. It is important to let go of attachment to that which is now passing. No matter if your ego feels humbled, The Tower is a card which brings divine blessings. The power of the bolt and its emotional intensity akin to thunder are a test of your spiritual acuity and readiness. The ability to draw upon spiritual and emotional discipline in an instant will bring the seeker divine insight.

The Reversed Tower

Similar to The Tower's usual position, the reversed card means much the same. The card warns that clinging to your old ways and outdated values is likely to lead to a downfall. If there is a difference, perhaps you might think of this as a 'smaller' tower. The seeker is not likely to fall so hard. Some decks indicate that, when reversed, the seeker might have the ability to make enough changes that The Tower will not be a destructive force. Because these interpretations can vary from deck to deck I recommend studying the notes which accompany your own deck so you better understand what is being specific in your own working Tarot.

The Magickal Tower

The Tower represents a magick which is masculine by nature, aggressive and demanding of one's attention. It may well leave the seeker feeling as though her naivety regarding the realities of life has been, perhaps, 'pillaged' by life! What we might try to remember is that, in classical mythology, when one was 'pillaged' by a God or Goddess it usually resulted in the individual being elevated to a divine or mythical state or becoming one of the immortals. The Tower represents raw power which lays waste to those things we've created for security but which now hold us back from enlightenment.

Interestingly, rather than the intense energy of martial herbes, the one which has been corresponded to this card is eyebright, an herbe which assists us in our outlook and perceptions. There are many stones and minerals associated with The Tower, including agate, bloodstone and magnetite (lodestone) as well as onyx, garnet and the metal iron.

The energy of this card is raw magick, perhaps the most activated of all natural forces. It is difficult to suggest a conceptualized ritual form other than to describe this natural energy as the most intense part of the Cone of Power. If working ritual to bring The Tower into your life, you are asking the Universe to bring change for the sake of change. You have requested a catharsis to shake you loose and bring the illumination of the lightning's flash of an even greater wisdom. In preparing for this ritual work, make adjustments in your life so that when this metaphorical earthquake might strike, your foundation is flexible and you are looking forward rather than counting your losses. This is not a card with which to work Magick if you are faint of heart, You are working with the great powers of the Universe.

XVII - The Star

Aquarius

The images for **The Star** card have great appeal to artists. There are many variations of this card. One of the most singular, Pamela Colman Smith portrays a picture of innocence. Smith presents a simple image of a kneeling figure, freed from the confines of clothing, who pours water from two ewers beneath a brightly starred sky. This image is filled with rich symbolism.

Whereas Temperance, the XIV trump, depicting water flowing between the two chalices represents a passive approach, here we see The Star taking an active, feminine role. With The Star, the water does not flow from one chalice to another. The figure pours from one ewer upon the earth, which responds with fruitfulness and, at the same time, pours from the other ewer into the wells of the subconscious from which dreams spring forth into reality. Some choose to interpret these two flows of water as the symbolic two pillars of the Tarot, here representing the solar consciousness of ego in balance with one's lunar intuition.

Stars with eight points, in numerology the number of death and rebirth, shine brightly overhead. The primary star may be considered a symbol of the seeker's own divinity. Within any solar system, star is the source of life and light, the center of being. A star is infinitely greater than the brief incarnation of a human life.

Elevated nearby, a tree grows, its fruitfulness evident. And perched upon a high branch a bird reminds me of the birds Aldous Huxley described in his book, *Island*, reminding us to pay attention. In the Tarot, a bird often represents the presence of an oracle. It reminds us that a voice is speaking, that we are to listen to our voices of inspiration.

The Star is a card of hope. It represents attainable goals if the seeker accepts guidance and nurtures her spiritual self in pursuit of future accomplishments. If you note the Star's posture, she is kneeling upon the solid earth but she supports herself by the foot which is resting upon the water. once again we are reminded of Temperance. It is from her subconscious, from her intuitive, divine self that she draws her strength. The Star offers one a path to the manifestation of dreams. The mountain in the distance is attainable.

Filled with inspiration, living the lessons and joys of this card is what the folk saying "hope springs eternal" means in its most positive perspective. What is important to realize is that the Star does not sit back and wait for inspiration to knock at her door. Rather, she is continually giving to both worlds, allowing pure, positive emotion to sustain the world of emotion and the world of dreams. This is a card of action, one in which the seeker learns to see herself as the source, as the channel of inspiration. It is the divinity within her which is the source of her ability to transcend the constraints of her mundane life. The Star offers insight into the transcendence of mundane reality.

This is a wonderful card to find in a reading. We are offered spiritual gifts, unexpected joys. Our good work has nurtured a creative, fertile environment. The seeker is shown that he has the ability to bring dreams into manifestation. At present her life may be blessed with good health and there is an aura of wonderment, of awe at the joy of life.

Just as we see in this card, despite the wonders of our inner vision reflected in the waters of time, we must remain firmly upon the ground. Only with your feet firmly planted in both worlds, with your mind clear as you fill your life with illumination, may you continue to reap the spiritual gifts offered by The Star.

The Reversed Star

When reversed, the self has been placed above the Divine and one's spirit becomes depressed. This results in disappointment, sickness and depression characterized by self-pity and hopelessness. The lack of spiritual balance can affect one's health and leave one's unhealthy ego in control of life. The spark is lost. Spiritual bliss is a void and the seeker forgets why she was pouring the water in the first place. In short, her ewers run dry.

The Magickal Star

The androgynous quality of this card leaves its sexual energy either not yet developed or not an issue, in this sense similar to that of The Fool. This may indicate having removed one's self from sexual activity. The polarities are present, portrayed by the two pitchers which are, symbolically, the two pillars in a fluid representation. The merging of the polarities occurs internally but are manifested externally, for the star is the center of its solar system. Yet we see that there is a comfort with the sexual self, inherent in the skyclad aspect. Despite the underlying androgyny, The Star is portrayed as feminine, implying an intuitive, yin magick.

The herbes of choice with which to stir the magick of this card are herbes of Aquarius: star anise and cloves, either whole cloves or ground cloves. The opal, rock crystal, amethyst and star sapphire are corresponded with this card as well as is the pearl.

Ritually, we might contemplate the fact that an ibis historically represents an Oracle. Ritual work might be planned so that the seeker has her feet in both worlds while seeking an answer from the Divine-within. Certainly one would integrate chalices into this ritual, either literal ritual chalices or perhaps a carefully selected pair of vases which might represent the two ewers. As with Temperance, the magick is to be worked in both realms, a combination of conscious awareness balanced with the astral senses found during trance.

In some ways The Star indicates a style of life rather than a formal ritual. One learns to function as a Priestess or Priest at all times, living in the mundane world of the job, family obligations and chores such as shopping yet even at those times embodying the qualities of The Star.

XVIII - The Moon

Pisces

This card of hidden changes is well known. The image of The Moon positioned in the sky between the two towers has appeared in many variations. But is it just the Moon? The lunar image appears to be superimposed directly over that of the Sun and may well represent an eclipse. If this is so, the background of this card is not night but only appears to be a time of darkness. The moon is covering the light!

In the distance is the mountain, that frequent symbol representing one's Highest Ideals and the pinnacle of achievement. The path is clear, but can be walked only if one is able to emerge past the fears and discomfort represented by the lobster, a crustacean crawling out of the pool. The pond is filled with the rippling waters of one's subconscious. Pincers raised, the lobster is ready to grab us, holding us back from forward progress, as are the dogs. With the waters stirred, we can no longer see the pond's bottom clearly.

The dogs are howling. Who let them out? First appearing in The Fool, the dog represented the words of doubt and caution voiced by a trusted and faithful companion. And now, far along the journey, the dogs howl. They are nervous. This is uncharted territory and things are not what they appear. The canines instinctively react based upon past memories. They do not trust the future.

The Moon represents the fears which lurk inside, particularly of those things you refuse to face. We can easily become caught by our own daydreams, worrying about those things which "could" go wrong. Sometimes we allow those dogs to bark so loud we are left too inhibited to move forward with our lives. Those internal, howling voices are represented by the lunar hounds. We hound ourselves and we hear our own fears echoed in the doubts of others.

Despite the overall anxiousness of this card, the period of time when The Moon reigns over the seeker's life could be one of initiatory growth. Those who are walking paths toward wisdom welcome this card. The Moon card is a time during which to peruse reality clearly, without emotion, a time to set aside those obstacles which are holding the seeker back from her dreams.

The Moon presents us the emotional web which accompanies the illusion of our dreams. Daring to gaze into the future we see all that is possible but yet we are gripped with fear, afraid that those fantasies of our hopes and dreams will be shattered. This is a card which may appear when one is clinging to a dream rather than facing reality, when one is looking for fulfillment and answers in all the wrong places.

Following The Moon is The Sun. In many ways, The Moon card is in polarity with The Sun. Whereas The Sun is a card of jubilant celebration in full view of one's peers, The Moon shows one's dark, inner insecurities. If this image is of an eclipse, the symbolism is clear. You must get your dark fears out into the sunlight. We must not allow the darkness of our anxiety to cloud our sunny optimism.

Failure to take control of one's lunar fears leads to paranoia, to feeling trapped, and to a life of unfulfilled longing. Self-negation will create patterns through one's imagination, stirred by foreboding It creates powerful images of things going wrong. But this is a strong card, one which warns the seeker that continuing to wallow in one's emotions is not the path to the light. If we allow our imagination to dwell on negative imagery it will become a self-fulfilling prophecy.

If the seeker doesn't change her attitudes, she is likely to encounter bad news or continued unhappiness. Learn this card well. It can be a very positive card. The Moon brings us a message which should never be ignored. This is a card of supreme divination.

The Reversed Moon

When The Moon is reversed, the position of the water has been moved to the 'top' of the card, a ready image showing what happens when your emotions take control. This may bring a great learning experience. The reversed Moon is also used to describe the the dark, murky waters of one's inner self and may appear in a reading when the seeker is mired in a morbid or deep imagination. Many authors consider the reversed Moon even more troubling than the Moon in its upright position.

The clinging of negative emotions may lead to mean behavior, actions which are inconsistent with one's Ideals. Your Highest Ideals are swept aside by the emotional currents. The reversed Moon can be used toward a positive and calm aftermath, but first the seeker must stop allowing her anxieties to affect her behavior. It may be useful drawing upon the wisdom of the card which sits on the opposite side of the zodiacal spectrum, The Hermit.

The Magickal Moon

Although not visible within the symbols of this card, the Moon represents the active magick when the Sun and Moon are conjunct. This is a true representation of the Union of Polarities. The further presence of the polarities depicted as the two pillars shows this card to represent strong, sexual energy, that magick which manifests when the polarities are conjoined. For this reason The Moon may be used when working to heal fears or anxieties arising from one's desire or the repression of desires.

Herbes one might select for work with The Moon would be elder and mugwort. The arrowroot growing at the edge of this pond may prove to be of magickal value as well. This card, associated with Pisces, has a number of stones associated with it including aquamarine, moonstone, quartz and smoky quartz. When using ritual to move through the Mysteries of The Moon it is essential to have the pillars present, whether set up physically as one might find in a Ceremonial Lodge or symbolically. With each of the Major Arcana, ritual work should seek to emulate the card to the best of one's ability.

Difficult for many to understand, this card works with the magick of fear. One pillar might represent working with the Moon card to confront and banish all fear, best done during a waning Moon. This pillar would represent the path to Perfect Trust.

The other path might represent conjuring up one's fears. What is there about horror movies which people find so delicious? Why do people like to experience fear? It is possible to work with both the light and the dark, allowing the Sun and Moon to illuminate *everything* within you. An excellent approach begins at the New Moon, the time for planting the seed. This will bring forth the bad along with the good. Such a profound working requires a complete ritual sweeping, including preparation not only of the ritual space, but of one's body. Be prepared to invest days of care preparing one's psyche.

The mundane interpretation of The Moon indicates the potential for manifesting your fears. If this is the situation, then a ritual to banish fear is called for, employing a methodical process of setting aside concerns as you banish them one by one. For those seeking to move within the magick of this card remember that The Moon card's magick is definitely operative. It will seek to manifest whatever images are stirring within you. This requires exceptional control over all aspects of your ritual work.

XIX - The Sun

Sun

As we near the end of our journey through the Major Arcana, the Sun card depicts the successful completion of one's Quest. The sun radiates brightly overhead, its sunny theme reflected in the row of sunflowers. The overall energy of this

card is that of joy. Life's joyfulness radiates outward freely, for all things have gone well. The obstacles of the past have been surmounted. The challenges have been transcended and the seeker returns from the journey holding the banner of success. The light comes not only from the sun above but from within the seeker as well.

The central figure represents childlike pride, a being who does not yet wear the fabrication of an adult ego. The exuberance is that of youthful joy, of a sense of rebirth born of one who has learned so much about life and of his self. There is no need for clothing. Only the wreath of victory need be worn. At this time, life is so wonderful it cannot be contained. One is so happy that emotion cannot be held within and the ability to allow this happiness to glow flows freely. Even the horse is free, without bridle or saddle. With both horse and child unencumbered, we can see that success is more easily attained when we are not weighed down by the motives of one's ego or the distraction of the reward.

When we last saw the white horse, it was being ridden by Death in the thirteenth card. Although life may have felt like death, the horse has long represented strength and vigor and in Death's distant backdrop the sun was rising, signifying that the period of darkness was leading to rebirth. Now, in The Sun card, the transformation is complete. Everything has been brought into balance and the seeker's faith in her abilities has grown.

The presence of a wall built by the hands of a skilled mason indicates that the seeker has returned to family and friends. The wall shows the presence of one's social environment. The Sun card indicates that your success and your happiness are to be shared and witnessed by those who know and love you. The sunflowers are ripening beneath the sun, a further indication that the harvest awaits.

The mind must be lit from within in order to radiate outward. This card shows us the value of freely expressed intuition. The Sun is a card of joy and happiness. It represents blessings and the attainment of one's goals. The seeker is not celebrating her own skill. The seeker isn't bragging about himself. There's simply a pure elation found through having learned the lessons, having moved forward and found success. Once the seeker has reached this point she has it all and fully deserves to ride high and be recognized as having done well.

The Sun is also a card of Perfect Trust. It represents the external expressions of reality and, when done well, the seeker will feel the world to be as great and wonderful as he feels. Not only will his joy be perceived by others but it will affect them and uplift them. When this card appears, the Tarot is communicating that the future is there before you. It is time to set yourself free.

Most often, this card will not appear in a layout until the seeker has created a successful circle in life. That circle includes having labored hard, recognizing that the process of working toward the goal is of greater value than struggling toward a self-serving reward. It is the internal change which is heralded by The Sun card. The child upon the horse shows that she feels exuberant and has been set free. The sacrifices were worth it. The process of learning and expanding is now ongoing. Because one chose goals of growth and wisdom, the ensuing freedom leaves us renewed and youthful. The Sun is one of the highly desirable cards, one which indicates a job well done both spiritually and in the real world.

The Reversed Sun

When The Sun is reversed, the light of one's inspiration has grown shadowed, quite possibly by the dark shade created by the desires of one's own ego. One's nature and one's relationship with the natural environment has grown disharmonious. The sound of cheering is now only a memory and, when recalled, leaves one only more dissatisfied with the present.

Did you become too attracted to the rewards? Did you claim too much the attention of others? Have you fallen off the wonderful steed, no longer moving in forward progress? Despite your disappointment, it is time to move forward again. The horse may have stopped but you can trust this steed for, if you restore your source of inspiration (it has not slipped away, only your ability to perceive it is astray) your horse will be eager to carry you toward new goals.

When The Sun appears reversed, the Tarot is encouraging the seeker to reclaim the light, to turn within and once again take up the staff of life, that joy found when life is lived with honor. Shed the constraints of one's ego, for that ego may be the encumbrance of heavy, musty clothing. Leave behind disappointments. Do not expect your friends and acquaintances to carry that banner for you. Other cards of the Tarot teach you that the harvest will be attained only through your own diligence and hard work. The rewards and the laurel of success will be had when you restore your faith. Remember, the horse cannot carry you through the boggy mire created by the burden of your negative emotions.

The Magickal Sun

This card is clearly associated with the planetary energy of the Sun, but this is the Sun in its vitality. The natural energy of this card is a sensuality which is youthful, a boyishness which has little to do with gender. That figure could just as well be a young girl riding upon the horse and, indeed, the figure drawn by Smith is undefined regarding gender. In mythology, however, horses often symbolize sexual and physical strength. The sexual energy may be present, but this card depicts the aura of celebration in a social context and, as a consequence, any sexuality would be removed from the activities of these events.

Bay laurel, the well-known herbe which creates wreaths with which to celebrate success, is an herbe which works with the magick of this card. Obviously, sunflowers make excellent herbal correspondences as well. Stones associated with The Sun card are amber, carnelian and topaz. The precious metal gold is also highly appropriate.

Ritually we endeavor to harness the power of our exuberance, to work with the forward drive of our internal magick. Whether we choose to work literally with a ritual staff or not, it is present as an archetype within the nature of the pure magick of The Sun card.

When using this card as a prototype for ritual, you would do well to shed all self-doubts just as the youth has shed all clothing. This card offers you an excellent symbol to represent the goal which your ritual will empower. It may serve as an image upon which to focus throughout your ritual, perhaps even the image which is transmuted when the energy of your work is spiraled upward to the Universe.

Approach your ritual as an act of joy. Engender exuberance. Use this card as an image to focus your energy throughout your work.

XX - Judgement

Pluto

Above the humans is the angel holding her horn from which waves a banner with the symbol of the four elements in balance. The Judgement card represents the creation of spirit. She is a solar angel, giving birth to a new light. Below are many people, all arising from within themselves. By sinking deep into one's self, the person is later able to re-emerge with a new, reborn self-identity and spirit. In the background are the elevated heights of wisdom. The people in the foreground, however, do not need to ascend those treacherous heights, for the Judgement card speaks of a great transformation during which the seeker has direct access to the energy of creation and recreation.

In the Judgement card there is no separation between the spiritual world and the world of manifest reality. This card represents circumstances in life in which the Underworld and the Above World are both present. The physical and spiritual forces of nature have been brought together and we have a union of polarities, a reunion of opposites. Spirit and Earth have been brought together.

There is a quality of rebirth about this card, much as a fertile garden emerges following the death-like period of winter. The period of withdrawal has passed. This card may sometimes follow a period in life which is not unlike the Death card or the Hanged Man card. Now the seeker may return to the world of activity, emerging into the realm of reality with a fresh and new outlook on life.

Is this 'judgment?' It is in the sense that this state of transcendence cannot be achieved without having embraced the lessons taught by the Tarot thus far in the Major Arcana. I have humorously suggested that this card represents receiving a high grade on your cosmic report card! Now what is needed is stepping forth into the light and fulfilling one's new destiny.

The Judgement card will appear in a reading when the seeds of a new future have been awakened, when one is prepared to respond to the sound of the clarion. That which has been lying dormant, deep within one's self is now able to emerge, ready to be brought into being, connected to the other facets of one's manifest life.

This is the only card in which creation is manifesting through sound, much as we see in the creation myths of most religions. One must remember that this card teaches us that ultimately, the angel is found within, much like one's inner child, but at a far deeper level. When we have brought our life into balance and when we have achieved the heights of wisdom, something within will be awakened and brought up from the deep. With an understanding that all of existence is interconnected, knowing that the Divine permeates the Universe and is also found within, spiritual liberation will be found.

The Judgement card is one which allows the seeker to be infused with wonderful, creative energy. But you gain even more if you let that energy flow out again into the world. Handled with wisdom, this card indicates good luck and health of body, mind and spirit.

The Reversed Judgement

When Judgement appears in the reversed position, it may seem that the seeker has retreated back into the inner confines of one's ego. One's self imposed limitations are, for the present, holding her back from emerging into the light. In an interpretation, this may mean that the attainment of goals may be delayed, a project may be put off. If rewards had been nearing, they are likely beyond reach, at least for the time being.

One way to remember this interpretation is to think of someone emerging out into the world from a period of darkness and withdrawal, only to see her own shadow and quickly retreat! If this is the situation, remember that the difficulties encountered are the result of one's own karma and must be addressed honestly, with changes made. When this card appears reversed one is often feeling out of control, thinking it due to something other than the self. It is difficult to recognize the source of the difficulties, of the challenges that may affect one's health, one's resources. With a disruption within one's being of the natural flow of energy between the spiritual and incarnate self, this separation leaves one scattered and out of balance.

The reversed Judgement may indicate that it is time to get back to one's roots, to return to the drawing board of your life plan. Yet Judgement is a difficult card to restore to its upright position. It may be advisable for the seeker to turn to a professional advisor, therapist or counsellor, depending upon the individual circumstances.

The Magickal Judgement

The natural energy of the Judgement card certainly includes the procreative forces. There is a sexuality present but it is not in its active, orgasm-oriented form. This is an awakening not only of one's spiritual and intellectual being but also of one's physical body.

There are not many herbes associated with this card. Chervil is one which is. Another is not an herbe so much as it is a fruit, one prominent in mythology, the pomegranate. The gemstones associated with this card include the opal, sardonyx and topaz. I have seen the metal tin associated with this card as well as the element of fire. Personally, I believe that this card moves beyond a single element, as is indicated by the equal-armed elemental cross on the angel's banner, which represents a blending of all four elements.

Astrologically this card is corresponded with Pluto, a planet sometimes difficult for many students of astrology to grasp. Its relationship with Judgement might help both students of Tarot and of astrology. Pluto represents the inner you which seeks to emerge and manifest in the outer world, a process which is dreamt of by the very young and sometimes achieved by those much older. In the Judgement card the music has sounded, awakening this inner being. If you have learned your lessons well, this card teaches us how to bring forth the inner, reborn self if we can but transcend our present, if we can liberate ourselves from the sarcophagi of our self imposed limitations and egos.

In this card the only tool of ritual to be found is that of sound. When working with a ritual form designed to bring forth this transformation, great care and planning are needed in order to allow you to move into the depths of yourself. It may be that an earlier ritual working with the Death card may be appropriate. The ritual action of Judgement may be what follows the inaction of the Death card. If working with both of these Major Arcana archetypes as ritual, I urge you to keep them distinctly separate.

When designing a ritual using the Judgement card, I recommend developing a form or script. Draw upon symbols which call forth from the seeker a sense of rebirth. One's conscious *and inner conscious* selves should be taken into the deepest inner levels. This is ritual work designed to bring forth one's internal and sacred dreams. This may not be so much shamanic journeying or astral work as much as it is conscious internal work. This activity could involve regression or rebirthing. You might also recreate a scenario which replicates a symbolic hibernation.

Whether a solitary experience or a ritual in which the seeker is the focus of group work would best be determined by the needs of the individual.

XXI - The World

Saturn

It has been a long journey since the Fool set out but she has now arrived at the World. When The World appears in a reading, it will generally indicate that the seeker is prepared to move in a new direction, the lessons of life (and of the Major Arcana) being well-learned. The World may be studied as a role model for the way in which life works. When you have lived the experience of each of the cards thus far on the journey in the Tarot, you now become the World.

The circle, a wreath of leaves not unlike those given to celebrate success, will carry the figure into the cosmos. She is moving beyond time and will carry with her the wisdom of an elder. In this card, learning to work within a ritual Circle and learning to embrace life as a circle leads to success as well as the ability to master manifestation.

At the four corners of the card are characters which represent the four elements. Some consider the representations to be derived from astrology. At the bottom of the card we see Leo's lion and the bull of Taurus. The human figure is sometimes interpreted as Aquarius, and the eagle is associated with Scorpio.

These figures are also interpreted to represent human mastery: In this view the eagle represents having achieved mastery of one's own mind and intellect. The lion represents one's drive, one's creative spark and pride in accomplishment. The bull indicates the ability to create a foundation and then move beyond it, leaving the past behind; and the human signifies learning to transcend the nature of being human, of coming to terms with the frailty of one's emotions and desires. And when the World appears, it is to let the seeker know that he has within himself the seeds of mastery. It is now time to become a role model for the way in which life works.

This card teaches us what is needed in order to embrace the world. It represents the balance of giving and of receiving, of learning that the circle of life carries us into the Mysteries. The figure is shown as timeless and represents the best of youthful enthusiasm combined with the humorous wisdom of the elder.

Balancing joy and discipline, this figure is reminiscent of the Magician, of the High Priestess, of many of the personalities we have met throughout the Major Arcana. The seeker is encouraged to transcend his self limitations, to come to terms with them mentally and to have the courage and desire to move beyond them. This card is not a reward for a singular accomplishment but indicates the potential to achieve major successes in life, of having the ability to grow and learn and make progress from the challenges faced at the onset.

The World is a card for one who understands and can work that divinity which is known to be within. She understands and can work with the divinity found throughout the Universe. The World is a card for those who recognize that the only boundary between one's self and divine knowledge is that which is self-imposed.

This may be one of the most difficult cards to emulate and yet it is the most rewarding.

The Reversed World

When the World card emerges in a reading in the reversed position, the stability and security which is a foundation is absent. This is the inner core of one's life, gained from having learned how to exist successfully in this incarnate world. Whether poorly learned or never learned, the situation addressed by this reversed card is a time when one is prone to stagnation. The individual may feel as if she is left going around in circles, with success slipping away.

One's work is imperfect and likely to remain flawed. Without gaining wisdom from past experience, the seeker is likely to repeat the past with continued negative results, unable to see how to step out of this cycle created by one's own doing.

The reversed World indicates an environment in which one is unable to attain success and, unable to feel the joy of progress, feels mired in one's own mental traps and self-doubts, none of which truly reflect reality.

Whereas the World itself represents a complete awareness and union with one's surroundings and the events in one's life, the reversed World indicates a situation in which the seeker is unable to see what is around her. One's lack of awareness and unwillingness to live the principles of wisdom push success beyond one's grasp, leaving, instead, the presence of difficulties.

This unhappy situation can be corrected, but it takes some serious work and a willingness to embrace change. Avoid shortcuts as a solution, for they can lead down the path to disaster.

The Magickal World

The energy of this card is not clearly identified by gender, although the creative feminine is usually depicted and Pamela Colman Smith's figure is clearly a woman. But we have moved beyond gender. Here, inherent in this image, is a union of the polarities and a balance of all four elements. In The World, all is within the capable hands of the individual.

Herbes which may promote an understanding of The World include lovage and mandrake (European mandrake). Other herbes associated with the lessons taught by Saturn may be appropriate. Copper, lead and lodestone (magnetite) have been corresponded with The World as well. The gems we might bring to this card are diamond and sapphire.

Ritually, The World requires skill in working with magickal imagery, having learned the four suits and how to balance them as the four elements or cardinal directions. We see them present in the card at the four corners.

The Circle itself is also in place and the combined symbolism of the card suggests a fully-cast Circle, within which the figure represents the development of control and of will. All the energy is to be placed into the image held within her mind and, although the energy of the Circle is active, within her mind she is holding the image as stationary as possible for as long as possible.

Her lack of a formal environment and ritual robe suggest that a more natural setting would be appropriate. She holds not one, but two of the magickal wands we first saw in The Magician. She does not stand between the pillars which represent the polarities, but she holds the wands to either side. She is able to manifest the polarities through herself. Magickally, she holds the whole world in her hands as she dances within the circle as the four elements are in attendance.

The World represents the ability to live and work a magickal life, having learned the lessons of all 78 cards of the Tarot. Live this card with joy.

The Minor Arcana

There are four suits in the Minor Arcana. Each suit has fourteen cards which are in the sequence Ace through King, one more than a deck of regular gaming cards.

The four suits have two layers of symbolism which are individualized in the specific cards. There is the 'suit,' itself, and there are the individual numbers. To give an example, the Seven of Cups share elements of the suit of Cups with all fourteen cards in that suit. And the Seven of Cups shares other elements of similarity with the other three Sevens. It is for that reason that the student is encouraged to study not only the 56 cards of the Minor Arcana but to devote some time to studying the nature of the four suits as well as the symbolic meaning of numbers.

The Swords of Tarot

This suit of the Minor Arcana represents the element of air, according to most Tarot adepts (there are a few who correspond it with the element of fire). A sword is an implement of survival, useful as a weapon or a tool of defense and, in its variations, something of great value in providing for one's needs. Swords address communication, the exchange of information and interaction of ideas. These are aspects of one's intellect. And life is filled with the challenges and problems which arise from the activities of one's thoughts, intellect and the ways in which we analyze and verbalize our feelings and ideas.

The issues of life which this suit depicts are much like air. They are intangible and can expand beyond belief. Ideas, words, thoughts, truths and even rumors are air-like: they cannot be contained without exceptional care. When teaching my Tarot Course I liken the spread of a rumor to the perfume molecules escaping from a bottle. Given time, all of the liquid will evaporate and be equally dispersed throughout a room. This simple experiment, often conducted in the early grades, demonstrates the pervasive quality of air. The cards of this suit depict archetypes which teach us of the values of honesty, forthrightness, of learning to use our words with care.

Truth is like the double-edged sword of this suit: it cuts both ways. When life taps you on the shoulder and tells you that "it's time to face the facts," there is usually some pain involved when we must confront reality. The double edge may also be seen as a symbol of there being 'two sides to every story.' Words can cause pain. It is not without reason that some people are referred to as "sharp tongued." Although we often speak of our emotions, this suit shows us that, to do so successfully, we leave our emotions in the suit of cups. When swords are too-frequently bathed in the waters of one's emotions, they quickly become rusted. There is far more pain when something must be severed with a rusty scalpel.

The sword is a tool. In order for a sword to be a worthwhile tool, it must be well-forged and tempered in order to endure. If not well-made, it will be brittle and will snap and break with very little force. In a basic deck of cards the suit of Swords is depicted as that of spades: a sharpened steel tool which is double-edged and tempered in order to cut through sod and soil. Swords may be used to separate things. We see how words can do this in our lives and this is shown in the cards as well. When it is necessary to sever something unhealthy, whether it be a gangrenous finger or an unhealthy relationship, this suit teaches us to bring down a well-sharpened blade swift and clean so that the healing may begin.

Swords are also used to confer knighthood, to crown a monarch. Many years ago, when performing a concert for a Cardinal's visit to a Catholic university, I saw a display case filled with the ritual swords of the Cardinal's and Bishop's predecessors. It was surprising for I had not been aware that even within the Catholic Church a ritual blade was an important tool. Swords are used to hunt for food, curved as a sickle for the harvest. They are closely related to the athame and phurba (ritual knives), to the arrow and the blades of cooking and horticulture.

The sword is not a light tool. It has substantial weight and requires strength in order to wield it with care. Similarly, one must have strength of character to wield one's words with care. The suit of Swords teaches us the controls needed for effective communication. We must speak with directness and be disciplined and strong, not allowing our emotional weaknesses to inflict pain upon others with our words.

This is not an easy suit. There are, arguably, more cards representing sorrow and discomfort in this suit than in the others, but they teach us essential lessons. They show us what is needed for mature communication. Through the swords we learn how to handle situations of difficulty. Swords are an essential suit and we cannot achieve maturity and wisdom without learning how to handle the swords of Tarot.

Ace of Swords

Perhaps the most significant difference about this sword from the most-famous mythical sword is that, unlike Excaliber, the Ace of Swords is being handed to you. It is not necessary to wrest it from rock, for the Universe is presenting you with this opportunity, its hand extending from the heavens. The sword is crowned, showing you that this reality offers the potential for crowning success, a success symbolized as well by the branch of laurel and an herb which I've never quite identified.

In the foreground is a tall mountain peak representing the potential for your pinnacle of achievement, but other mountains are visible as well for, if handled with wisdom, the life-changes of this card could bring skills allowing you to accomplish many great goals in your life.

An event such as this would seem to be brought by divine intervention (some might see this sword as being presented by the hand of their divinity). It is important that you take this metaphorical blade in hand and make time and make space in your life, for without either you'll find yourself unable to bring forth the rebirth of life and creativity represented by the Ace of Swords.

Because this Ace and suit deal with facing facts, you should be able to develop a clear understanding of what's taking place. As soon as you know that this series of events will be coming into your life, begin by taking stock. A full accounting of your assets and abilities, your skills and what is lacking in order to achieve your goal will give you adequate control over the situation. The ability to wield this sword is essential, for it heralds a major change, the beginning of new directions capable of cutting away old patterns.

Embrace the Ace of Swords. Accept the fact that some pruning will be essential, that some degree of what may seem sacrifice is called for. What is needed in order to create time and space and perhaps redirected resources is a small price given the potential for a triumphant conclusion, one which is able to bring you a new awareness not only of life but of yourself and your ability to manifest success.

With rare exception, the Ace of Swords does portend success. Only in the least frequent of circumstances might the Ace of Swords herald a winning situation which is unpleasant. In those rare scenarios, it speaks of conditions which, from the hindsight of the future outcome, one would still be glad for what has happened, even if victory exacted a painful experience.

With this in mind, you have no cause for worry although events will be likely to happen with swiftness. The sword is a large tool with substantial weight and when brought down, it chooses to mark a clean and sudden departure from one's past patterns. Prepare yourself. This is a wonderful card, an exciting card. If you can let go of those mental attitudes which hold you back, you should be able to embrace a brighter illumination.

The blade of a sword is sharp. It is necessary that it cut through the old, quickly and cleanly. The more you resist these changes, the more pain and anguish you must experience. Let go quickly and you'll be able to take the sword in hand.

reversed

When the seeker is unable to take the Ace of Swords in hand, one is left in an uncomfortable position. Progress is not being made and yet one is aware of the potential. The resulting stagnation leaves one in a mental and emotional stew and what is brewing in that internal cauldron is not pleasant. The reversed Ace of Swords must be turned around. Although it will not be easy, making change is the only solution and the rewards will more than compensate for the effort needed to bring a sense of rebirth and restoration to one's life.

There are many adjectives attached to the Ace of Swords when reversed and not a one is flattering. The types of behavior manifested by someone who is at the mercy of her own unwillingness to take the sword in hand include the symptoms of depression and anger, obsession and compulsion. Typically these are scenarios in which one is unwilling to face reality and manipulates the facts in order to avoid embracing real life. What should be a crown for one's achievements becomes a shackle to one's destructive stubbornness.

The import of the Ace of Swords is, like its energy, direct and swift. Yet the wise student would spend time with this card for it introduces all the swords of this suit.

Two of Swords

The Two of Swords depicts someone who has taken pause from activity. Seated upon a bench, the blindfold upon the figure reminds us of the archetype of Justice. The figure in this card has stopped the process of examination, of recrimination, of judgement. Detente has been established although the issues have not disappeared. Represented by the two swords, they are held by the crossed arms of the seated woman.

The bench is placed somewhere along the shore and there is nothing to obstruct your view. As you can see, 'the coast is clear,' but this is temporary. The Moon has risen above the horizon, a thin crescent. The waters of emotion will rise again as sure as the tide. When that happens, they will splash against the large rocks, obstructions which indicate that one cannot travel safely upon the surface of those emotions. The waters off shore cannot be safely navigated. Although some rocks are visible it is very possible that others lie beneath the surface making the journey perilous.

The Two of Swords is a card of detente, of temporary reconciliation. In the recent past, there has been considerable discord in a partnership or relationship. Many of the differences appear to be reconciled and the situation appears calm. Do not allow the calm waters to be misleading: changes by all parties must yet be forthcoming.

There is another aspect to the blindfold. It indicates that this is not a time to examine the 'other' party's faults. At present there must be no recrimination. Peace will be sustained if we close our eyes to the faults of the other parties and, during this detente, turn our examination inward.

Breathe deeply. Find peace seated upon this bench. It may not seem so long ago that those swords were at odds with each other, the dueling of opposing views and aggressive words. Now, during this temporary reconciliation, you are removed from discord and can use this as an opportunity to create a breakthrough, manifesting the Ace of Swords which brings much needed change to *all concerned parties*. Without this major level of change, the storm may return when the blindfold is removed.

reversed

When reversed, this is not a comfortable card. What usually appears as a safe place to sit peacefully during self-examination is now a source of concern. Although one may *wish* this period of peace to be safe, the horizon is about to break into emotional ill weather through misinterpretation or possibly the spreading of false information. Things being said should not be taken at face value. The seeker may have a desire to be trusting, a feeling motivated by a wish for peace. But the reality is that at least one of the people involved is emotionally tense. Those emotions are ready to be set off at the least likely provocation. The reversed Two of Swords is an alert that the situation could be hazardous.

The solution? Caution is needed. If possible, work to return the situation to the respite depicted in the Two of Swords. This Two offers an oasis of calm from which the ultimate reconciliation can be created.

Three of Swords

When looking at Colman's image for the Three of Swords, we see a heart pierced by three swords, all point down with their hilts to the sky. From the clouds we see rain. There is nothing truly of substance other than the pain. No mountains, no gardens, no solid earth is to be seen.

The nature of swords in this card describes the arrival of some news which causes great sorrow. Or it may indicate the divisive nature of a sword which, when brought down, cuts apart something (such as a friendship or relationship) which was previously whole.

Although popular thought is to react to this card in great horror, the reality is that the time and space created by the Three of Swords is a most important facet to the healing which is needed for the seeker.

As Waite's design indicates, the sorrow at hand is very heartfelt. One feels 'cut to the deep,' as if the pain is too much to bear and is cutting one's very heart asunder. The image of the card reflects the seeker's feeling that the events are far beyond her control. The swords have come down from the realm of the Divine. Our *feeling* is that there is nothing we can do but be burdened by this debilitating pain.

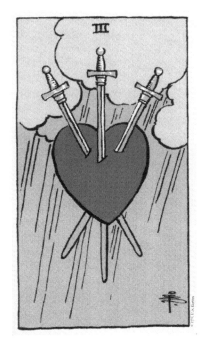

What type of pain might this card be describing? Although a few decks may differ, it is nearly never the death of a loved one so much as the death of a relationship or of a situation. The Three of Swords has much more to do with our response to the severing of something we held dear. Emotions associated with this card might reflect our disappointment or, perhaps, a sense of loss over the separation between people who have loved.

With nothing visible but cloudy skies and rain, it is obvious that the sorrow has made it impossible to see anything but one's pain. The Three of Swords wishes to remind you to have your sorrow but to become mindful that down below, just out of sight beneath the card, the rain is bringing much-needed nourishment to the gardens of your life.

This card teaches us that it is important to become objective and not let one's heart get in the way. The situation is not the end of the world, even if it feels that way. It is not uncommon for this card to appear in a reading when the separation or parting of ways is but temporary. If you allow your perceived pain to become magnified and dominate your life, this card cautions you that your actions will be motivated by your emotions. This could lead to immature behavior which could make the break much greater in scope. To be sure, many of your plans for the future were based upon this shared endeavor and now you must wade through the difficulty as you either go it alone without your friend or partner or you must create new plans.

The Three of Swords is descended from the Ace. These swords show you that the Universe is teaching you to take the sword in hand and cut away your pain. This is not the same as cutting the person or situation permanently out of your life. It is a reflection of you and your need to handle your own attitudes.

As is true with all cards of the Tarot, the Three of Swords is teaching you to work change creatively in your life. It is your choice. You can continue to be doom and gloom, raining on your own parade, or you can part the clouds and the sun will begin to shine.

reversed

In most decks, the reversed Three of Swords indicates that your emotional response to the situation is getting out of hand. It may be causing you disorientation and confusion, even leaving you with a significant imbalance in your abliity to manage your life. When reversed, the Three of Swords usually indicates that professional help is needed. You are so dominated by your own painful emotions that you are unable to maintain a perspective on life.

What has caused the pain or delay is not the problem. Your reaction to the event is the problem. The sorrow with which you have swaddled your life is unlikely to go away by itself. The voices in your head are caught in an endless loop, chanting a litany of woe as your emotions exhaust themselves on a treadmill. A helping hand is needed to bring you back into balance.

Four of Swords

Frequently misunderstood by those who do not know the Tarot, the figure in this card is not dead. The sword which was presented in the Ace has now been positioned upon the side of the figure's resting place. He is lying upon the sword, symbolically, and is taking a break from the activities of this suit: this is not a time for talking nor allowing one's mind to run on endlessly.

An conscious decision has been made to seek repose. All physical action has ceased. The situation is now one for taking time for meditation, for going on a retreat. The image of the church window shows us that the figure is being blessed by the light coming through the stained glass, that she is taking sacred time in a sacred space. This is one of the lessons taught us by the Four of Swords: Let the light shine upon you. Indeed, rather than seeing this as a stone figure, I look at it as someone bathed in the window's light.

What reasons might there be to cause one to seek retreat? Recovery and healing are in order. It might be a need to take rest from strife. Swords, at times, may represent the process of verbal battle. Perhaps the figure is in need of rest from these struggles, choosing to leave the situation and set aside unpleasant events so as to regenerate his spiritual self. The other three swords have been hung up on the wall, taken out of action and put away. One might be in need of taking relaxation following a period of anxiety. Another might be convalescing from an illness.

We see the figure of the person above the fourth sword, the foundation of her beliefs. This state of meditation may indicate an important phase of working toward a goal. The image of what may also be seen as a tomb represents a sense of hibernation, a return to the earth and a sense of being grounded. The figure is moving into the underworld of the inner self in order to seek rejuvenation. During this time all activity is very conservative so that as little energy as possible is expended, allowing him to recreate the foundation of his beliefs. In this manner might one return to the beginning of the suit and, having tempered one's beliefs as one tempers a blade, claim anew the strength and joy of the Ace of Swords.

reversed

When the Four of Swords appears in its reversed position, the above mentioned need for rest and recuperation is still important, but the seeker is unable to retreat. Caution is now needed and one ought be guarded when interacting with others. Care is needed in how internal thoughts are processed.

Continued stress or illness are likely without this much-needed rest. It is possible to transcend the apparent limitations of the situation. Do your best to conserve your energy and go about your business without allowing emotions to affect how you wield the four swords.

Five of Swords

When the Five of Swords is turned over in a reading, it is time to set aside your ego and self-pride whether you want to or not. What was once a tool of great promise and power extended from the heavens by the divine hand has now become many swords, each controlled by a different intent and will.

Why have difficulties befallen the seeker? The lessons of this suit were not well learned. The hope of the future lies at the tops of the mountains, across the watery abyss, but no one gazes toward the source of inspiration. No one is looking toward the ultimate goal. They are tired, their heads hang down and they are retreating from the situation. Above we see storm clouds. It is rare to see a Tarot character's hair and robes blown by the winds of change but the Five of Swords is not an easy card. Yet it represents a catalyst for change. In the science of numerology, a five is akin to raw magick and requires considerable skill if one is to manage it.

The character at the forefront does not have the most loving of facial expressions. The realm of swords is that of the spoken word, of the intellect. No one has been physically hurt although the potential is there. A primary player in this situation, the primary character is holding three of the five swords. This makes it clear that he is not holding all of the facts. He relies upon the negative desires of his ego in order to wage a verbal battle. It is not pleasant.

Traditionally, this card indicates that the situation is likely to lead to loss. The seeker will face humiliation and defeat for a five is a card of karma. Even should a skirmish have been won, ultimately the battle will be lost unless the seeker can embrace the spiritual meaning of a five and make strong and immediate internal changes in her outlook on life and the way in which others are treated.

Those who have not attained wisdom and strength through spiritual growth tend to perceive the fives of Tarot as negative cards. They are not, however, no more than a storm with thunder and lightning is inherently negative. The Five of Swords as shown contains considerable energy and it is through this primal power that any tendencies we have to wish ill of others, to use our mental powers to inflict harm in an attempt to become the victor, will ultimately come back to us. Each of those swords represents there being two sides to the situation. This card compels the seeker to learn to see and to accept the views of others as being valid.

reversed

When reversed, the Five of Swords may be even more of a challenge. In interpretation it is not so different than its usual position, perhaps indicating that more time may have passed. Some decks indicate that it is not so intense when reversed.

The majority of decks convey a meaning of being brought face to face with the realities of the Five of Swords. Having fallen under the wiles of one's ego and manifested some of the above undesirable qualities, one now suffers regret. Now one begins to realize that any victories are empty and hollow. The gains one thought to have reaped are not worth it and the losses take a heavy toll upon one's soul and one's heart.

It is too late to change what has happened but not too late to take responsibility and to change the course of one's future.

Six of Swords

The sword, once crowned and held so proudly in the Ace with its blade erect is now joined by five others, subdued, as they pass over the abyss. The message in this card is one of a spiritual passage, a journey and transition moving the seeker into a new stage of life. Whether it be difficult or not depends upon how you handle the journey. The seeker is shown shrouded, sitting in repose, allowing her mind to be at rest as she trusts the force moving the boat.

What is waiting in the future? We see trees atop gentle hills, perhaps the promise of a more lofty mountain yet unseen. Is it perhaps the Isle of Avalon? This is the card which is so often described as a 'journey by water,' although these are the waters of one's spiritual evolution. In this card, however, the abyss is not so deep. The pole of the boatman must reach the bottom, allowing him to guide the boat forward.

There is a lesson in this. The seeker is being propelled forward by the events in his life, just as surely as this card shows the boatman moving the boat from the past toward the shore of the future. The boat, itself, is characterized with the six swords, each set into the craft's bottom. These are the facts of the situation, the truths of one's life. They should not be toyed with. To do so would cause the boat to fill with water and you are still far too distant from the shore! It is time to trust the boatman. This guide represents skilled counsel and is a wise guide who knows the crossing.

Be calm and accepting and, as is often said today, 'go with the flow.' Enjoy the ride. When this spiritual passage has been completed, you may reflect upon your journey and find yourself upon the solid shore. Contemplate your reality and accept the facts. Someone else is the mover of the situation These events will change the course of your life. Acceptance of this reality means you are likely to achieve success. Your role is to focus within yourself. Allow the world around you to change as you make changes within your consciousness. Make your journey within your mind, within your soul. Yet I should add that now and then this card does fit the stereotype seen in movies. For a few, this card may indicate a real voyage.

reversed

When reversed, the Six of Swords generally means there is no forward progress. The seeker is stuck. Perhaps the boat is caught on a sandbar or perhaps the boatman's pole has become mired in the seeker's lack of maturity.

Rather than an evolution of spirit, the seeker is likely to be experiencing anxiety, possibly even becoming dysfunctional when confronted with the facts. Rather than accepting them with calm maturity, the anxiety and reaction to the news is causing the boat to slowly take on water and sink with weight. Why did she pull those swords out?

The reversed Six of Swords will sometimes appear when we receive news which comes as a shock. When the facts are revealed to us we realize that our ignorance of the reality provided us with a comfortable denial.

Effort must be made to transcend this reversed card. The seeker must embrace the wisdom and maturity available. Then will he be able to accept all of the facts and begin making significant internal change. It is only with this growth that the boat will right itself and the positive journey offered by the Six of Swords be once again available.

Seven of Swords

The suit of Swords examines how the archetype of air functions internally as well as through the external mediums of communication. What we see in the Seven of Swords is complex psychological behavior. It is unclear which of these swords is the divine progenitor we saw in the Ace. The seven swords are actually in three groups, two upon the right shoulder and three upon the left, which could readily be interpreted to represent imbalance. And two more remain behind where the nature of the cutting edge of a blade brings into manifestation another quality of the sword: separation.

Although the sword-carrying figure dominates the scene, it would be wise to study the background detail to better understand the nature of this card. In the far distance we see the mountains of wisdom, but it is not to those heights that the figure is stepping. There are three or more figures gathered together in the near distance but whether they sit around a campfire (we cannot tell whether we see smoke or clouds behind them) or are at a game, we cannot be certain.

Colorful tents stand just behind the two remaining swords. But there are more. An enlarged deck shows, just at the crest of the horizon below the mountains (look beneath his tunic for this), what appear to be three more tents with small flags blowing in the breeze. Typically, these tents would indicate a fair or a gathering where games and the marketing of wares is taking place.

But what is this figure doing? He is not participating in the activities with the other people, but appears to be departing. The image is open to more than one interpretation. Is he a trickster? Could he be making off with swords belonging to others? This possibility would bring a somewhat different interpretation to the card. Some authors consider this figure to be capable of trickery and, yes, even thievery. Is he sneaking off with stolen goods? Could he be a spy, making off with the plans and tools of others so as to favor his own enterprise?

Others suggest that those are his own swords and that his lack of perseverance and shortcomings are such that he is holding back the truth. Swords are strongly symbolic of truth. The adage, 'truth cuts both ways,' is one we see as a recurrent theme within this suit. Perhaps the figure has gained many truths at this gathering but is taking leave early, unwilling to stay until he is able to handle all of the available information.

These possibilities lead to the card appearing when the seeker may be attempting to quit while ahead, even though that is neither the mature nor wise decision. The image convinces us that this is not appropriate action. Reminiscent of the potential for conflict found in the Five of Swords, the seeker is urged to stop and make adjustments. It is time to fix the situation, to work with and gather *all* of the facts and to look at them realistically.

Quitting now is playing with the facts. Some of that information will surely create a barrier to the seeker's ability to return and again interact freely with the others. If change isn't made now, the lessons will surely be painful when they are once again encountered.

reversed

With the Seven of Swords, the reversed position is far healthier than the above. The seeker now has the opportunity to embrace wisdom. One of the phrases I have found to be a recurrent theme is one which makes me feel a bit *odd* quoting to a client. It goes somewhat like this: "you are getting very good advice and ought to be paying close attention."

The reversed Seven of Swords indicates that the seeker has changed the path. Rather than attempting to leave without being noticed, she is now experiencing something being restored. The Seven of Swords may indicate that one is now finding wisdom restored, that the 'facts' are again being brought together. Yet another aspect of this card reverses the potential for 'thievery' which *may* be indicated by the Seven. Sometimes this card appears to indicate the return of one's property.

With several possible interpretations available, check the instruction book which accompanied the deck you are using for the best option.

Eight of Swords

Alas, the beautiful, shining sword offered by the divine hand in the Ace has lost its promise. The seeker is now held in the harsh grip of reality, standing blindfolded with the eight swords which create the illusion of a prison.

In the distance we see the wonderful image of a mountain. Not only does it represent the recurrent theme of achievement and promise we see throughout the cards, but there is a magnificent castle upon it. Were the difficulties of this card transcended, one might again be on the path of this suit, bringing into manifestation the promise of the Ace which leads ultimately to the honor of residing within that edifice.

But she cannot see the mountain. She is unable to even turn her mind toward such lofty goals. Right now

she believes she cannot go anywhere. It is obvious to us, looking at this image, that this is not a prison. The Eight of Swords is an archetype for the self-imposed prison we create when our thinking process is trapped, when our self-limitations keep us from seeing that there are ways to set ourselves free.

This is a card which may appear in a layout when we are forced to face our own negatively-created images. When things you have said which are hurtful or which lack honesty come back to you, there you stand, trapped by your own words or trapped by what others might be saying about you. If you pardon the folk sayings, the chickens have come home to roost, leaving you with egg on your face. Now you feel bound by reality just as the image in the card stands in the bondage of her own creation. Mentally preoccupied, you can no longer see beyond the situation at hand.

Pamela Colman-Smith's drawing shows water which appears to puddle at the figure's feet. The seeker's emotional response to the situation is a further restriction and has insinuated itself into her thought processes. This leaves her helpless and feeling unable to make any choices. The situation at hand leaves one struggling with internal emotions and the intellect goes 'round and 'round listening to the mind's voices repeating statements over and over again without any learning and subsequent changes taking place. It is like the prisoner pacing in circles around his cell in endless agony.

And yet, this is an Eight, a card which promotes change-making. Indeed, without a change the Universe will continue to intensify the situation until a crisis may well bring about mental exhaustion or an illness which provides the semblance of freedom.

What the Eight of Swords calls for is facing the crisis. Transform the self, transcend the patterns of negativity. By resurrecting the purity and promise of the Ace of Swords and by embracing the lessons this suit teaches us, the situation can be so changed that the path to the castle again becomes clear. The moral of this card? Set yourself free.

reversed

Generally speaking, most authors and deck designers treat the reversed Eight of Swords as having moved the seeker closer to a crisis. At this point the distraction is so strong that things are getting out of hand.

The reversed Eight of Swords is a warning. Unable to break free of his mental bondage, the seeker now faces a crisis. We can only hope that these events prove cathartic, breaking him free of his sorrow.

Nine of Swords

No longer do we see the beautiful blue heavens from which the Ace has emerged. With the Nine of Swords we are in the dark of night, a time when the restlessness of one's soul can wake us to face our nightmares. It is as if the figure in the Eight of Swords, unable to extricate herself, is now caught up in her own darkness.

Nine swords pierce the night. The bed is inviting, the coverlet of the zodiac and plants offering warmth beneath which to snuggle but, pulled back, comfort is not available. The carved figures on the bed appear to be at odds with each other, one possibly wielding a sword in a combative pose. This is not a happy scenario. From the swords above to base of the bed, this is an image of grief. Reality has pierced the dark and the central figure is awakened, eyes covered, filled with the dreaded sounds of 'woe is me,' sometimes accompanied by the melody 'nobody loves me.'

What we have here is a figure who is unable to get on with her life. This is a situation in which the seeker is having great difficulty accepting reality. The degree of disappointment or sorrow is forming an emotional quagmire.

If the sorrows are self-induced, then we are likely to see someone wallowing in his own misery. The promise of the Ace seems lost. It is time for the seeker to face the facts and see with a clear eye what he has done to himself. Only then will he be able to begin moving forward.

There are times when this card may appear in a layout indicating that the grief one is feeling over the loss of a loved one seems overwhelming. The Nine of Swords encourages the seeker to take the Ace of Swords in hand and cut through the despair in order to move forward with life. When the seeker feels that death is unfair, he is likely to find himself caught in this darkness.

The unhappy Nine of Swords teaches us what befalls the seeker who is unable to keep her woes removed from her consciousness. When the intellect becomes trapped in one's own woes, life becomes one of self-imposed martyrdom. For these individuals, life can become filled with disappointments, a miserable, lonely existence.

This is the card of the unloved, but the Nine of Swords appears when it is time for an awakening. The seeker must face the lesson that her suffering is self-imposed. The seeker has been living under the illusion that things are much worse than they are. The heavy weight of emotional pain is ready to be thrown off and the seeker is to rise and face a new day.

reversed

In many decks, the reversed Nine of Swords indicates that the situation is less permanent and, perhaps, more readily changed into positive momentum.

On the other hand, some authors perceive the reversed Nine of Swords to be an indication of the seeker's reaction to life's disappointments and a continued inability to accept his own role in that sorrow. As he continues to perceive his reactions as the reality, feelings of shame are likely, as well as a suspicious nature and the tendency to place blame upon others.

Several authors suggest that this reversed Nine cautions us that it is time to be wary of other people, that the difficulties might enter our lives from the ill doings of another person whose unhappiness inflicts pain upon us. If there is a conclusive view of the reversed Nine of Swords, it might be that our fears may or may not have been reasonable but now it is time to work through them and get on with life.

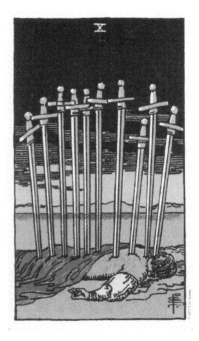

Ten of Swords

Oh my goodness! If you thought the Nine was troubling, this is clearly one of the more unpleasant cards of the Minor Arcana. Although the darkness has not left and the sky at the horizon is bright, the seeker cannot see the dawn. One who is unfamiliar with the Tarot might panic if this card appears in a reading, for the figure in the card appears mortally wounded by the ten swords. But this is not a card of death. The Ten of Swords is a card of metaphor.

A popular and humorous phrase begins a work of fiction with "it was a dark and stormy night." This, however, is no work of fiction. The brightness of the horizon with the sky overhead looking dour and gloomy indicates the darkness of a storm. But rather than raining drops of water, the storm has rained down swords.

Remembering that swords can indicate facts, this is a card depicting someone who has been impaled by reality. They feel stuck, pinned to the ground. Past actions or things they have said have come back to haunt them and can no longer be changed. My father's mother might have described this as "one's chickens coming home to roost" which should mean something good for the farmer. But, as we saw with the Eight, this phrase was always used to describe a situation in which one had to face the reality of one's own negative behavior.

Once the Ace of Swords offered the promise of a new, fresh start. But the seeker has stumbled, falling over her own mistakes. Her sense of failure at being unable to change the past is overwhelming. The sense of grief and desolation are a heavy weight. The past has been analyzed to death and indeed, right now the seeker feels as if she is in a living death. At present there is a major wallowing in one's own pain.

But the pain of the present circumstances is shown in this card as something which must not be permanent. What's done is done. It is time to call an end to this period of numbness, of emotional suffocation. The seeker must embrace his pain and begin to see the entire situation from an objective perspective. There are two sides to every story, two edges to every blade. The pain which exists is not the realm of the seeker alone.

Healing must begin and the potential for renewal offered by the Ace of Swords must be again claimed. If there was ever a time, it is now to 'pick yourself up' and 'start all over' with a new and improved attitude and set of ethics. It is time to see past the swords, to look beyond the pain of the present for there, along the bright horizon, the mountain tops of our aspirations sit waiting. The Ten of Swords may look dark, dreary and filled with sorrow but clearly we are offered a strong and positive future if we can but move ourselves forward.

reversed

The creators of Tarot decks seem to be fairly consistent about the reversed Ten of Swords. The light has now been elevated over the dark and the bright rays of hope begin to emerge over the horizon. With this shift in the energy of the situation, the seeker is urged to take advantage of things. The time is opportune. And the appropriate action begins with taking responsibility for one's own behavior and for one's self. The final note about this reversed card is that there must be no delay in embracing this mantle of honesty.

Page of Swords

Now we begin to meet the Court cards of this suit. The sword first seen in the Ace is now held by the youthful Page, the watchful messenger who stands, poised, waiting to see which way the wind may blow. High over head birds fly. Whether they are carrier pigeons or not, we can see them as part of the information gathering process, perhaps bringing news. The Page is observing all of these signs, noting the patterns of the birds, observing the shapes of the clouds and watching the direction of the wind blowing the distant trees.

We see the page, androgynous, dressed in courtly fashion. There are no symbols which indicate being taught the early lessons in the Mysteries, nothing to indicate that he will ever take an initiatory path. Hair blowing in the breeze, the page is a youth, one whose role at this time is in the service of those who protect the community, the village, the realm.

The Page of Swords has removed herself from the distractions of people. It is in the larger environment that she is seeking information. The mountains in this card are distant and do not obstruct the horizon. It is not a mountain upon which she stands, only a rise, yet the Page has chosen a site which allows her to scan the horizon.

The sword held aloft as it was in the Ace and as we find it held by Justice indicates physical strength, even in this youth. We see by this card the wisdom of the Page. Information gathered must be used wisely. The sword has risen. The page is observant yet objective. Keen of mind he knows that decisions cannot be made rashly. The Page is a person of sharp insights. There is a sense of grace found in this figure, one who appears able to move with the very wind. The Page is someone able to discern and glean information which others might easily overlook.

Holding the double-edged sword, the page looks in both directions. The Page also knows that the truth she may retrieve from her search may have the ability to cut both ways. Truth may sometimes cause pain. For that reason she lives an ethical life, clearly keeping the message and the messenger separate.

Watchful, alert, the page will fulfill his role as he does in society as a message bringer, as an instrument of learning for those whom the page serves.

reversed

When the Page appears reversed, the news is typically not good. The Page now indicates a situation (or a person) which has been 'in the clouds' - a reality which was inappropriately trusted. Perhaps assumptions were made. Perhaps information was withheld or presented in a misleading manner. There may be issues of trust which were either misplaced or not honored.

Pages are the messengers and the reversed Page of Swords may indicate that news will be forthcoming, news which may catch the seeker off guard. The moral of this card is that someone has not had his ear to the ground! The circumstances in the seeker's life will let you know whether there is time to make adjustments. The layout and position of this card combined with information from the seeker will indicate whether it is speaking about events already passed (and too late to change) or whether there is time to change one's mental awareness.

At the least a valuable lesson is to be learned.

Knight of Swords

Unlike the Ace of Swords which looks promising and filled with Divine Magick, the sword held aloft by the Knight stands out against a background indicative of stress and concern. The trees lean to the right, pushed by an unseen force. The clouds in the sky look anything but peaceful. And the Knight is riding directly to the source of this disturbance. This is a card of action. The alarm has been sounded. Did it come from the Page?

The birds seem removed from the immediate environment. Flying high overhead, they are safely away from the trouble. Often depicted to represent the bringing of information found through an intuition attuned to the natural environment, these birds depart from this role. The Knight pays them no heed. Whether they signify alarm I cannot say.

What we see indicates the need for action. The butterflies and birds which adorn the horse's gear seem incongruous with the Knight's readiness for combat. The horse charges forward with speed and the Knight is a dashing figure. The time for the gentle exchange of words and sharing of ideas which are one aspect of this realm of air is well past.

What we learn from the Knight of Swords is that it is time to be strong, to be armored and armed. Decisive action will be needed and the seeker is encouraged to have her defenses readied. Although the Knight requires the presence of strong, aggressive male energy, we can strive to emulate the positive characteristics of knighthood.

Does this mean physical combat? Swords are tools of air so this card is more likely to indicate a battle of words and of ideas. One is likely to encounter an individual (or group) who may be ruthless, who are more than ready to oppose the Knight of Swords. Whether the card indicates the seeker, someone who will provide defense and support for the seeker, or whether it represents the opposition, can best be determined in the context of the specific layout and neighboring cards.

In many ways it does not matter. The Knight is strong, brave and willing to dominate the situation if needed. Skillful and clever, among the Knight's arsenal is the ability to be persuasive. This card alerts the seeker that mental alertness is essential and, if not already present, the seeker must either take on the Knight's personality or find a Knight who will aid in his defense. The victor in the forthcoming struggle will most likely be the side which rallies to best meet the challenge.

reversed

If the Knight is reversed, the cards caution the seeker that the situation is likely to dominate the Knight rather than the other way around. There are chinks in one's armor leaving one ill-prepared for action. Under these

KNIGHT of SWORDS .

circumstances it is quite possible that one's rivals or those in opposition will hold the upper hand and it will be nearly impossible for the seeker to gain victory without seeking out the help of experts.

Indeed, the stress and pressure of this struggle could easily take too great a toll on the seeker, leaving her susceptible to greater difficulties as her emotional and mental strength are burdened. The moral of this reversed card? Seek qualified and capable help without delay.

Queen of Swords

Alas, the poor Queen of Swords. She always appears less pleased than her three queenly sisters. The Sword extended with such magnificence in the Ace has proven to bring difficult challenges for a woman in her role. She sits upon her throne, holding the sword aloft somewhat reminiscent of Judgement. Yet unlike Judgement, the Queen is not so readily able to be completely objective. In this card, she is not surrounded by a loving family, for the lessons of separation taught by this suit of blades are among the more painful of life's realities. One might imagine that the King is off defending a more distant region and she must now embrace the role of protector of their kingdom.

In today's world there are many women who can relate to this figure. She is perceptive and she is intelligent. Life has brought many lessons and she has grown from this knowledge and learned from her own pains. Many professional women have gained success in contemporary society They achieved prominence, political and economic power. Yet these gains have not been without their costs. Unlike her sisters, this Queen's path has taken her away from the domestic joys and the pleasures of mothering children. Oftentimes the responsibilities of the throne supersede any personal desires. It is not easy but it is her path and she would not have it otherwise.

Her crown is beautifully adorned with butterflies, seen also upon her throne which bears a cherub's face. Clearly, the suit of Swords arrives on the wings of air. Her robe is woven to look like shimmering clouds, but her role is to wield the sword and a sword may well bring with it pain. This is the role of a woman who must be strong enough to brave the storm. Indeed, in the background the trees appear to be blown and a huge mass of clouds is gathering at the horizon. She holds forth her hand, sensing that she must strengthen herself emotionally. Nor all of what she must do will be pleasurable yet it must be done for the good of those around her.

The Queen of Swords is a wise woman, one who is perceptive and intelligent. Her path has taught her of human suffering. She is able to bring a keen and sharp perspective to the situation. Despite the downturn of her mouth, she does not bring the distraction of her emotions with her. We might imagine her sad but we might also see her expression as one of resolve. Her visage reflects her knowledge of the pain which all individuals encounter in life.

This woman has knowledge of the path many women must take, one which may bring them encounters with sadness, with disappointment, but which leads toward wisdom. She knows that occasional sadness should not hold one back from her life's work. The role of this Queen includes the ability to wield the sword, whether in defense of those for whom she is a protector (in the absence of the King) or when she might be called upon to make a swift and painful decision, cutting swiftly and cleanly but never with pleasure. While it might be emotionally safer and professionally 'easier' to retreat behind the illusion of feminine gentleness, the Queen of Swords only empowers our view of the realities of life. Traditionally this is thought of as a man's role but that view is only within the stereotypes of the human imagination. A full understanding of womanhood includes the Queen of Swords and all women should honor her.

There are times this card appears in a reading with a message, encouraging the seeker to seek out spiritual perceptions from a skilled person or counselling from a professional on the matter. Similarly, we can readily imagine that this Queen might seek solace and comfort from the High Priestess.

The images in this card may be communicating that you, also, are too aware of the pain you must endure to become strong and wise and are encouraged to seek advice in severing yourself from that emotional sorrow. Perhaps this is the message being brought by the bird?

reversed

When this Queen appears, her sword of truth now pointing downward in the reversed card, we find a situation in which someone who is in a position of power, who should be highly regarded by her community, has turned her values upside down. The sword no longer represents judiciousness. It is no longer being used wisely. The throne has been elevated over the Queen, herself, perhaps indicative of a person who seeks status rather than finding fulfillment through being of service to the people of her realm.

This lack of humanity is typically found in someone who may also manifest a calculating approach to the handling of others. She may be manipulative and, given her position, used others in ways which further the Queen but do not benefit those being used.

Be wary of this individual. This is someone who will leave people emotionally drained. She may well be prone to deceitful ways, someone who makes unfair judgements (inevitably in her own favor) yet someone who is, after all, upon a throne and who wields power. This is not someone you wish to deal with and, if you must, seeking counsel from someone with knowledge and skill in handling a situation such as this would be to your advantage.

King of Swords

KING of SWORDS.

The Sword first presented to us in the Ace has been passed card by card through the suit and is now held by the King. Unlike the Queen, who rests it upon the arm of her throne, the King demonstrates his considerable masculine strength as he holds the large, heavy sword steadied by his mental concentration.

The King is a good husband and protector and works well in the partnership he enjoys with the Queen. Like the Queen, he also has butterflies upon his throne. His crown and throne depict winged cherubs. Like all the kings, he is removed from the social and domestic life of the court. He must be prepared to defend even the furthest reaches of his realm. Yet from this view can be seen the distant mountain, the pinnacle of wisdom, a place with which he is not unfamiliar.

The King of Swords appears somber. He has an unemotional demeanor, representing a mature individual who understands the mysteries of the sword. The King must be able to wield the sword with a sure and certain hand. At times he may be called upon to administer justice. He must be sharp of mind when visiting the borders of his land, far removed from Justice herself who remains back in the city. When the King must bring down the sword of truth, he wishes the blade to cut swift and clean.

The King is considered wise and brilliant. For the seeker this usually indicates someone who is knowledgeable in a field or profession. Whether this person represents the legal field, a skilled communicator, decision maker or manager, there are times when we must seek the advice and counsel of he who has the ability to be a judge and healer as well as knowledgeable when parrying with words or leading people through discord. The King of Swords will typically appear when the Tarot advises the seeker to consult a person with considerable mental agility, able to think clearly yet quickly, a person able to be decisive without being rash.

This King is able to use his sword to separate fact from fiction, truth from falsehood. He is a skilled strategist. Some authors of the little books which come with decks suggest that the King of Swords may be alerting the seeker that a lawsuit or similar situation requiring the King's skills may be at hand.

reversed

The reversed King of Swords is not someone you would wish as an adversary. In this reversed card the absence of emotional involvement indicates someone who acts without compassion. This might be someone who is cold and calculating, someone who even derives pleasure or personal power from seeing others suffer. Wielding power with little care for those in his way, this King may be considered dangerous, someone to avoid if possible. He is a king, after all, and even if not a kind king, it will take a lot to depose him.

When this card appears in a layout it may suggest a situation in which the person represented by this card may be prone toward cruel behavior. If legal action had been contemplated, some believe it may best be set aside until later. Having to face this King brings one into circumstances in which the adversary is likely to be stronger, enjoying toying with the seeker as the brunt of his cruel mental games.

If this card addresses the seeker's own personality it is a clear and strong word of caution. No longer deserving of the throne, professional help should be sought at once to bring about changes in attitude and behavior before the consequences are dire.

The Wands of Tarot

The element of Fire is represented in the Tarot with the suit of Wands, save for the minority who correspond the wand and/or staff with the element of air. In many decks the staff, the larger version of the tool, is represented. To help you see how this correspondence with fire makes sense, pause for a moment and think about sitting around a campfire. It is very difficult to resist taking a long, thin branch - instinctively shaped like a wand - and using it to control the fire, to play with it. In larger bonfires one uses a long pole-shaped branch (which is the 'staff') to manage the fire. And there are so many other tools from every day life through which we can see the properties associated with the wand or staff. One of my favorites is the long, pole used by a tightrope walker with which she maintains balance as she crosses what to us is an abyss. Aspects of the balance needed when working with the archetype of fire is shown in several of the cards in this suit.

In traditional playing cards, the wand is the same as the club. We see wands and staves (the plural of the staff) throughout our lives. There is the baton of an orchestra conductor, whose role it is to provide the spark, the drive and the energy of a performance to the musicians. And we often see the leader of an expedition with a staff. He must provide similar qualities for those who follow. Then there is the shepherd's staff, the tool of one who conducts and leads, through whose guidance others can achieve their goals without undue wasting of their own resources and energy. By following the example of the wand or staff, we can learn how to provide ourselves with fuel, how to control the 'fires of life' and to carefully transform our own fuel.

In my experience teaching Tarot and Ritual Magick, it seems that more people have difficulty with this element than with the other three of air, water and earth. This is because fire burns, it is difficult to control. More people seem to have a fear of fire than they do of water, or wind or of earthquake. Then there is the folk phrase which describes well one of the lessons taught by this suit, 'burning the candle at both ends.' Many of my students have had difficulty with this lesson as well.

Fire is a challenging element. From a metaphysical perspective, fire is a symbol of energy. Working with this element successfully requires learning how to maintain and utilize the energy for as long as possible. Despite the very active nature of this suit, wands teach us to be conservative. These cards teach conservation of fuel, particularly of the fuel of one's own life. By working through the cards we should learn the importance of self-control, or learning how to harness the power of our wills. We are taught the need to have discipline in order to accomplish a goal. Wands and fire teach us about stamina and endurance, the ability to utilize your strengths over a longer period of time without suffering 'burn out.' And they show us when to seek a little help from your friends.

Beginning with the Ace of Wands which embodies the 'staff of life,' the cards of this suit show us what results when we maintain self-control. They also show how we feel when our lack of self-control and discipline lead us to being somewhat embattled. The wands of those cards look much like the long staves used in martial arts, capable of fending off aggression. The wand, descendant of the club, can be a tool of aggression. The cards in this suit caution the seeker to avoid inappropriate aggression against others.

Returning to the reference of the 'staff of life,' in some decks the wand is depicted representing the polarities. The slightly knobbed wand used by The Magician is a prime example. In many decks there are buds, sometimes an occasional leaf, which show that the wand was derived from a living thing and contains yet within it a living, vital force. This is enlightening when we compare this suit with the other three tools. Those are created by humans from metals and forged and tempered with great skill.

The wand, representing the polarities of Yin and Yang (witness The Magician), may function as the lightning rod, drawing energy to it, that creative energy and drive which will be available to the seeker when she turns to the great, divine powers of the Universe.

If we are unable to manage this element in our lives, we are likely to encounter burn-out, a very appropriate and accurate phrase. Our passions and our desires must be harnessed. We cannot let them burn out of control and we must learn how to gather and utilize the fuels we need for success in our lives.

Ace of Wands

As do all aces, the Ace of Wands represents the birth or rebirth of a situation. It offers the seeker a renewal and a sense of beginning. What a great card! Depicting the fertility of a new cycle in one's life, the Ace heralds the time for a fresh start. This is somewhat like a divine relay race in which the gods have handed you the wand. Now it's time to utilize this energy wisely for much power and creativity are available. Events are able to move so quickly that it seems like the hand reaching through the cloud represents a breakthrough of sorts.

We know that the situation is fertile. Traditionally, the wand is shown with leaves, sometimes even a flower to remind us that the wand or staff is filled with vitality and the forces of life. The seed of one's desire has germinated and new life bursts forth. But all of this momentum requires focus and we are reminded that the suit of Wands brings us face to face with the lessons of discipline and of controlling one's will.

There is much which you can accomplish at this time. Success lies before you, indicated by the large, towered edifice atop the mountain of wisdom, one which is attained only by crossing the river of a deep, internal transformation. But to embrace these creative ventures, physical action must be initiated. This card serves the seeker notice: the time is now. This is not a time for procrastination nor for wandering aimlessly in the abstract mental realm. Take the wand in hand and put things in motion. Now.

The wand is the only tool of the four which has been a living being. Chalices, blades and pentacles are all created, traditionally, from metal, forged by humans in fire. But the wand has been cut from a living tree. It can only work with fire when it is the tool in control. This reminds us that the physical world is very present and involved in what lies before the seeker. It brings to mind an important religious action. A living thing has been *sacrificed* in order to manifest this change. To effectively handle this tool and to reap the potential benefits will also require sacrifice, but this mystery teaches us that true sacrifice brings elevation.

The Ace of Wands is a card of power and activity. It takes considerable strength to handle the wand, not just physical strength, but that of character as well. It is not uncommon for the proper handling of these events to lead to a position of leadership. Appropriate sacrifices offered toward positive goals will prove wise investments.

The Ace of Wands symbolizes the masculine half of the Universe in its creative aspect. It is fair to say that there is a phallic aspect to this tool. The energy is dynamic and, if used inappropriately, can become aggressive in ways detrimental to others and to one's spiritual health. When this happens, the wand becomes more like its mundane cousin, the 'club.'

reversed

The reversed Ace of Wands is a clear warning that your life is not in balance. All the creative potential discussed above is now in jeopardy and may be facing destruction. Because wands teach us of the mature handling of one's will, it is likely that the seeker does not understand what is taking place. We rarely do when we are out of control. This card offers clear notice: you can begin to turn things around by taking responsibility for your misspent actions.

Avoid rash behavior and, certainly, take control over emotional reactions to the situation for that will only lead to further negative complications. When this Ace is reversed, it may indicate the imposing or forcing of one's will upon others. Frankly, the implications of this card are not pretty. Someone whose behavior has brought about a reversed Ace of Wands is someone likely to misuse power, who is without spiritual balance. If you want a convenient way to interpret this card, that reversed wand reminds us of the 'ten-foot pole' with which you wouldn't wish touch the person or situation represented by the reversed Ace of Wands.

A reversed Ace of Wands may indicate a situation in which someone is handling this tool as a weapon rather than as the means of supporting one's self. Be very cautious if that is the scenario. If this card indicates the seeker, failure to remedy the situation can have drastic consequences.

With misdirected physical and emotional energies, the person in question has lost the ability to grow. Irresponsible behavior has cost the strength of character needed to hold the wand in its healthy position. But this reversed card can be restored if the person is willing to make the needed changes.

Two of Wands

The wand which had emerged in full creative potential from the Universe has now become two. When two creative endeavors, two wills or two desires, have been brought into manifestation it is necessary to pause and reflect. The two staves are not in balance with each other and it is that which is the crux of this card.

Looking at the card designed by Waite and illustrated by Pamela Colman Smith, we see a figure who holds the elements of the world in her hand. Sometimes when teaching my course we break into a refrain of "He's Got the Whole World In His Hand..." Looking toward the horizon, we see fruitfulness upon the land. Within walking distance is the shore is a large body of water, symbolic of the depths which might be crossed as one undergoes transformation. In the distance to the right are the mountains which represent pinnacles of achievement in the realms of spiritual and intellectual growth. A careful examination of the figure's head indicates that he is not studying the globe in his hand so much as he is gazing out to sea, perhaps wondering where this quest, that of the staff in hand, might lead in the long-term future.

It is that staff which has been raised. In the moment of the card, it is likely favored over the other, which has been set against the wall. Note that there is a brace near the base holding it in place. It is quite possible that the second staff will not be brought into use in the immediate future. As the figure examines his situation, one option is apparently favored over the other, but it is not yet appropriate to take action, for this period of study indicates that there is something to learn.

The Two of Wands is frequently a card of positive developments, but it is important to read the other cards in a reading with care. In some situations this card indicates that there may be some degree of tension between the two staves or forces. In this card both wills are not functioning together in harmony. One will prevail and the process leading to that dominion may not always be comfortable for those concerned. Some artists create decks in which the Two of Wands describes a situation in which there is some degree of friction between those involved, or there may be disharmony within the individual who must choose within herself. There are times in which this card can indicate a contest of wills to determine who ends up with the controlling power.

It should be noted that the figure has not yet set out on the journey. Still hoping for an answer, the character is hesitant, possibly wondering if he truly wishes to move forward. There is a moral sense to this card, for the situation is not one of happiness yet, at this time, there seems to be a lack of fulfillment. One staff must be chosen and that course of action followed. Initiative must be taken and the journey begun.

reversed

The reversed Two of Wands indicates a lack of control, a lack of understanding the situation. The loss of awareness creates threads of paranoia, uncertainty regarding one's unhappiness. The loss of self control gives others the upper hand. The Two of Wands in this position may be alerting the seeker that events might be changing in favor of others, urging an evaluation of the situation and a change in one's approach and attitude.

The reversed Two of Wands might indicate to the seeker that her own internal response is out of balance. This card appears when feelings of resentment over someone else having the upper hand may lead to an aggressive or hostile response. The Two of Wands in this position is a card implying oppression, hostility, and a lack of control over one's will. It can be restored to the thoughtfulness and caution of its upright position. There should be no delay in making immediate changes in attitude and behavior.

Three of Wands

Who is that, standing upon the hill overlooking a large body of water? It is difficult for me to see Pamela Colman Smith's image and not wonder if she is not listening to the strains of "I saw three ships a-sailing." This figure is typically that of the person seeking advice through the reading, she who is seeking counsel through the Tarot, framed by the presence of the three staves.

The staff, emerging from the sky only two cards ago in the Ace, has now evolved into three, one at hand and the other two firmly set upon the hill. The wand or staff represents a strong will and the discipline necessary to utilize the available resources in a most fruitful manner. Two are positioned on either side of the cloaked figure and, with the person, recreate the two pillars which frame the High Priestess. This symbolism of the two pillars and the third, the middle pillar, is echoed throughout many cards of the Tarot. But the 'three' which is most interesting is that of all three staves as a whole.

The natural energy of a 'three' is that of progressive change, one which evolves through stages and leads to a new level of understanding and ability. A three is the number of the trinity, of complementary energies which are yoked together, in this case through some commitment to an undertaking of business. There is strength in numbers and there is business strength in this suit's third card. It is not coincidental that one's own staff is extended to stand outside kÂp   p u † the two. Th kA pport from one's associates is an even greater source of strength and more relevant to the achievement of your goals than you may realize.

In the distance we see mountains, those mountains which represent the potential for success and achievement. Yet one cannot reach the mountains without crossing the vast stretch of water, ever-present symbol of the abyss. There is no other way to reach the goals of those distant shores. How would the seeker cross the abyss? The crossing might be taken through shared effort, not only blending the three staves or separate wills into a common energy but doing so in both worlds. The Three of Wands alerts you to the need to make progress in crossing the abyss (the spiritual realm) and to work within the manifest world utilizing labor, money and time. No one's will can dominate the others, for what lies before you is a harmonious, cooperative effort.

If the sailing ships are any indication, this is too great an expanse of water to cover in any vessel which would move by solitary power. The size and shape of the ships indicates that these are not pleasure craft, but are vessels of commerce and trade, representing the interactions and dealings of people working in society. Through working well with others, you will not only reap tangible rewards but you will also make significant spiritual progress.

If there is any doubt that this card represents working in cooperation with others, the presence of the two staves, held by unseen hands, further represents this concept. It is not the identity of the individuals which is the moving force helping you toward your goals, but it is their combined wills, their desires, which are paramount forces.

If the figure represents your self, take note of where you stand. You have already grown and accomplished enough in life that you are depicted standing on a hill or prominence. It is through your own gains that you are now working with others and through your own 'prominence' that you can see the potential of the future, symbolized by those distant mountains. The very position which has been achieved allows you to gaze into the distance and see with clarity. The Three of Wands is communicating that you are in a position of advantage.

The Three of Wands also brings this message from the suit of Wands: success can be had through working in cooperation with others toward a common goal. Implied is that the goal is not easy, there is much water to cross and there will be heights to scale. It is not something you could do without the help of trusted and wisely-chosen associates.

reversed

Of course, there will be times when the Three of Wands appears in its reversed position, cautioning you to avoid building your expectations upon potential help. Under these circumstances, it may seem as if you'll have all the help you need, yet those individuals may prove unreliable. Perhaps the coalition of the three staves will be unable to sustain itself. It may be that those upon whom you wish to rely will be unable to back up their good intentions with action. Some authors consider them potentially untrustworthy. But do not only look at others as the potential source for difficulty. The reversed Three of Wands could well be indicating that your own weakness of character might be your undoing in this cooperative effort. Rather than three separate wills able to blend and work harmoniously toward the common end, they are likely to be at odds with each other and the labors not as fruitful as you hope. Do not allow your desire for the end goals to affect your ability to clearly assess the present.

Four of Wands

That fertile, creative Ace of Wands extended by the heavens has taken root and multiplied. Four wands are strung o'erhead with lush fruits and vegetation. These staves stand in pairs, reminiscent of the two pillars, as a framework through which we see a highly desirable scenario.

A couple stand, their heads wreathed in garlands, arms raised bearing flowers or herbes or other symbols of celebration and joy. Guests are gathering in the background. To the right is a bridge, the same design which appears in the woeful Five of Cups. The abyss of one's dreams may easily be crossed. The bridge is lush with fertility to welcome those who would come to the home of the couple.

And such a home it is! Rather than a tall, erudite mountain in the background, we see one of the finest castles to appear in the Tarot. The Four of Wands represents the fruitfulness one can have when the four elements are kept in balance through will and perseverance. The staves represent success but they also provide support in order to sustain success.

This card is among my favorites, not only because it is a card of goodness, of hard work rewarded with fruitfulness and abundance, but primarily because it has long been the significator for The Rowan Tree Church.

Not seen in this card - yet indicated by its numerical value - is the nature of a four. The lessons one must manage in life are not only those of the suit of

Wands, but of all four suits. The mysteries inherent in the numerology of a four are those found when one manifests the wisdom within all four and keeps it in balance. The achievement of such a perfection in one's work brings forth the simplicity of the Four of Wands: "and they all lived happily ever after."

A card of peace and joy, the Four of Wands provides the foundation of one's creativity. These ethical values are structural, and it is upon them that one creates the castle of your desires brought into manifestation.

The aspect of prosperity often indicated by this card may sometimes appear in a reading when the acquisition of a new home or a real estate transaction is being successfully completed. Because of this, there are some who wish for the appearance of this card, not realizing that all of this bounty does not arrive by chance. The structure of these four wands indicates that these achievements have been through a cooperative effort. Hard work, discipline, a will focused toward these goals, all of this has provided an established space within which to be creative and joyful.

The appearance of this card in a layout is like receiving a high grade for your hard work. The Universe has rewarded you.

reversed

Those for whom the Four of Wands appears reversed are very likely enjoying a significant degree of success. However, there is the sense of the work and success being incomplete. One might imagine hearing Peggy Lee singing, in the background, "Is That All There Is?"

The reversed Four of Wands offers the same degree of potential, but the card in its reverse position contains a cautionary message. Without embracing self-control and taking seriously the lessons described above, incomplete happiness will keep one from the joy which should be available.

Five of Wands

There is a look of disharmony about the Five of Wands. Although an occasional artist will depict this card with strong overtones of battle, the Five of Wands does not represent open conflict as much as it does a situation in which different people are unable to reconcile the differences in their wills and egos. Looking at the image of the wands, we see energy moving in many directions without harmony. It is as if five individuals, attempting to place their staves in a workable pattern, are completely at odds with each other.

The promise of the single, fertile wand extended from the divine hand in the Ace is now caught up in the immediacy of the situation. We do not see mountains in the distance, only a small hillock. The events of the present distract us from thinking about the long-term future. While it may be desirable that these individuals learn to work with cooperation, this is a situation in which there is a lack of harmony, in which each wand represents a desire for control or to move in a different direction.

Individual egos and desires struggle among themselves and, to emerge from this card feeling good about the outcome while enjoying success, it will be necessary to approach the situation with determination, prepared to stand your ground.

The Five of Wands cautions you about a period of strife. This card portends ordeals, is typical of office politics and may even indicate the need for legal action. You will be tested and will face competition, but the archetypes of the Tarot are wise and, if you have learned your lessons well, you will pass the test.

Fives are not generally welcomed by seekers, considered neither easy nor desirable cards. You must be able to rely upon your instinct and, if you do, will emerge from this situation changed. It will not be easy but, like the fine metal of an exceptional tool, you will be tempered and strengthened by all which takes place. Events will move quickly and you'll not have the luxury of withdrawing to contemplate and make logical plans. You face fast paced action alone with your instinctive response as your primary defense. If your instinct is based upon wisdom, compassion and spiritual maturity, you are in good shape. If not, you may feel yourself under attack, tired and frustrated from facing chaos while lacking in self-discipline, self knowledge and self-control.

Although this may not be the most comfortable of situations, it may be just what is needed in order for the Universe to temper your will, showing you how to be strong and decisive of character without becoming emotionally entangled in the situation. Be prepared to be assertive when needed, but in a mature, calm manner. Prepare yourself quickly. This is a fast, hard-hitting and tricky situation. Should this card appear in a reading, waste no time.

reversed

The creators of Tarot decks are not always consistent with the reversed meaning of the Five of Wands, perhaps indicative of the nature of this card. It will be necessary for you to check the instruction book which comes with your deck.

The situation before you may well involve trickery and fraud. But with many decks the ordeal may be changing for the better. On the other hand, some decks indicate that things may have taken a turn for the worse. In any case, things are in flux.

Those who have a healthy love of good competition and bring maturity and wisdom to the situation are more likely to have a good outcome. They are apt to feel exhilarated by the vitality of the events and able to have the upper hand.

Six of Wands

When the Six of Wands appears in a layout, take joy! The strong, fertile wand we saw in the Ace, sprouting leaves and creative energy, now bears a wreath. We see a second wreath worn upon the head of the rider. Perhaps she encountered the Five of Wands but had learned well her Tarot. Her horse is cloaked in a garment, which further represents the celebration of victory and success. The Six of Wands depicts the potential of being rewarded for a yet-incomplete endeavor. Thus far there is success. The work has been well-done, the energy created in the process is positive and growth oriented.

In addition to the crowned wand, the other five staves are carried by one's companions. These might be fellow warriors or coworkers. They also have a share in the victory, having contributed their efforts to those of the seeker. They raise their wands high and cheer their leader.

There are no buildings, no mountains, no trees. The scene before us in the Six of Wands is composed entirely of the small group of compatriots who have shared in the efforts thus far and who will continue to follow the rider as they collectively face the next challenge. This is not the final card in this journey of life, for the lessons the seeker must embrace are those of this suit and the lessons of any other cards which represent the next challenge which lies ahead.

This card of Wands represents the numerical value of a 'six.' These events are an evolutionary process. The horse is also indicative of the need to sustain the current momentum while it is favorable. Horses are often symbols of fertility, of regeneration and of movement toward the goal. Although horses are sometimes symbols with overtones of sexual fertility, this horse has been draped, indicating that its energy is used only toward the goal at hand. Perhaps much later will this horse be allowed to run and frolic in some pasture, but for now it is part of the concerted work toward success.

There are times when the Six of Wands appears in a reading to indicate that the hard work or 'battle' is at hand, that success is possible should the seeker follow this course of action. The rider remains upon the horse, ready to spring into action. In such circumstances, the immediate wisdom is to remind the seeker that she has the support of her group of close friends or coworkers. The seeker is reminded of the need to be flexible, to be alert to the events at hand and able to make creative adjustments as needed. The situation will require an understanding of other cards in the layout. The interpreter may wish some feedback from the seeker to be clear in deciphering whether this card speaks of the celebration as a current event or whether it speaks of the need to wear the laurels rather than sit upon them. One must be strong of will, able to fend off attack, ready to remain astride during the fast-paced action.

No matter whether the major battle has already taken place or is at hand, the Six of Wands is considered a card of good news. The seeker should embrace the lessons of this suit in order to prepare for the laurel wreath.

reversed

When those lessons remain unlearned, when the seeker is unwilling to set aside his ego or to bring spiritual balance and wisdom to life, then the reversed Six of Wands has a contrary meaning. It may now easily represent the opposite of success. The rider of the horse may feel thrown off balance. It is time for retreat. It seems as if things are going astray.

Opposing forces may well have the upper hand. The wills of others are likely to be imposed upon the seeker who is paying the price for poor preparation. This may translate into poor judgement manifesting as indecision, inertia, laziness, or an unwillingness to make changes and prepare for the challenge.

The reversed Six of Wands indicates the need for immediate caution. Reactionary behavior may lead to one being thrown off the horse. However, a willingness to embrace the wisdom and lessons offered through the Tarot is essential to avoid slipping back into the disharmony and pain of the Five of Wands. Although at least one author sees the reversed Six as positive, check your deck's book to be clear about the interpretation for this reversed image.

Seven of Wands

The wand which began this suit in the Ace is now held as a staff. The man stands near the edge of a precipice, his demeanor indicating that the six remaining staves are not considered friendly and supportive.

The terrain presents an interesting feature for not since the Fool have we seen someone standing so near the edge. However, unlike the Fool, this figure does not seem ready to take the plunge. The precipice is also an indication that the figure in this card has achieved some success in life. She is elevated over those who would challenge her.

A lack of self-confidence might erode one's will. After all, the seeker is definitely outnumbered. But this suit instructs us in the inner values we must have to achieve success in life. The wand represents will and that aspect of the card is essential in the Seven. This card shows that the seeker must draw upon his inner sense of strength. There is no one else upon whom he can rely and the Seven of Wands is a reminder that holding fast to his convictions and standing strong for what he believes will lead to victory.

The figure in the card stands solidly upon the earth. Similarly, it is essential that you stand firm upon your beliefs. You must trust yourself and feel comfortable relying upon yourself. Do not expect someone else to come along and fight your battles for you. Keep your feet well-planted upon the earth but remember to remain flexible yet sure-footed. You cannot retreat. The only path before you is to face this challenge and, done wisely, it will crystalize your inner strength. This is a card representing the potential for growth and these circumstances will be a catalyst.

This card represents many virtues, strength and valor among them. This is a time for facing challenges. Emulate the lessons of this card and you will be pleased with the outcome. A positive card, it is time to feel encouraged, for the Seven of Wands assures you that you do have the upper hand. Holding the staff in hand, it provides you with balance. Use it wisely and you can quickly make adjustments. Be decisive if necessary.

Should you panic and run, you will lose. The Seven of Wands is here to assure you that what you hold in your hands and within your spirit is your strength. Your character and your positive virtues will bring you to victory.

reversed

When the seeker does not trust her own principles and is fraught with anxiety and indecision, the Seven of Wands is likely to appear in a reading as a reversed image. When will and self-reliance are eroded by doubt, one is left vulnerable to those who would oppose your progress. This gives the upper hand to those who do not have faith in you. Your own cowardice will lead you to feeling badly over what is likely to be a failure.

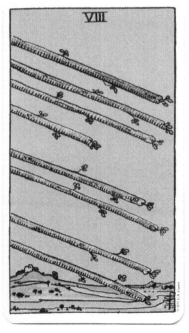

Reversed, the Seven of Wands attempts to warn you that your lack of will power is going to be your undoing. Take this warning seriously. You are about to be nudged right off the precipice, falling away from what should be a major step forward toward greater success. Changes can be made but require that you act without delay to empower your inner strengths.

Eight of Wands

The Ace of Wands, once held proudly by the hand of Divinity, would now seem to be shown as having become eight facets of the one desire. But this card is not the will of one individual, representing instead the momentum of will happening on many levels of reality. It may further indicate will and direction within a number of individuals.

In the distance atop a small mountain is a sizable building. The achievement of success awaits the seeker but only when having crossed the wide, meandering river of the abyss. No bridge is visible yet the seeker's eye does not look for the means to traverse the flow of the subconscious. In the immediate foreground eight wands are moving with great force and momentum.

There is no stopping the Eight of Wands. As an eight, it is a powerful card, one which can bring about transformation of the seeker at a deep level. Anticipate change at the mundane level within the events of one's life and also expect change to take place within the astral or spiritual. Expect your soul or spirit to feel the impact of change as well. Eights are cards of transformation.

And oh, if you could but remove yourself from the situation, gazing peacefully from the perspective and security of the hilltop ... but that wish is not to be. The Eight of Wands indicates a considerable amount of activity. Indeed, there is so much action you might, metaphorically, 'fasten your seat belt.' The human tendency, by nature, is to grasp at one or more of the wands, trying to control them separately. The better approach is to embrace change so that it is integrated into all aspects of your life. Stepping back from the details allows the seeker to see that everything is moving with a sense of purpose toward the desired goal. There is no conflict indicated.

This card may appear when there is too much to handle and when the seeker is likely to become too caught up in her own ego and its willfulness. Things are moving so quickly that it is difficult to feel in control. The luxury of having time with which to make an objective judgement is not found within the Eight of Wands. Wands represent the creative force and this is a card of swift regeneration. The seeker may well be getting what he asked for (even if he now wishes the results to be otherwise).

As an eight, this card shows us that there are others involved. All the seeker can do is to expect events to move so fast one shouldn't waste time reacting. As a footnote, it is believed by some to be not uncommon for this card to appear when a person jumps into a hasty marriage or intense love affair, one which will shake the seeker's life at all levels.

reversed

The reversed position of the Eight of Wands indicates an absence of the harmonious energy portrayed by the parallel tools. No longer moving in concert toward a common goal, a conflict among wills arises. Harmony of purpose is replaced by disharmony.

The reversed Eight is indicative of discord and disruption, quarrels and disagreements sometimes arising from envy and jealousy. The reversed Eight might suggest that an intense project becomes seriously delayed, increasing the potential for one of the parties involved to be unable to control his or her physical energy. At the extreme this card indicates a potential for physical violence.

Speaking to us of the problems which arise when people are unable to control their egos, these situations are definitely not fun. There is generally too much negative energy for the seeker to handle. It is to be hoped that the surrounding or adjacent cards in the layout might provide information useful in carefully working through this situation.

Nine of Wands

The fertile Ace of Wands extended from the heavens and sprouting promise is now held before the wary, tired seeker. Learning the lessons of this suit has been a challenge. The joy found in the Four of Wands led to disruption. The path of this suit has been one of victories and of skirmishes. The seeker stands there, a bandage about her head. Behind stand the eight remaining staves, readied behind a wall or terrace and, in the distance, we see the rise and fall of the Tarot's symbolic mountains.

The Nine of Wands is a card of self-discovery. The images of this card convey information about the seeker. Although the seeker may feel she is facing too much adversity, the card is telling her that despite any 'battle scars' she can build upon her past success. Some difficulties have already been overcome and she does have the strength to see this through to victory and success.

At the same time, the Nine of Wands cautions the seeker. This is a time to focus one's will. The eight remaining staves stand straight and orderly. They have been prepared and are organized, a lesson for the seeker. Some interpretations of the traditional imagery describe these eight representing allied strengths of the seeker, but some see these as adversarial. In either view, if the seeker uses this time well and prepares himself, he will be the ultimate victor.

The reality of this card is that the seeker, feeling a little bruised, will recover from his past wounds. The events at hand will show the seeker that he is more resilient than he believes. The process of rising to the challenge will focus his will, a process which requires drawing upon learned skills.

The distant mountains offer the promise of growth in strength and wisdom. Now is the time to remove any feelings of isolation, of separation from one's support systems and skills. In a metaphysical perspective, the seeker must become one with the wand and embody the principles of this suit. Channeling this energy through one's physical and spiritual being creates a catalyst for assured success.

reversed

In the reversed image the eight staves are likely to be adversarial. The seeker's inability to transcend feeling weak and sorry for himself are likely to give the upper hand to those who do not have his best interests in mind.

The seeker has now lost touch with his will and no longer believes himself capable of victory. Because the seeker thinks himself incapable, he is likely to fail in his goal of making progress. Unfortunately, he will manifest his negative belief.

Rather than the strength of victory, the reversed position cautions the seeker that a lack of preparedness allows the will of one's adversaries to dominate the situation. What can the seeker do when facing the reversed Nine of Wands? Trust yourself. Gather yourself together quickly and take control of your self, your emotions and your will. Build upon your strengths and take ethical action.

Ten of Wands

What a heavy burden life has brought our seeker. The Ace of Wands, which offered so much promise, has expanded into an armful of staves, the weight of which causes the seeker to be painfully bent over.

This should be a joyful journey, for there are fertile fields, verdant trees, the warmth of community and, most likely, family awaiting. But the load is heavy and the seeker's gaze is not upon the end of the journey. He appears to be gazing into the nexus of the ten staves.

The fiery creativity of this suit exemplified by the wands and staves has been overshadowed by the burden. The labor and responsibilities have outweighed the joys.

Unable to see beyond his armload, the seeker clings to his burden as if it is his source of strength. We can see that, although there are others waiting at the end of the journey, the seeker has not yet found a way through which to share the work. It is not that others are not willing to help. The very lesson of this card provides notice. The situation grows increasingly difficult to manage and control unless one is willing to allow others to become involved. Ask for help.

While it is true that this might require relinquishing some aspects of control, the Ten of Wands encourages the seeker to set aside the ego's belief that she alone must bear the burden. This card encourages her to share. It reminds her that it is essential that one's labor must also bring self-renewal, must recreate the joys of being creative.

This card indicates the need for change and, as a ten, is a card which shows us that this level of manifestation is not a solitary venture. The seeker must learn to share the work and share the rewards lest his labors become so oppressive that the toll overwhelms him. The need to go it alone may sometimes cause this card to appear when the ego believes that one's self-sacrifice is essential, perhaps at the expense of one's family.

Although the Ten of Wands usually appears at a difficult time in one's life, it is also a card which is supportive, reminding the seeker that he has done well, should persevere and continue, just not alone.

reversed

If the Ten of Wands has appeared in its upright position then no matter how difficult it may seem, it remained a card of encouragement and support. It is not so when reversed, for then we might imagine that the figure in the card has tripped and fallen right into his burdens. Their weight became too much. He lost sight of his goals and did not lighten his load when life brought that suggestion.

The reversed Ten of Wands becomes a card of self-defeat and loss. Seeing what has happened may be too difficult to bear, but it is important to learn from this Ten: the seeker has brought this upon herself.

Some decks offer differing interpretations of the reversed Ten of Wands. At least one artist suggests that the card means the situation is actually less of a concern, which is at odds with the majority but may work well in that deck. Check the manual which came with your deck you use when choosing an interpretation for this reversed card.

Page of Wands

A well-dressed Page stands at the center of this card. Androgynous in appearance, this might be a young man or a young woman. The position of a Page is usually that of someone of a youthful age. Her boots have flame shaped tops. A curious red feather or flame adorns the front of the hat. Her robe is embroidered with salamanders, the elemental creature associated with fire.

The Page stands in a large open space, mountains readily visible in the background. This is quite possibly a higher elevation, dry during the summer. The foreground does not offer us flowering trees or fruiting fields. The colors of this card are the colors of the desert, shown beneath a cloudless, blue sky. Even the distant mountains are a sandy brown color. The only green found in the colors of this card is that of the leaves, sprouting from the life-giving qualities of the staff. The Page's attention is held by these leaves. It is not the heights of achievement which hold her attention, however, but the staff, which obviously shows the life qualities which permeate this tool.

The wonder in the Page's face might be that of a young man who is dazzled by the miracle of life. "It's growing," the Page says. The awaited news is not that of external events so much as it is indicative of the energy of the situation, the fertility of potential and of the qualities needed to bring this new endeavor to fruition.

PAGE of WANDS.

The Page is traditionally seen as someone who is a faithful friend. After all, he is willing to put forth great effort to bring information back for the good of the realm. A creature of fire, this is someone who could be very dynamic, with a vital personality. This is a good thing when the card is in its healthy position but not so desirable if reversed.

Wands, staves and the element of fire are all indicative of the principle of action. Pages represent the activity of gathering news and information. This card usually indicates good news, positive news, but that which will require making adjustments in one's life and priorities.

Some who create decks see the passionate nature of fire and staves with a sexual, romantic overtone. The good news of which those Pages of Wands may speak might well be in the realms of love and sex! No matter what the news, wands speak of action and whatever the message brought by the Page, this news will require activity. It becomes the seeker's role to accept this news and be prepared to make these good events manifest.

reversed

The wand and the staff are commonly perceived as symbols of the discipline one has over *will*. The appearance of the reversed Page of Wands often coincides with events indicative of a person who has poor control over her behavior. Temper tantrums are like the sunspots of one's ego as it flares out, wastes fuel and negatively affects the self and others.

This is an unstable card showing that the individual is unlikely to be handling bad news with maturity. If it refers to the seeker (the card's position in the layout will indicate this) the advice is to get help. If it describes the actions of someone in the seeker's life, then he is advised to treat that out-of-control person with great care and give them as much space as is reasonable.

Knight of Wands

Like the baton in a relay race, the divine wand of the Ace would seem to have been handed off to the Knight, who is now charging forward. Wearing armor adorned with what looks like flames at his knees and elbows, the plume flowing from his helmet is also much like fire. The Knight is wearing a bright robe adorned with salamanders, the mythological figures representing the spiritual essence and life of fire.

The red-hued horse may be the most active of the four Knights' horses. Rearing and ready to go, horse and rider represent the great potential of energy being released. This dynamic card represents action and impulsiveness, warmth and passion.

Generally a positive card, the Knight of Wands represents someone who can be impetuous and unpredictable. This is a Knight who prefers dashing off to tilt at windmills, seeking dragons to slay, and romping through far and distant lands. There are no long-term goals represented by the mountains, frequent symbols of wisdom. I like to think that the background shows three pyramids, for the Knight has travelled far from the Page, who stood with three mountains at the horizon. Pyramids indicate a great cause, one which was achieved only because of those who shared the labor and embraced a common will. The workers and builders were honored for their labors and their rewards were far greater than simple self gratification.

The Knight will pursue a cause only when it is as sacred and meaningful as the wand found in the Ace. There is honor among Knights, and at her best, she seeks to represent it. The wisdom this Knight may gain from her quest is that found in the patience of others. She is happier burning her candle at both ends as she often flirts with danger.

Regardless of gender, the Knight represents an aspect of the masculine principle. An appealing individual, this dashing figure is attractive and represents much of the appeal humans find in fire. Alert and active with the quickness of fire, the Knight would love to remain home and fan the flames of his favorite romance(s) but the thrill of the quest has won.

This card indicates a need to emulate many of these qualities. An alert mind and quick, creative approach to problem-solving will help avoid battle. A skilled rider, the Knight and horse together can change direction in an instant without losing momentum, so long as the goal is kept in mind and the drive to succeed shines bright. This card shows the enthusiasm and passion with which one can manifest faith through the tools of one's will.

reversed

Those fiery, attractive qualities must be held in control by the Knight's honor and will to be fair. When out of balance, when the animal nature of passion is allowed to rule,

KNIGHT of WANDS.

the reversed card positions the horse above the Knight. Now the Knight represents an individual more than able to impose his will upon others and for whom the reward is so appealing that he can use his charms and guile to manipulate others in an attempt to bend them to his will.

What were battle skills and the ability to defend his lord and lady in the honorable Knight's path appear now as a tendency toward cruel and malicious behavior in the reversed Knight. Unable to control his passion and emotions, lacking the wisdom to see the greater view of life, the Knight's ego and selfish desires now rule. This card indicates a need to be extremely cautious when dealing with this individual. Immediate action may be questionable for it is important to avoid fanning any flames or aggravating someone able to react with violence. If at all possible, give that person space until he cools down.

If the card indicates the seeker, then advise the person to seek counselling at once to make changes and avoid what could be serious consequences.

Queen of Wands

Holding in her hand the handsome and powerful staff first manifested in the Ace, the Queen of Wands represents all that is good within this powerful, feminine presence. In her other hand she holds her scepter of a sunflower, but it is not the these symbols of authority which hold her attention. She appears to gaze elsewhere, her awareness turned to the more important matters of her realm.

The staff is fertile, having sprouted leaves, and the sunflower is organic and in harmony with nature. This is a fruitful and loving Queen. Even her crown is adorned with leaves. She is a wonderful, affectionate and powerful woman. She accepts her position as a role model. The Queen of Wands prefers the role model image to that of a woman with power over others. She is charming and inspiring yet she has been taught to handle the staff not only as a symbol of authority but, if necessary, to use it to defend her honor and throne.

The lions upon her throne are indicative of someone who represents great power, but what about that curious black cat? It is one of my favorite symbols found in the Waite-Smith deck, and one which is quite singular. Is there something about the Queen of Wands which no one is telling us? Personally, I like to think of the black cat representing this Queen's ability to be well-connected with the world of spirit. Perhaps she has far more ability than her skills as a manager and her ability to rule with a firm yet loving hand even when her devoted partner, the king, is elsewhere.

While the lions adorn the throne of someone with a stable, yet commanding ego, the suit of Wands reminds us that this Queen has her ego in control. This quality gives her the freedom to be warm and affectionate, sharing the fruitfulness of her wisdom with those who turn to her. Whether encouraging people to pursue the heights of their dreams found upon the mountain tops or holding fast to their ideals, she represents the quality of wands found through a positive, affirming determination. She is supportive of people, of their creative endeavors and their work. She is a benefactress as well as a leader.

Her will is steady and she is a warm, trustworthy person. The Queen of Wands is secure upon her throne, her position assured by the love and admiration of those who live within the kingdom. She knows what it has taken to hold the position of Queen. It has not been easy but it has made her strong and allowed her to extend her loving gaze to all who come to her.

The layout and cards near the Queen of Wands will indicate whether this is to be your role, whether this is an important influence in your life by another, or whether this is someone to seek out, to whom you should turn for guidance during the coming events.

reversed

The reversed Queen of Wands is someone who has great difficulty handling her staff of power. With a temperament easily described as that of a person with a 'short fuse,' the staff can quickly be used to impose her will over others. This card is indicative of someone who would not hesitate to misuse her power and whose emotions, when out of control, could easily lead to an abuse of power.

When reversed, she has placed her material desires before any spiritual wisdom and is now quite contrary by nature. Unable to control her willfulness and ego, this is someone who cannot be trusted, someone far too ready to manipulate others and attempt to bend them to her will. Do not expect fruitfulness to be found in this situation. The life created by the reversed Queen of Wands is one which will lead to a most unhappy conclusion. If this card represents another person, be very cautious with any interaction. If this card appears in a reading and is speaking of the seeker, then immediate and profound counselling is imperative.

King of Wands

The wand which initiated itself in the Ace is now standing before the King. It has made its journey through the suit and arrives transformed, representing a powerful will, one which is perceived in its role of leadership as an act of love.

With the salamander, a creature symbolic of the element of fire, near the king's feet, numerous kin of that elemental amphibian are seen upon both the King's throne as well as his robe. These salamanders are variations of the Ouroboros, the serpent which has taken its tail in mouth, representing the circle of creation and rebirth.

The mountain top in the distance indicates that the King has attained a noteworthy elevation. Certainly he is a man of fine character. He is honest and true blue and, despite the lack of greenery, he and his Queen represent the presence of fertility, of a couple who are closely tied to the land. He is held in high regard and he is someone easily loved not only by the Queen, but by all as a role model and a leader.

The King of Wands is a man of passion and this card is sometimes considered indicative of the potential for a strong and passionate partnership. Some see it foretelling an affair or a marriage. The King knows how to work well as half of a partnership. He is a good lover, he is conscientious. This card often represents a man who has an admirable character as well as being a desirable partner.

The suit of Wands is one representing the fiery nature of masculine strength. It can be strong and appealing yet, at times, behaving impulsively. By the time the wand reaches the King, however, his fiery nature has been tempered with maturity.

Although not readily visible other than through the Ouroboros, the King of Wands is a man of spiritual awareness. Although he carries considerable physical power and his will is one able to lead his people, the control he learns through his spiritual disciplines allow him to wield a power which is warmly extended and available to all who live in his realm.

reversed

The reversed King of Wands carries a big stick but does not speak softly. He is heavy-staved and wields a lot of power but does so without compassion and without the loving respect found in the card's upright position.

Controlling by nature, he not only attempts to maintain too much self control for his own good but he will be excessive in his need to exert his will and control over others. He can be demanding, someone who threatens others with his power when they do not do things his way.

If this card describes the seeker, then advice and counselling are in order. Not only is the personality of this reversed card unpleasant and hurtful to others, left unchanged it is likely to be the undoing of the 'King' himself.

Be careful of this individual. This card represents someone who is masculine by nature, someone who has lost the ability to control his temper. This personality may even carry traces of cruelty, taking a quiet fulfillment in the dominance of his power over others. Your caution in dealing with this person is important. Be temperate and avoid arousing his wrath.

The Cups of Tarot

Each of the four suits in the Tarot is devoted to one of four divisions of a person's reality. Swords address the element of air: ideas, thoughts and communication. Fire is concerned with one's reserve of energy as manifested through will, passion and desire. Pentacles teach us about our relationship with the manifest world: our ability to purchase needed resources. But cups cover possibly the most illusive of realms: that of our emotions.

Elementally speaking, cups correspond to the element of water. The cup is the tool which teaches us how to handle our ever-fluid emotions. It is through studying the 'tool' of each suit that we gain insight into the aspects of our own elemental natures.

Pause for a few moments and contemplate the nature of water. Water will take the shape of its container, but unlike air does not require a 'closed' or sealed container. So long as the container has sides and does not move too quickly, gravity will keep it in place. Water evaporates relatively slowly, and an open container will do just fine. Yet, emotional issues being what they are, positive and negative emotions alike definitely require a container.

A chalice is a wonderful container. Basically a goblet, it is representative of the traditional drinking vessel. There are a number of wonderful, romantic expressions sprinkled throughout poetry and literature which describe drinking as an emotional experience. What first comes to mind is the old song, "Drink to me only with thine eyes." A chalice is a suitable container for our emotions. We can gaze at the surface and see reflected some variation of reality. When perfectly still, it is a mirror but add motion to those fluid depths within the liquid and we lose our sight of reality. And the bottom? We can see and imagine those deeper levels of reality as we choose.

The element of water brings with it an interesting quality. Water distorts reality. No matter how clear it appears to the eye, water bends the refraction of light and even when pristine and pure, things are not quite what they seem. When disturbed and roiled, the muddy bottom of reality can be stirred up, creating a murky depth. This clouded water enables us to perceive our emotional sensations as a reality, for the true reality is hidden from view by our troubled emotions. Even our joyful memories tend to be rose coloured. Water is illusive. You can not grab a handful of water. It slips through your fingers. Our emotions are not the medium through which we ought gauge reality.

The vessel for water is the cup. It is interesting that the sword or the staff and wand are capable of being used as weapons. The pentacle is also a shield, useful in defense. A chalice or cup appears to be neither. Perhaps a chalice need not be a weapon because our emotions are weapon enough. Ah, but then there are those times when a poison was slipped into another's drink. A person's vile emotions are not unlike a toxic poison which inflicts harm upon whomever it is splashed. How different our social world would be if we could but contain our emotions.

The cards of this suit teach us much about handling our emotions. Years ago when teaching ritual arts, I had my students carry a filled chalice of water while walking around a Circle. Now *there's* a lesson in life! If you wish to live with a full range of emotions, then you must move carefully, steadily. Emotions are very fluid. When our lives are out of control, the cup's contents splash forth and eventually we are left feeling drained.

Some of the cards in this suit speak of pain, of loss and sorrow. These, too, are part of the rhythm of life. The suit of Cups teaches us that our feelings are not improper. Difficulties may arise, but that is through inappropriate behavior or expression of those feelings. Living with your chalices means learning to handle your emotions in a mature manner, yet learning to *have* your emotions and allowing them to bring you life. Just as the tides of the ocean have their rhythm, each of us is a chalice. The suit of Cups can teach us to live with our emotions, to have them and embrace them and use them as a tool with which to bring joy to others and through which to find our own fulfillment.

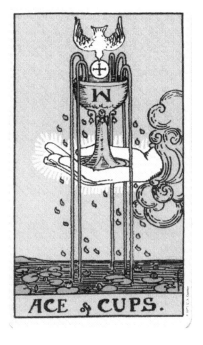

Ace of Cups

What an image! Frequently a favorite card for artists and designers, the Ace of Cups is a blissful abundance of joyful images. The hand is extended from the heavens offering blessings from the Divine. Five streams of water, for spirit and four elements, overflow down into a pond upon which float water lilies. A dove which represents the purity of spirit and peace holds the bread of manifestation. Through this manna one communes with the equal armed cross which represents reality. Truly it seems like gentle music in the background should be playing "my cup runneth over with love..."

If you understand the lessons of this card and manifest the spiritual awareness and balance implicit in its images, then you, also, can have this perpetual flow of the waters of life coming into manifestation without any disturbance. It is essential to not just count one's blessings, but to see simply being as the means through which they constantly overflow and are a source of inspiration for others. The strong, religious imagery depicts this principle: your life is not just for your own happiness. Live so that you can bring inspiration to others so that they, also, may find inner fulfillment.

This card indicates that your life is overflowing with emotional renewal. What lies before you is further symbolized by the small 'tongues' which represent the presence of divinity, not just within the hand, but gently coming down to earth.

This gift of the gods does not arrive from the unexpected. One cannot experience this sublime reality unless your life has been prepared. How can this be accomplished? We must understand the principle of recycling. Water flows from the chalice into the pond but the chalice is ever full. You cannot have overflowing joy unless you are constantly renewing your soul through a direct connection with the Universe. And the water flowing down into the water below creates not a ripple. The lily pads represent grace and fertility and yet, there is a mountain in the distance which shows that we can, indeed, achieve the heights of our ideals through this card.

Is it possible for the Ace of Cups to appear when you are *not* feeling an awareness of abundant joy? Certainly it is, and then the card is reminding you that you have all the blessings you could possibly have. It is time to make a major shift in your awareness so that your inner self can sustain its renewal.

Many might overlook the tiny bells hanging around the bowl of the chalice. Bells are traditionally used to dispel any negation. The Ace of Cups is a radiantly positive card and one of the most desirable in the deck. If you'd like to see it appear in one of your readings, then study it well. The Ace of Cups offers you lessons and images with which to evolve your spiritual and emotional self. Learn to live so that your emotions are a calm, fertile pond within which grows the lotus. Learn to open your inner self to the spiritual strength of the Universe, so that the cup of your emotions can be ever filled to overflowing. Learn to live your life so that your blessings overflow and touch the lives of those around you. This is not something which will 'just happen' to you - it is something which awaits those who make it happen.

reversed

As we might expect, when this lovely cup is reversed, it leaves us wanting, feeling drained as if we're running on empty. Why might we feel this way?

Because we have lost touch with the true source of happiness. Perhaps the seeker has experienced a severe loss and forgotten that no matter how great one's personal sorrow, life goes on and the Universe continues to proffer blessings. Only infrequently might this card indicate symptoms of depression such as that experienced when one has lost a loved one and is without a spiritual foundation for sustenance. The reversed Ace of Cups does *not* indicate the death of a loved one, only the person's inability to handle such a situation.

Some situations cause this card to show up in a personal reading, indicating that the seeker does not have a connection with spiritual elevation. In this scenario the Tarot is trying to alert the seeker or the interpreter that one's spiritual vitality is drained because of misplaced values, perhaps because one is unwilling to grow emotionally.

When one is emotionally bereft and the reversed Ace appears, it indicates that one does have the ability and potential to restore one's spiritual and emotional health and vigor. Such a renewal and restoration can occur only with hard work and with sacrifice. But look at the image of the Ace. Could anyone not embrace the growth necessary to hold that card dear?

Two of Cups

What was, in the first card of this suit, a stunning chalice extended from the heavens, has now manifested as two chalices, each held by a figure. The energy of the two figures and of their cups is given shape as the twined serpents which arise to the divine, winged lion, a symbol of creative force which leads to success. The traditional caduceus (a herald's staff) belonged to Apollo but was given as a gift to the messenger Mercury, hence the wings we usually see which, in this card, include the lion.

The couple stands upon a flat plain with a perfect horizontal line, indicating that human forces have brought change to the immediate landscape. In the distance we see a home upon a hill, representing the fruits of their success. It is a visible, attainable goal.

In order for the joys of this card to come into being, friendship and harmony are essential. The potential for success will be found through a mutually-supportive endeavor, one in

136

which each partner respects the other. The fact that the male figure's hand reaches out and the woman's does not is likely a reflection of the times and should not indicate that one figure takes precedence over the other. Both partners wear wreaths upon their heads. Each will contribute equally in this venture.

This card does not appear only for romantic unions. It is equally representative of unions which are based upon business goals but which may also hold a spiritual and emotional bond. There is great reason to share a cup of celebration when our lives enter this phase. We might raise these cups to toast each other. Handled in a mature manner, working together will greatly enhance the friendship. Being cooperative and understanding will bring to the situation increased fruitfulness and improve the odds of success. The Tarot perceives each partner as having the needed maturity and poise to carry a full cup, the ability to maintain emotional stability. Each is able to make adjustments, to cooperate in the give and take of such a joint venture.

reversed

As one might expect, when the Two of Cups meets its reversal, the relationship is troubled and there are likely to be misunderstandings. The human response to such discomfort is to withdraw from the working relationship, and this card may indicate such a division or parting. Everything seems turned around but, this being the suit of Cups, the problems are likely of an emotional nature and can be resolved with maturity and openness. If you encounter a reversed Two of Cups, remember to hold your chalice steady.

Three of Cups

The cup initially extended from the Divine with which to celebrate emotional joys has evolved into three cups, each held aloft by a dancing woman. The three cups together represent a type of trinity, a religious symbol of manifestation. In the foreground we see the fruits of the harvest, which looks much like a pumpkin, perhaps with grapes, and behind them an abundance of other fruits.

One of the women is clothed in a white robe, her hair garlanded with flowers as if the Maiden. To the right of the three is a woman with fruits in her hair. As she dances, she holds a bunch of grapes. She represents fruitfulness and fertility and could well represent the Mother. With her back toward us, in an autumn-colored robe of russet cloth, is a woman whom we might choose to perceive as the grandmother of the maiden. In the autumn of her life, perhaps she is the Crone.

A joyful card, and one greeted with pleasure when it appears in a reading, the Three of Cups represents fulfillment both in the manifest world and in the spiritual world. The seeker is being shown that abundance and fruitfulness are present in her life and it is now appropriate to take time and space within which to celebrate.

Recognition by one's friends of this good fortune is important. The seeker has integrated lessons learned and brings spiritual awareness to the celebration. All aspects of life are touched by the spirit of wonder and of the divine, and are in the process of being transformed to a new level of awareness. The Three of Cups indicates that the seeker is being rewarded for his good work and is now entitled to some gifts from the Universe. The spirit is feeling elation, having grown. The corporeal body is likely to be enjoying good health and healing. And the world of the seeker is bringing rewards and good further into manifestation.

For some, this is a card of Women's Mysteries. More than once a woman in one of my Tarot courses has suggested that this card may indicate pregnancy.

Whether you see the three figures as the three aspects of the Goddess or the Three Graces, there is cause to be dancing in joy. Typically, this card will appear in a reading when you have worked very hard to achieve your goals.

reversed

However, should this card appear reversed, it indicates that the seeker may be desirous of this type of celebration, but the perceived success is not genuine success. You are celebrating when you shouldn't be. The lesson of this reversed card is the need to finish what you are working on. Avoid the temptation of indulging one's sense of wanting. If you remain too focused upon the rewards and the desire to party and take pleasure without embracing the spiritual lessons at hand, the rewards (which have only begun to manifest) are likely to come to a halt. One's pleasures are likely to be transformed into the pain one encounters from having ignored the fullness of reality.

Should this card appear reversed, a careful and honest self-examination allows the individual to take the proper steps so that the immediate work at hand will lead to the dance of joy so favored by the Three of Cups.

Four of Cups

Reflective of the Ace of Cups, we again see the hand extending from the heavens. It is offering the young seeker a cup, but the seeker is not looking at this wondrous gift. I am reminded of two old, popular songs. "The fool on the hill" is the young man. He's not paying attention and, instead, is humming the lyrics to the song Peggy Lee made famous, "Is That All There Is?" No, he's not paying attention and gazes not at divine opportunity but at the three cups sitting just below.

We wish he were embracing the view from the top of this hill. In the distance are easily seen the mountains of achievement and spiritual attainment. Instead the figure leans against the tree of life, oblivious to the spiritual wisdom it contains.

The Four of Cups is a card of mixed blessings. It alerts the seeker that there is much goodness in life, but an apathetic attitude leaves one feeling that spiritual gifts and inspiration are beyond one's reach. Once again, an emotional reaction has left reality beyond one's grasp.

When counseling clients and this card appears, I inevitably quote from the Charge of the Goddess (attributed to the late Doreen Valiente): "Know that the seeking and yearning shall avail thee not unless thou knowest the Mystery: that if that which thou seekest thou findest not within thee, thou shalt never find it without thee..."

The seeker believes that she has the desire to bring change into her life, but she is unable to see the whole picture. She cannot appreciate the simple things in life. She has forgotten to count her blessings. Now, her emotions weigh her down and her life is without momentum.

The Four of Cups teaches us about the foundation of our emotions. If we are too concerned with immediate gratification, with self-promotion, with financial windfalls, our emotional health and well-being are subject to the whims of life's transitory nature. There will be many periods of boredom and ennui in life. One's gifts are not appreciated and there is no joy to be found in daily life. The seeker, unable to see the potentials of his life, will be plagued with dissatisfaction, with a sense of restlessness but without the clarity of emotional vision to recognize that all that he needs is being offered to him. It is right there before him. Those four cups are the foundation of his future.

This card, embodying the cornerstone of the numerical value of a four, teaches us that our emotions create a weak foundation: do not base your decision upon them, particularly when feeling despondent. The seeker's posture is not one found in yoga: it clearly depicts frustration but not the type of unrest which might lead to a positive solution.

Wanting things to be different but doing nothing about it causes the blessings to be ignored rather than counted. Something wonderful is about to slip away or evaporate. Don't allow yourself to wallow in this emotional pool but, rather, face the music and take that cup of spiritual blessings being offered.

reversed

The interpretations of this card may vary among decks. The more popular version is that it represents a positive change in energy. Something good may be coming. The seeker is likely to see the possibilities reflected in the offered chalice. New possibilities can be perceived following a change in attitude. Decisions are being made from a foundation of mature judgement.

And yet there are some decks that treat the reversed Four of Cups somewhat as a 'little Moon Card,' suggesting a sense of premonition and foreshadowing that things may be turning for the worse. You will need to read the little book which accompanies your deck to determine the appropriate interpretation for the reversed position of this card.

Five of Cups

The figure we see in this card is not a happy camper. Wallowing in self pity, we have an image of someone crying over spilt milk. Indeed, three cups are tipped over, their contents seeping into the earth. Despite this immediate scene of sadness, there is so much being offered to the seeker. Two cups await, sitting securely, their contents intact. If the seeker could but get past the sense of loss and regret, the path across the flowing abyss is clear. A bridge spans the water, sometimes perceived as reminiscent of a rising Full Moon. The promise of the Ace of Cups remains, but only if the seeker is willing to transform herself.

If this were a musical card, we might hear Simon and Garfunkle singing, "Like A Bridge Over Troubled Waters." Certainly the figure is troubled, wearing a black cape of depression. Unable to see the good which remains in her life, the disappointments (sometimes over friends or family) are not reality-based. The seeker must transcend her expectations of others and let go: they have the freedom to pursue their own lives. As long as one clings to emotional losses, life cannot be enjoyed. Progress cannot be made. The river needs to be crossed for there, upon the hill, is the castle of one's dreams.

The seeker may well be filled with a sense of despair, wanting to give up. But just because you're not having fun right now is no reason to give up and chuck it all! The words written by most authors of Tarot decks indicate that the seeker expected more than he got and now is acting childish. It's time to focus your attention upon the two full cups. Drink from them and you can again experience the renewal which emanates from the Ace of Cups.

When this card appears in a reading, it's time to count your blessings! You alone are the cause for your present emotional pity pot (as one of my students called it). Quit wallowing in your misery. Pick up those two full cups (which are as much as you could carry, in any case) and cross the bridge into the dreams of your future.

reversed

There are some curious interpretations associated with the reversed Five of Cups. Overall, it reverses the above negative outlook on life. The 'yuk' of the Five of Cups is replaced by hope. Sometimes this card implies that there may be some reunion with those from whom we have been unhappily separated. When the Five of Cups appears reversed, there is reason for a sense of hope and every reason to take courage. It is time for moving forward with one's life.

Six of Cups

The cup once offered us by the heavens in the Ace now sits upon a pedestal, filled with flowers and given a place of prominence. The Six of Cups is in an urban setting. Full of imagery, six cups are surrounded by large buildings, paved walks, formal planting and human figures, from the youths in front to the guard walking toward the tower.

This card may be seen as a reflection of the harvest, for each cup has been filled with flowers, including those lovely five-pointed-star types. Four flower-filled chalices create the foundation of this card. One cup is being honored on the pedestal and the sixth is being proffered by the woman gardener to the figure in the fool's cap. (Or is it the other way around?) These figures are often described as representing children yet the female figure seems a child only because of the lack of height. The younger of the two in appearance would seem to be too tall to be a child. It is a mystery!

This is a curious image. It is also possible to interpret these figures as the jester offering the chalice to the woman. Yet, in the context of the harvest, it would make more sense to see the woman as the one who planted and nurtured the seeds and cultivated the flowers, now offering the chalice to the jester who is smelling them. Jesters and fools are frequently found in association with the harvest. Not only is there a sense of the male fertility image (as in Puck) but the celebration of the harvest is a time for gaming. I could readily imagine someone chosen to embody fertility dressed for the harvest festivities, costumed larger than life with a jester's cap. It remains your decision whether you see the two as children or as jester and gardener. The mitten on the woman's hand may be the gardener's glove or it may be a further variation of the glove as symbol of something present yet unseen which has appeared in other cards.

Regardless of their stations in life, the two figures represent reflection. Cups are the Minor Arcana tool which is that of water, of emotions and the subconscious. It is time to reflect upon all the good which has been manifest, to count one's blessings and enjoy these simple pleasures. The energy of the number six permeates this card as well. This is a time to reflect upon the growth and to contemplate what changes would be appropriate in order to continue manifestation into the future.

But the Tarot is never so simple. If one's guard has been let down (the guard is, after all, walking away!) we might be brought into the illusion of our memories and dreams. It is the illusive nature of elemental water which permeates this suit. Each cup may be perceived as filled with memories and memories are wont to become daydreams. A gardener knows that daydreaming does not bring forth the harvest. The garden visitor is apt to dally with the daisies, smelling the flowers and allowing the many-hued scents of the abundant flowers to evoke endless dreams. But the gardener is ever attentive to the water content of the soil, the presence of weeds and the health of the plants.

The Six of Cups may be a card of abundance, but whether it represents actual manifestation or the illusion of abundance is best determined by the neighboring cards in the layout. When the Six appears in a reading, you know that your life goals are best served if you take the emotionally responsible path. Be mature with your emotions, adjust your desires, and tend to the 'gardens' of your life.

reversed

Should the Six of Cups appear reversed, it is likely speaking of a situation in which one is avoiding the lessons of reality by clinging to the sweet scents of one's memories. Clinging to the past is keeping you from embracing the future. The 'good old days' weren't as good as you remember. This card may indicate that attempting to water the gardens of your life with the illusions of the past is not a path to success. The reversed Six of Cups has sometimes been an important warning of an impending learning experience, one which may be some form of 'crop failure' about to happen among your expectations. I will again state that emotional maturity is essential.

But there is another less-frequent possibility which may be found with this card. Now and then the reversed Six of Cups is said to herald the appearance of an old friend from the past.

Seven of Cups

In Smith's depiction of this card, what was once a single chalice of inspiration offered by a divine hand extended through clouds has expanded into an assortment of cups. Whereas the clouds in the Ace indicated the heavens, the clouds we see in this card show us that all the wonders before the seeker are without substance: they are not based upon the manifestation of earth.

The Seven of Cups speaks of the role imagination may have in one's life. Imagination is a most valuable tool for it can give shape to our dreams and assist us in finding the way to bring them into manifestation. But when imagination is not accompanied by will, by a faith in one's self, then it may become the fantasies of someone wishing to avoid facing reality. When imagination is not accompanied by a willingness to labor toward those goals, then one is left clutching at pipe dreams.

Each cup holds a different fantasy. We see public recognition represented by the wreath of laurel. There is a fine residence, one which is many stories tall and appears to be more castle than home. There are symbols of lust and desires, images which show a hunger for wealth. It is not wrong to daydream about sensual joys, to imagine what your life might be 'if you won the sweepstakes.' And what is the figure in the center cup, draped in white? Perhaps an unknown savior.

But the Seven of Cups addresses the situation when the seeker has lost her focus. Her dreams are so desired yet they remain unaccompanied by wisdom and hard work. Her life has grown stagnant with little if any progress being made.

There are a number of similar situations to which this card may speak. The man who becomes so lost in his daydreams that he is not meeting the goals necessary to do his job well is one. Another might be someone who spends too much time self-indulgent in pipe dreams. And we have situations in which one is deceiving the self, using his imagination in order to believe that his pursuits are worthy. It is even possible that there is some sense of success in the seeker's life or it may be that she is able to *imagine* that she has adequate success.

The Seven of Cups may well appear in a layout, for example, when the seeker is playing with destructive fantasies. He might be imagining that a friend or co-worker has a genuine, romantic interest in him. He is subconsciously and emotionally recreating reality to support that belief. The ending to this story will not be happy.

This Seven may also appear when the seeker suffers from a variation of what may be called 'welfare mentality,' dreaming of all the wonderful things which should somehow appear in the seeker's life, expecting that life, itself, will be generous. The seeker believes she will be rewarded with love and wealth and power simply because she desires those rewards.

This is the card of wishful thinking. This scenario is a lot of "I want, I want, I want..." without any idea of how to make it happen. This is dreaming of a lottery ticket without putting food in the cupboard. The seeker's fantasies are working against her for the Seven of Cups shows no desire to work. It is time to face emotional reality. It is time for the seeker to realize that good intentions do not pay the bills, that wanting success and imagining it is not the same as earning it. The time and energy being spent on creating these visions represents the same skills which would be useful in bringing those dreams into reality. Now, if the seeker could be willing to embrace hard work and find joy in that as well, this card would indicate a happy ending.

reversed

When the Seven of Cups is reversed, the seven chalices are no longer so filled with the stuff of dreams. There is a subtle shift in the tide. This is a time to stop being self-indulgent. Now the seeker has the ability to succeed if will and determination are brought into the picture.

Emotional discrimination is essential. You must choose where to place your desire and use that as a motivating factor. Follow through toward the achievement of your goals. The manifestation of one's dreams may be a reality, but only when we carefully choose our dreams.

This reversed card indicates that the seeker has the ability to regain control of his life. The spark of one's work ethic has returned and it can be used to light the fire of one's passion. Should you make this important transition, the Universe will reward you.

Eight of Cups

No longer is one cup extended from the heavens. Now the lessons of the cups teach the seeker that handling one's emotions is not always an easy task. Indeed, the seeker is retreating, leaving eight cups standing in the foreground. Just below the barren rocks upon which the seeker ascends is the flow of water, the abyss, subject to the tides of one's life. The landscape carries no indication of fertility, rather presenting an image which seems forlorn.

As a eight, the energy of this numerical position represents the presence of very strong energy. Above, in the sky, we see what appears to be an eclipse. Despite the presence of such intense natural forces, the seeker is withdrawing.

The promise of the Ace of Cups once created a wellspring of hope for the seeker, but his expectations have not been met. This card indicates one's emotional response to life within the context of the reading. Other cards will provide information about those circumstances.

Although it would appear in some artistic renderings of this card that the seeker has said, "It's too much ... I've had it and I'm out of here," the Tarot teaches us that there are times when it is, in fact, necessary to take space and then count your blessings. The cups in the foreground are far from empty, but the current lack of spiritual fulfillment inhibits the seeker's ability to partake of them and be renewed. The emotions surrounding the present situation are very complex and may be beyond the immediate grasp of the seeker. The time has come for emotional regeneration and for the recognition of one's potential in line with new goals.

Abandonment of the old can be acceptable if it is replaced by a Quest for a (sensible) new goal. The seeker is holding a staff. Although it may be as simple as a walking stick, it also holds within it the potential of being a ritual tool. The staff also shows us that the seeker has more personal power than she may realize. Right now the power is internalized, swirling around in the emotional sorrows rather than emerging as creative energy to be used toward accomplishing one's goals.

The nature of the complex magickal energy of the eights is found in this card as well. The actions being taken have a tremendous impact on the future. If the seeker does not do well with this card, then she may be destined to repeat her mistakes until she learns that withdrawal must be for the correct reasons.

At a more mundane level, there are times when this card may indicate that one is feeling a deep and painful disappointment with one's family or offspring. There are some circumstances in which an individual is faced with overwhelming emotional difficulties and must simply walk away in order to recreate a new life.

reversed

The reversed meaning of this card, in most decks, suggests an improvement. It indicates that the path has been reversed and now the difficult times are likely to be behind. A card of encouragement, it urges the seeker to raise the cup or, perhaps, empty some of the cups of their sorrows. Perseverance and continued emotional and spiritual growth can lead one toward fulfillment and happiness.

Nine of Cups

No longer is the Ace's cup extended from the heavens. Now we see nine identical cups - but these are at rest sitting upon a draped stand behind the seeker. Although the seeker feels good, there is a sense of complacency. The cups are no longer active and neither is the figure! Although most seated women and men of the Tarot are shown upon thrones or seats indicating honor, the character in this card is sitting upon what looks to be more like a table.

The cups represent her emotions and they are elevated. They reflect the seeker's feelings of everything being fine, of having successfully transcended life's challenges. Life is good. A sense of satisfaction is evident. The seeker appears willing to settle for the rich rewards from past accomplishments, a path which leads to an out-of-balance life. The cups, set above, are out of reach and the seeker is no longer gazing into the waters of future dreams.

And yet, despite the blissful smile upon the seeker's face, she sits upon her laurels and has obviously been enjoying the celebrations of success more than what would be good for her health! A lack of work has increased her girth. We might well interpret the seeker sitting because she's become lazy and it's easier to sit than stand.

The Nine of Cups wants the seeker to realize that it is time to raise the curtain. While it may be easier to enjoy the fruits of past labors, the Tarot teaches us that we must always strive toward our Highest Ideals. Draping a curtain over the table of success obscures the view into the future. Goals have been met and material happiness is abundant. Yet the Universe offers more. Draw back the draperies and see what new mountain tops are waiting.

Rather than one's success becoming self-serving, the self will be better served with work to increase one's self awareness. Use the wisdom one has gained in order to resume growing. It is time to draw back the veil and drink of one's wisdom and experiences, to gaze upon the potential of the future and again seek the joys of spiritual aspirations.

Rather than leaving one's emotional depths upon the shelf in order to sip and sup from superficial rewards, consciousness of one's spiritual wealth will help the seeker sustain her good fortunes in coming times. It is time to use the cups as tools. It is time to embrace exercise of the spirit and, perhaps, of one's self at all levels.

reversed

When the Nine of Cups appears in its reversed position the seeker should be cautioned. Life is tipping out of balance. The lessons of the Nine of Cups have been disregarded and they are about to come tumbling down. The seeker has been seduced by material rewards, His satisfaction has allowed him to ignore signs that changes are needed. Continued focus upon the rewards which pleasure the physical senses is likely to lead to serious loss.

Ten of Cups

If you contemplate the suit of chalices and see it as a journey toward wisdom beginning with the Ace of Cups, when we arrive at the Ten of Cups we should have learned the lessons which have been offered. This is another of those "and they all lived happily ever after" cards although even this card contains images of lessons and wisdom without which joy would be far too transitory.

The perfection and celebration represented by the Ten of Cups has not been a solitary venture. The symbols clearly show that we have accomplished our goals with the help of another person. We know that success is indicated, for what may seem like a distant mountain in some cards is now close at hand, crowned by a Tree of Knowledge. And upon the hill to the right we see the roof of the home or manor, the physical indication of material success. Flowing down from the hill is a river. It will be easy to reach one's home and not so difficult to transcend the waters when walking to the pinnacle.

Each of the lessons guiding us toward emotional maturity and responsibility are raised aloft. The lessons well-learned, they form a rainbow overhead, showing the promise of the future. A further promise of future success is echoed in the children holding hands and dancing. Indeed, if the seeker works hard to embody wisdom, perpetual success may be available.

Although the goals have been achieved and one feels emotionally fulfilled and complete, the presence of the children indicate that the work is not done, nor will it ever be done. One must integrate into life all of the lessons learned and pass them on to those who will continue the work. Thus will the seeker be the beneficiary of continued benevolence from the Universe.

And as you prepare yourself for the future, enjoy the peace of mind and spiritual elation which are indicated. Having done well, you have before you a good life. You have accomplished what you set out to achieve and have the blessings of many friends and family. Many people have been with you knowing that, as they help you, you are one who readily gives back to them.

Your spiritual treasures and peace of mind are great gifts. They are rewards - but with them come responsibility. Now, if you keep it all together, you can sustain your success well into the future.

reversed

When the Ten of Cups appears as a reversed card, you might think of it as the flow of water in the river being cut off. One experiences a sense of emotional emptiness, emotional poverty, for the cups are draining and along with them goes the ability to sustain any sense of joy and fulfillment in life.

This sense of loss and unhappiness is generally not understood by the seeker, for if it were there would be no need for the reversed Ten of Cups to sound its alert. A lack of emotional maturity may lead to misplaced emotional stress, such as anger, directed toward others. The seeker (or the person indicated by the card) is experiencing considerable unhappiness and does not yet realize that the changes needed must take place within the self.

The situation can be changed. It is reasonable to expect that this card can be restored to its joyous state, but there is work to be done. That work begins with one's own emotions and the way in which we handle them. Study all of the cups and see how the seeds planted by the Ace can guide you to that emotional maturity needed to achieve your dreams.

Page of Cups

The Page stands gazing at the chalice in hand. Wearing a beautiful tunic with a design of what look like lotuses, the Page's hat is adorned with a blue scarf which appears to splash from the hat and flow forth, draping over her shoulder. This is a well-dressed Page and she is holding a large, fine chalice. We can see that the Page of Cups is comfortable with the element of water.

The suit of Cups teaches about our own internal emotions. Whereas the other three Pages are all looking externally for information, testing the wind, studying the growth on the staff, or seeking the wisdom of the pentacle, the Page of Cups looks within her emotional self for answers. And what does she find when gazing into the chalice? Unlike the Ace of Cups which shows us the sacred host as manna, now we see the fish. It is possible to formulate an analogy based upon 'loaves and fishes,' appropriate for understanding this fish. It does represent rejuvenation of the spirit and the ability to multiply. Yet another interpretation of the fish is that it represents the potential for manifestation within the astral.

PAGE of CUPS.

The symbol of a fish is often interpreted as the ability to receive news which, in this situation, will be found within the realm of emotions. If one is sitting back, enjoying a landscape which includes a river or lake and sees a fish leap up from the water, it is perceived as a good event or a good omen.

Standing against one of the most curious of backgrounds, we can only guess that perhaps the tide is coming in. The water is undulating, in contrast to the man-made foundation upon which the Page is standing.

The Pages are those who bring us news and the Page of Cups is likely to herald information which may lead to the birth or rebirth of an opportunity. The circumstances may involve a spiritually-sensitive person whose contemplative nature may prove very helpful. The card may also be speaking of a situation which is reflective, indicated by the Page gazing into the Chalice.

Just as the Page is able to see eye-to-eye with the fish, it is important that the seeker trust his own emotional response. It is important that he not let emotional misgivings and old baggage cause the seeker to ignore the message of this card.

This is a "help cometh!" card and the seeker is guided to trust the new direction this help may bring.

reversed

No matter how wise one's internal emotions may be or the good advice they may be offering, a reversed Page of Cups indicates that the fish is swimming away. The seeker is not paying attention and a good opportunity is slipping out of one's fingers.

Having your life out of balance has caused the cup to be tipped. It is no longer filled with potential and emotional fulfillment. It no longer offers an environment for the fish. The seeker is advised to become more sensitive to the situation (or individuals). One's lack of sensitivity is causing difficulties.

It is important to change your priorities or get a new perspective. It is quite possible that one's ego has gotten in the way. Hoping to see your self image reflected in the cup only causes it to be tipped over, leaving you stranded, like a fish out of water.

Knight of Cups

Unlike the Knights of Swords and Wands depicted in their active, masculine roles upon charging steeds, the Knight of Cups stands in repose, a counterpart to her cousin, the Knight of Pentacles. The suits of Cups and pentacles, water and earth respectively, represent the feminine, the yin or receptive, polarity. Despite the repose of these reflective suits, the Knights of Cups and Earth still embody excitement and have great appeal. The exhilaration of the Knight of Cups is not the valor and fighting skills of the Knight of Swords nor the fiery dash of the Knight of Wands. The excitement which is aroused by this Knight is romantic, stirring one's emotions.

The chalice, once extended from the heavens in the Ace, is held by the Knight who gazes into the cup at the reflection upon the water's surface. It is this vision which the Knight offers to the seeker. Seated upon a white horse, the Knight represents one who is sensitive, one who wishes to pause and reflect, then to dream about the future. In traditional Tarot symbolism, white horses will often represent a strong, sensual and physical energy. The figure of the horse might lead one to expect the situation to be filled with vital, forward momentum. If this is the seeker's belief, then it might be appropriate to change those expectations. This Knight is not ready to spur the horse forward.

With wings on her helmet and boots, and with fishes upon the robe covering her armor, we might expect movement from the Knight. The horse stands poised, eager to move forward but it is held in place, reined in by the Knight. In the distance we see the mountains which represent the goals and aspirations of the seeker, yet the path across the river is not visible. There is no bridge by which to cross the river. Unknown waters waiting to be forded symbolize unseen challenges. The seeker may wish to move forward but the Knight is not ready. Progress and success will require action which may be beyond this peaceful figure. The Knight is holding the chalice steady, so as to see clearly what course of action might be best.

This is a card likely to appear in a layout when one encounters an appealing situation, one involving another person who may be in the role of the Knight. The Knight is, in some ways, a messenger, but here he brings the offering of a chalice seemingly filled with the joy of the Ace, yet it also contains the stuff of dreams. This is a loving Knight, one who is gentle, sensitive and, yes, a dreamer. This Knight balances intelligence with his love for the emotions found within dreams. He is an adept at the magick of daydreaming.

Should you believe what the Knight offers? It is exciting to contemplate the potential future found in this enticing situation or proposal. Certainly the opportunity offered the seeker is a good one. The mountains are real. But is it realistic to join the Knight, climb aboard the horse and expect to reach the mountain's height? Perhaps, but the Knight of Cups of the Tarot wishes you to know that, although you may well enjoy the journey, if you are to depend upon the Knight to achieve this success for you, then you're better off going it alone. Although the situation has great appeal, it will take more than the Knight to bring it to fruition.

This card cautions the seeker to make certain of what is real and what is illusion. It reminds us that it takes more than enthusiasm to bring a dream into manifestation.

reversed

When the Knight of Cups is reversed we see a Knight who is unstable. This is not a good time to go along for the ride. Doing so might get you into the waters of one's imagination which could be over your head.

Many authors suggest that this is not a good time to place your trust in the person who is offering the seeker this proposal. As a messenger, she may be talking pipe dreams and this is likely to be a project unable to come into manifestation, one in which the seeker will encounter emotional instability and find that he has been caught by the seduction of a dream.

The reversed Knight of Cups offers great allure but allowing one's self to be caught in this illusion could well lead to the Devil Card further into the future. Be very cautious with this situation.

Queen of Cups

The Queen of Cups is seated upon a throne which is a stunning representation of the element of water. Set into the solid throne are cherubic figures holding shells, yet these are not angels but creatures of both land and sea. They will grow up to become mermaids. The throne is substantial, yet we see it removed from the court, allowing the Queen to sit at the water's edge. Emotions are often private.

Almost as prominent as the Queen is the large, ornate chalice held in her hand. It has certainly evolved from the simple cup which overflows in the Ace. This amazing chalice has winged beings standing on the handles, representing the polarities which bring into manifestation the dreams within this covered chalice. And yet, they are shadowed, even as the chalice has a large, ornate lid. In addition to her role as Queen of her realm, this Queen also sees herself as one who holds and who protects the Mysteries. They are not for viewing by the public.

Despite the chalice being covered, the Queen has the ability to see within it to the depths of the cup.

When she looks at you she sees far more than your surface appearance. Wearing her crown and a robe which mirrors the patterns of water, she is wise and to be trusted. She is able to move and adjust with the ebb and flow of life, knowing the inner spirit of the element water.

Like her sisters, the Queen is someone who is partnered. In fact, some of

153

the handbooks published with decks offer a divinatory meaning that this card might well indicate a happy marriage.

More importantly, you are reminded that this Queen is comfortable in both the spiritual world as well as the material world. Her throne is one representing riches, yet it sits at the edge of the waters of one's emotions and visions. The Queen of Cups represents a feminine, Yin being, one who is emotionally stable and able to bring her visions into reality.

This is a card of inspiration, emotion and intuition. The Queen is someone who is sensitive, a woman who trusts her dreams, but who remains grounded in her environment. This card speaks of trusting your inner feelings, indicating that knowing what they are in the present circumstances will benefit the situation in question.

There is a beauty about the Queen, even as she is deeply focused upon the inner Mystery of the chalice. The scalloped throne behind her hints that the Queen is knowledgeable of the Rituals of Aphrodite. Despite the weight of this large and heavy chalice, she is able to hold it steady. She has control over the chalice. She is able to work with her dreams and intuition because they arise out of the calm pool of stable and mature emotional depth, unlike the emotions of the reversed Queen.

reversed

The reversed Queen of Cups is not to be trusted. She is lacking the depth of the chalice, too easily lost in the confusion of her emotions. She is unable to distinguish between her daydreams and the reality of life about her. This Queen is superficial and tends to create visions which satisfy the desires of her ego. She deludes herself into believing that those visions arise from the Universe. She is lost in the waters of her fantasies and her dreams become unreliable. Now upturned, the babies of her throne represent the Queen's immature nature controlling her actions. Out of control, she claims a position of power but she is not enthroned because of merit. This woman holds power over others because they fear her.

If this card represents another, treat them with great care. The woman is prone to capricious behavior and cannot be trusted. If this card speaks about you, then pay close attention and make significant change in your behavior, attitude and morality without delay. One who emulates the reversed Queen of Cups will find that one's daydreams will turn into nightmares. Reality will, in fact, become those frightening dreams.

King of Cups

The chalice extended from the Universe completes this suit, held in the King's hand. The suit of Cups is brought full circle. The King sits upon his throne. Its construction is interesting, with the wave-like back to the throne and the base a solid square. That base is emblematic of social order, with its solid foundation though surrounded by the deep waters. The throne appears as if it is a raft. Even though the waves are in motion, the fish leaping and boats sailing, the King's throne is secure and the contents of his chalice will be held steady.

Traditionally this King is considered to be someone who represents the good qualities of a professional in business, law, or even divinity. The jumping fish represents his ability to sense what lies beneath the surface, and yet the ship of commerce is clearly within his realm.

The very throne of the King of Cups is of water, and this King is a man of deep emotions. But they are held steady as the chalice. He is able to do his work despite the unpredictable emotional environment caused by others. A man of quiet power, the fish pendant may be a symbol of his ability to trust his intuition. He is the epitome of a male figure in touch with the depths of his own emotions and inner consciousness.

The King of Cups is considered compassionate. He is interested in the creativity of others. Being in balance with his emotional and intuitive self allows him to have power, yet it is a strength which is not always apparent. His inner reserve is not easily visible nor is he wont to show his inner self readily to others. It is only during a crisis that he might draw upon his reserve. For this reason, do not be quick to judge the King of Cups for you may be misled.

The King has a sense of vision, represented by the fish. There is a union between the one on his pendant and the one at the horizon. Yet this vision is not one to further his personal goals, only to ensure that the harvest will provide enough fish to feed his kingdom, that the trade between his realm and others may flow smoothly.

His cup is offered from a loving hand, for his compassion toward others bestows generosity. The depth of his inner control can be remembered if you think of him as able to control the direction and movement of his throne no matter what condition the waters may manifest.

reversed

When this King has been turned upside down, his throne is sinking. It will take very little to stir up the waters of his emotions and bring a storm to those around him. Seeing this card upside down shows you that he has lost his emotional control. The upside-down throne may also be seen to represent someone whose sensitivity is shallow, who has hidden agendas, and someone who can easily be roiled.

A man in power who cannot control his emotions, who is not in balance with his own feminine energy, is likely to be temperamental and something of a chauvinist, insecure about his own masculinity. Given to mood changes, he does not trust his inner voice and may treat others with suspicion and distrust. This King is able to submerge the truth when it suits him, using hidden information to manipulate others.

Without working to correct this card, his throne (representing the individual's desire for power) is likely to sink him. His unethical use of a tool as honored and sacred as is the chalice only reflects his lack of morality. This is not a good-hearted man.

The Pentacles of Tarot

The suit of Pentacles is oftentimes both misunderstood and misinterpreted. Sometimes referred to as 'coins,' that paradigm offers a very limited view, one which misses the most important concepts of the suit.

A pentacle is the fourth of the four basic ritual tools, the others being the blade, the wand and the cup or chalice. Blades deal with ideas and communication, things of the mind but intangible. Wands teach us about will, desire, passion and what it takes to keep our energy going. Cups include the realm of emotions and feelings. All of these areas of one's being are intangible. Pentacles, on the other hand, refer to those things in life which are definitely tangible. By their very nature, tangible things are those which have substance and, in our modern world, this means they can be traded, bartered, bought and sold. Yet the suit of Pentacles is not about cash.

The suit of Pentacles corresponds to the classical element of Earth. Earth is the most stable of the four elements. It is, for example, very difficult to contain air. You cannot grab a handful of it. Air may be contained in a completely closed container but even the slightest opening and its molecules will quickly slip right through. Fire is quick to start burning wherever it has fuel. Fire is not easy to contain. Water can slip right through your fingers, but water can be contained in a basin. An open container will still lose some water to evaporation, but water is more easily managed than the first two elements. Earth, however, stays put when you set it down. In some places it will not move until the Mother Planet sets loose an earthquake!

Pentacles embrace that level of reality often referred to as the 'earth plane.' Earth is the element from which tangible reality emerges. Both the suit and the element deal with tangible things, things which have substance. Pentacles offer you guidance so that you can learn how to manifest the resources you need in life. The various cards of the suit portray perseverance and patience. They depict learning to do quality work. They present the element of time in combination with elements of discipline and control. There are lessons regarding the harvests of life. The suit shows you how to fill your cupboards and your closets. Learn your lessons well and you may have a bumper crop. However, we are taught that despite the glitter of wealth, greed will inhibit our progress. Pentacles discuss the necessity of work and of a good work ethic.

Dealing with resources, all of which can be purchased in modern times with money, Pentacles do refer to money, to dollars and cents (or pounds and euros). It is for that reason some authors call Pentacles 'coins' choosing (perhaps unwittingly) to limit the suit so that it refers only to cash (and credit!). But money is a tool and all tools need control.

In common playing cards, this suit corresponds with diamonds. Certainly a symbol of wealth, diamonds represent earth in one of its most beautiful, concentrated forms. Although we are more accustomed to perceiving the sword or the staff and wand as weapons, in armory the counterpart of the pentacle is the shield, which is not a weapon per se, but is used in battle to defend one's physical being. This sense of protecting one's corporeal self is also part of the suit. Food and shelter are purchased with pentacles and they, also, provide protection.

At the level of the most sublime, we see a modern day version of a pentacle in religious services such as those of the Roman Catholic Church. A gold paten is used as a ritual tool when the communion wafer is served. In the Major Arcana, ritual pentacles are found with only two cards, The Magician and The Empress.

Of the four elements, earth is very dependant upon the other three. Without them it cannot manifest fertility. Without oxygen freely mixed into the soil, without water, roots cannot survive. And, without the fire of the sun, plants cannot grow and generate chlorophyll. The suit of Pentacles is, for many, the most elusive. View the suit as dealing solely with money and you may miss the larger lessons of generosity and of work ethics. Life in today's society makes the study of pentacles one of utmost importance.

Ace of Pentacles

As with the other three Aces, the image of a hand arising from the realm of the spiritual symbolizes the energy of a new or renewed beginning. And below, the realm of the element earth is clearly visible. In the foreground we see the lushness of green fertility from which grow lilies, always a symbol of spiritual rebirth.

A path leads to the hedge, but before we follow the path consider the hedge, itself. Lush and green, fruits or flowers are indicated by the very small spots of red color. We know that the foliage of the hedge is thick and vibrant. But unlike annuals and perennials, the presence of the hedge is a clear indication of the passage of time. Such a fine hedge could not have grown in one season, not even in a few growing seasons. The archway has been created by one skilled at topiary, a feat requiring the passage of a significant number of years as well as the adept handling of a pruning blade.

All of this brings us back to the path which leads beneath the archway. Through this opening, beyond the enclosure of the safety and fertility of one's gardens, lies the rest of the world. A considerable journey must be taken before the seeker can reach the tops of those distant mountains, before enjoying the view one has upon achieving maturity and wisdom and having an enlightened understanding of reality.

From an artistic perspective, we see that the hand is much closer than are the lilies, closer than the portal in and out of the garden. If we look into this card as if it is a window of reality (as one ought with *all* the cards of the Tarot), the size of the hand indicates its proximity.

Dominating this card is the single pentacle which is held by the Divine hand. As we have seen, pentacles represent living with all four elements (air, fire, water and earth) in balance so that we can use our spiritual energy in order to bring the tools we need in life into manifestation, whether they be money for rent, food to stock the cupboard, or a budget able to afford books for learning.

As do all Aces, this card symbolizes beginnings and what is singular about the Ace of Pentacles is that the Universe wants you to know that many resources are being made available. The hand is presenting a boon from the Universe, manna from heaven or, at least, indicating the presence of the substance or means by which to acquire what you need.

Material and tangible results will be manifesting in your life. You have the ability to achieve your goals. Having learned to work with the other three suits and having grown spiritually, your soul is prosperous and this will now be reflected in the mundane world. Yes, this is a very good and desirable card to have appear in a reading!

Now note the position of the hand. See how it holds the pentacle? All five elements, shown by the five-pointed star, are poised and in balance. They are visible and available for your use. And there are no strings attached, no hidden easel holding the pentacle which is balanced with such skill. The Tarot wants the seeker to know that the work already done has prepared the seeker for this new phase in her life. The time is ripe, just as are the red fruits and flowers growing in the hedge. You now have the ability to manifest what you need for your progress toward the top of the mountain. This is truly a wonderful card!

reversed

But what do we see when we take this image and reverse it? The foundation of this imagery is now based upon monetary values rather than one's life-long quest toward the spiritual maturity and wisdom depicted by the mountain. With one's value system out of balance, the desire for the rewards is now too strong. In excess, it could be described as greed.

When the Ace of Pentacles is reversed, counsel should be given to avoid taking risks lest the Universe be tempted to offer the seeker a sharp lesson. Think about this image in the reversed card. The pentacle is almost like a yo-yo, about to descend. Your ability to draw upon resources, to have a workable budget is about to take a decline. Avoid taking risks and begin working, immediately, to restore balance in your life. Fix your priorities and do what is necessary to restore this card to its rightful position. Failure to pay attention will lead to some hard lessons which will be the result not of bad luck but because the seeker has been putting the earth plane before that of the spiritual. The advice? Become financially conservative and, while avoiding rash action, contemplate what changes are needed - and then make them.

While not a highly desired card, the reversed Ace of Pentacles arrives to indicate that change can be made and that the product of such changes will be highly fertile ground for the future.

Two of Pentacles

The figure stands poised, one foot raised as if to quickly make an adjustment in his balance should he have difficulty juggling the two pentacles. The foreground is flat. The immediate horizon which separates the moving waves from the foreground is a straight line, one which could only be created through human construction and commerce.

The theme of commerce or trade which, in the Tarot, indicates the managing of financial affairs and business dealings with others, is repeated in the two ships, each riding crests of the waves.

In the Ace of Pentacles the hand, extended from the heavens, offered the pentacle as prosperity of the spirit. In the Two of Pentacles the disks are managed by the hands of the juggler, who uses not only physical dexterity but also his spiritual, creative will.

That will is indicated by the elongated symbol which may be interpreted as a moebus band or the symbol for infinity. It is within this flow of energy that the two pentacles are balanced.

Events in the seeker's life have been undergoing considerable flux but, at present, harmony is restored and life appears to again be in balance. Despite the suit of Pentacles often perceived as stable due to its correspondence with the element of earth, this card suggests that there has been considerable movement. The ups and downs of life have been affecting the seeker's life and fortune just as the waves have moved the ships. And the juggler must keep the disks in motion in order to maintain the flow of energy which keeps the pentacles in their appropriate positions.

Although depicted as a solitary person, the nature of this card indicates that the seeker is not alone. There is a connection between the figure and the ships. The issues addressed by this card, typically, speak only to the seeker and not to one's business partners. The Two of Pentacles will often appear in a reading when a collaboration is supportive, when partners work well together and when the effort has brought stability into the seeker's life and improved his circumstances.

But all has not been permanently fixed. The sense of balance is, in large part, dependant upon the partnership or the help from the other person(s). And yet the waves move up and down and the ability of the captains to keep their ships on the crests of the waves is not known. One of the lessons of this card is to caution the seeker that mood swings, the waters of one's emotions if left unchecked, could threaten the stability of the partnership.

At present give and take are working well and adjustments are being made. The seeker may believe things are better than could have been expected, but balance must be maintained. It will take hard work to develop any permanent harmony. Assumptions should not be made nor should one take others who may be involved for granted. The juggler is shown alone because he must develop the skills to be able to manage all affairs in his life without depending upon others. Only then will he be a healthy, contributing partner.

reversed

When the Two of Pentacles is reversed, the ground beneath one's feet is no longer solid. That wonderful harmony and balance depicted by the juggler is threatened. This may indicate the possibility of conflict and of friction. It is possible that the seeker has not yet become aware of the growing difficulty and continues to assume that everyone involved remains supportive and that her life is just fine.

The reversed Two of Pentacles urges the seeker to look below the surface and to do so without becoming emotional at what may be found. As true of the entire suit of Pentacles, remaining focused upon the necessary work ethic can make all the difference. Do not take your self so seriously that adjustments *within the self* cannot be made to restore harmony.

At present the support upon which the seeker is counting is tenuous and a careful examination of the situation is needed. It would be desirable for the seeker to contemplate the entire suit of Pentacles in order to develop the skills and attributes needed to restore this card to its more favorable position.

Three of Pentacles

The primary figure of this card appears as a stone mason, standing upon a low bench, his tools in hand. Nearby are two individuals, showing him plans for work. Tradition leads us to believe that they are seeking the craftsperson's skill for a new and different project.

A very desirable card, the Three of Pentacles is the Tarot's way of offering a compliment for having done good work. There are many values indicated by the craftsperson. She has done superior work on previous projects. She does her work with the creativity and skill of an artist. She takes her training seriously and is becoming a master craftsman. Tradition tells us that she should enjoy the rewards being offered her. She must draw upon all of her talents. She will be earning those rewards. The commission or new project being offered will require all of her skills and will also require much hard work.

The stone mason's life is a balance of the spiritual and the mundane, brought down to a practical level. We see three pentacles which were created in the stone tracery of the religious setting. These three represent a trinity, symbolic of the process of manifestation. Indeed, even as the mason brings the project into manifestation, so too does his embodiment of a virtuous work ethic bring his future into manifestation. A further aspect of this sacred setting is that the stoneworker treats his work ethic as sacred. He sees his talents as a divine gift and is both humbled and appreciative at the work before him.

Whether the appearance of this card in a reading refers to an actual project or to one's ability, the suit of Pentacles embraces the material endeavors in one's life. The situation described by the layout is one of gain, potential and the ability to grow in one's skills.

In the Major Arcana we learned that a throne is a symbol of community stature. In a simpler fashion, the bench upon which the stone mason stands represents the fact that her work ethic and skills have given the craftsperson prominence in the community. When the religious figures come to seek her skills, they are looking up to the stone mason.

In learning the underlying lessons of this card, we have a glimpse into the future if we but embody the work ethic. The Tarot teaches a willingness to learn our skills and to work with them until we are highly skilled and worthy of the rewards promised by this card.

reversed

As would be expected, the reversed meaning of the Three of Pentacles indicates work of poor quality. The results are slipshod, speak of mediocrity and reflect upon the poor work ethic and value system.

Incapable of doing quality work, the subject is likely to be looking elsewhere for the causes, placing the blame upon others. The reality is that the contracts and agreements are likely to be delayed. Opportunities may well be lost due to a lack of discipline, commitment or perhaps simply due to general laziness and the inability to remain focused upon the work at hand.

Failure is on its way unless the seeker heeds the lesson offered by the reversed Three of Pentacles. Return to your lessons, organize your skills, embrace commitment and discipline and, if you work hard, success will return.

Four of Pentacles

The pentacle so graciously offered from the divine hand of the Universe is now greedily clutched to the figure's heart. The heart chakra is now diverted, focused upon clinging to money. And the other three pentacles? Two are placed so as to represent his path, his foundation. And the fourth is perched upon his crown. Obviously, he has money on his brain!

The Four of Pentacles teaches us of the potential danger encountered when the ego becomes too impressed with the power money can have over others. This is always a hazard in today's world in a developed, social economy. We see images of an urban area in the background. Simple barter of field-grown goods or labor is no longer adequate. In the business world people may forget that money is a mere symbol of exchange. Those familiar mountains, symbols of achieving one's Highest Ideals, are present, but one must first work through all the lessons of urban life before leaving it behind to ascend the heights.

The crown and the throne upon which she is seated clearly state that the figure has achieved some measure of success and stature within the community. This is not the throne of royalty. Rather, it is a 'mini' throne. Whether it has been earned or inherited, the issue at hand is that the woman is too impressed with the power of these rewards. It has not been easy to acquire this status. If earned, it has been a painful struggle. If inherited, perhaps the death brought extreme emotional pain. The events which led to one's status and wealth have caused the central figure to lose sight and perspective. What should be considered gifts are now hoarded.

The Four of Pentacles carries a very clear moral. Placing the power and status of material rewards above one's spiritual growth and ideals carries a harsh price. The figure is an image of unhappiness. Clinging to his goods, his body is bent over, a posture which will lead to a future of pain. The Tarot urges the seeker to avoid being dazzled by money, to rearrange one's priorities and assess one's values. Money and goods are merely one of the tools of the Tarot.

reversed

The lessons become imperative when the Four of Pentacles is reversed. In this position, the Four of Pentacles is likely to indicate that it's now time to face reality. The lack of spiritual balance when placing money above other values exacts a toll. This card indicates that the security of one's money and resources is now in peril.

The desire to hang on to one's money and status has turned the figure upside down. One's funds are likely to be dwindling. No longer will you be allowed to turn to your money as a source of security. This card will often appear when possessions or money are lost due to an inappropriate attitude or spiritually-bereft behavior. It may also appear in a reading when someone has been counting her chickens before they hatch, hungrily anticipating the arrival of money and possibly spending it before it manifests. The Four of Pentacles may be letting the unwise investor recognize that there will be no return. It may teach the borrower the pitfalls of living on credit. Hope of easy money is turning into painful, yet essential, experiences.

The reversed Four of Pentacles alerts the seeker that it is now time to pay your dues and learn some essential, if difficult, lessons in life about what is truly important.

Five of Pentacles

Continuing with the self-induced sorrows of life depicted by the fives in the previous three suits, the Five of Pentacles shows two individuals walking past a church. There is no personal interaction between them. Although it is frequently assumed that they know each other and must have some type of relationship, there is a sense of personal isolation about them. They are walking through snow, so caught up in their misery and weighed down with the problems of their lives that they do not even see the beautiful stained glass window immediately beside them.

The figures before us embody their struggles. Their clothing is torn and patched. They are images of poverty, of those in trouble with the material world. This card may appear when some difficulty has come up, even the loss of one's job or status. The Five of Pentacles is a reminder that, when one becomes so focused upon his pain and suffering, he forgets to look beyond the ego's plaint.

The beautiful, shining pentacle which was offered in the Ace now sits atop four additional pentacles, representing the presence of hope and the ability to restore a faith in life. Earlier we also saw the Three of Pentacles as part of religious architecture. Many see a most curious quality of this suit: that relationship between pentacles and spiritual evolution. But the lesson of this Five is shown in this card. The solution to the couple's destitution can be found through seeking the light within the foundation of one's spiritual beliefs, here shown as a church.

Their misfortune is as much a product of having abandoned their light, becoming so involved in their own woes (for this is one of the 'woe is me' cards!) that they cannot see the solution shining upon them. Although difficult to imagine, there is a curious type of negative strength derived from seeing one's self as a victim. These two are avoiding the difficulty of change by escaping into their negative view of life. If they embody this martyrdom, they can avoid taking responsibility for their fate.

The Five of Pentacles is a card indicative of those times when a person pursues a path of negative escapism. This provides the illusion of the freedom from avoiding the taking of responsibility for self-induced woes. Despite the ills of this card, it certainly indicates that they will survive. It calls for an end to spiritual impoverishment through looking outside one's self and seeing that help is available if you but take the steps and once again enter the edifice of your spiritual beliefs.

reversed

Unlike some of the other cards which address our pain and tell us to grow up, in the majority of decks the reversed Five of Pentacles does not bear an improved message. Indeed, now the beggar's bell rings more loudly. The obstacles grow larger. This card is a clear message that one should seek help, no matter how strong the ego's pride.

But you should study the deck you use and refer to the author's notes which accompanied it, for some decks are created to indicate that the light through the window now shines more brightly, and it is time to feel renewed courage. Events are taking a turn for the better.

Six of Pentacles

In Waite's deck, Pamela Colman Smith provides a very graphic representation of the life lessons encompassed by the Six of Pentacles. Holding a suspended balance scale in the left hand, a well-dressed (fairly androgynous) figure stands in the center of the card. With the right hand, coins are being given to the two

persons who are upon their knees, depicting those who are less fortunate and in need of alms. Are they the two from the previous card?

The horizon depicts trees and vegetation, a recurrent symbol of fruition and fertility. It also shows an urban setting which represents interactions with others, business and dealings which extend beyond one's personal realm. The upper area of the card contains the six pentacles, filling the open area which might otherwise be sky, creating a pattern certain to intrigue those who study the Hebrew mystical system known (in all its spellings) as Kabbalah.

The lesson depicted by this card is one frequently difficult for the average person to learn. In the sense of the most practical karma, we can see graphically another brick in the foundation of Pentacles. This card shows what is necessary for us to have material success in the world. When the Six of Pentacles appears in a reading, it brings a strong message that, no matter how tight you think your budget is, adjustment (indicated by the scales) will enable you to be generous and give to those charities which merit your support.

For those who believe they don't have enough money with which to give to their church, their schools, to the needy, the Six of Pentacles offers us one of the Mysteries in life: if you wish to be able to increase the flow of pentacles (resources) into your own life, then you must demonstrate to the Universe your ability to handle money wisely and, with generosity. If you cannot recognize that you are more fortunate than others, then the Universe is unlikely to freely bestow upon you further bounty. This card teaches you about karma: if you want more in your life, then learn to 'do unto others.'

It is not a coincidence that, with almost no exception, families which have great wealth are also known as philanthropists. Although they describe their giving nature frequently in terms of humanitarian efforts, it may often be paraphrased as a variation upon 'sharing the wealth,' despite the cynic who believes they do it solely for tax purposes. Those families with 'old money' treasure the virtue of philanthropy. Those unable to part with their hard-earned money are usually first or second generation wealthy, who still remember how painful their labors, and who are not yet wise in the long-term processes by which one can sustain wealth. The Six of Pentacles attempts to teach a person that, if you wish to continue having your assets, then you must be willing to count generosity and a giving nature among your most cherished possessions.

What does this mean on a more practical level? Nearly two decades ago I learned a valuable lesson. If my income was inadequate and I needed to stimulate some paying clients for as an astrologer and interpreter of Tarot, the most effective means was by doing some gratis work. Today I do as much pro bono and gratis work as I am able and yet continue to meet the responsibilities of my budget. The Universe provides.

One of my favorite images for this card is found in the 'Sacred Rose

Tarot' designed by Joanna Gargiulo-Sherman. In her rendering, we see three pentacles above the earth and three below, also creating a design which could readily be interpreted as sephiroth on the Tree of Life. One hand reaches down from the heavens and one reaches up from below, showing that balance in one's life, in manifest reality, is achieved through giving.

Pentacles do not represent coins and money alone. They represent resources and the Six of Pentacles could indicate giving of yourself or of your time. Perhaps you might look through your closets and remove clothing you've not worn in the past year or two so it can find a new home where it will be loved and admired and worn on a regular basis with immense appreciation.

In the simplest of interpretations, applying the Tree of Life structure to this card we learn that the phrase, 'as above, so below' could be directly interpreted in the context of the Six of Pentacles. If we wish to receive, then we must be willing to give. Monetary justice in your life will be achieved only when you are wise enough to understand that you can readily prune some of your spending in order to be benevolent to others.

reversed

Should this card appear reversed, the Universe is giving notice. Your attitudes toward money are unhealthy. Whether you have adequate money or not, an underlying cause of your difficulties is a lack of understanding that money is only a 'tool.' Your attachment to it means your financial future is in question. Those without money may be generating envy rather than making internal changes. Those who feel entitled may find the flow of resources decreased. The bottom line is that the Universe is warning that your lack of sharing is not well-founded. Your selfishness is based upon your own insecurity. You may be suffering self-doubt in your ability to generate enough resources with which to be generous. When the Six of Pentacles appears reversed, take steps quickly not only by simply giving something, but by making a major change in your attitude.

This is a wonderful card. The Six of Pentacles has taught me much in my life. Coming from a poor, dirt-farm background, I did not understand the nature of pentacles and, if anything, my childhood poverty left me wanting to hang on so tight to every dollar. My ability to purchase happiness was kept in check by unwise spending which soothed feelings of deprivation. I am grateful to this card, for sixes bring the numerical energy of organic evolution. Worked wisely, a Six brings permanent, fulfilling change into one's life. Once we learn to work with the Mysteries of the Six of Pentacle in our personal lives, we can then see the role we might play in humanitarian efforts as churches, organizations, and as a political culture.

Seven of Pentacles

The suit of Pentacles began with the Divine Hand offering the wisdom of manifestation through the Ace. Pentacles teach us the lessons which are essential for manifesting our dreams in the real world. It is one thing to manufacture your fantasies of words, or to create them in the illusive realm of visions. It is quite another to bring them into tangible reality. In the distance of the Seven of Pentacles we see mountains, far across the plain. But the seeker is not gazing into the long-term future. This card is teaching us the principles of manifestation at a far more practical level. And yet, the symbol of the mountain is clear, indicating that the wisdom of this card brings with it long term benefits.

The lesson offered us with the Seven of Pentacles is found in many popular images. If ever there were a 'money tree,' this might be it! But this is no magickal tree one might find growing, laden with currency just waiting to be picked and spent. The lush plant growing in this gardener's field does not contain the DNA of a winning lottery ticket. What has brought this crop of pentacles into being was considerable labor, seasons of hard work and now, patience.

The Seven of Pentacles represents fertility. The seeker had no silver spoon in his mouth. Rather than the gift of inheritance, he was given the gift which taught him how to cultivate success. It is a hoe which he holds. A hoe is a tool made of a handle like a staff and a metal blade which may be thought of as a variation of a sword. We may well believe the gardener carried water to his plants, as well. He has cultivated this plant, tilled the soil with vigor. He has tended his crop, seen to the weeds.

Knowing that, if he does all his work well, he should be assured of fruitfulness. His crop must have adequate moisture, sufficient light, and abundant nutrition. He did not wait to see if Mother Nature would provide all of this for him but willingly embraced the field laborer's tools. He understands the nature of fertility. In a very practical sense, this tree of abundance is the seeker's 'Tree of Life.'

The Seven of Pentacles shows us that even having cultivated your harvest, having invested considerable personal labor, there remains one cornerstone to the manifestation of one's success. Patience and faith. You must be willing to wait, knowing that your work is not yet ended. This Seven advises us to take care of our business. Things don't grow any faster than they grow. The wise seeker will avoid the temptation to harvest the rewards before they are fully ripened. It takes time to grow not just the immediate harvest but what will be next year's seed as well. What will bring success? Hard work is a way of life and patience is truly a virtue.

reversed

The fruitful harvest of the Seven of Pentacles is not in one's future when the seeker has been too concerned about the size of the harvest, perhaps spending his rewards even before he has been willing to labor and await their maturity. Impatience, the placing of money as a priority above more spiritual concerns, and an unwillingness to work hard, may all contribute to this card appearing reversed.

Now, there is a warning. No longer does the seeker have her feet upon the ground. Her values have turned topsy-turvy and now she frets, worrying that the harvest will fall short which could leave her stranded amid budgetary woes.

All of this indicates that the reversed Seven of Pentacles might presage financial loss or a harvest shortfall. Continuing to worry is not the solution. The harvest will not grow well when it is surrounded with the magick of anxiety and doubt (all of which create extremely counter productive images).

Be careful! It is time to replace your impatience and worry with a careful return to the values of which this card speaks. And whether it is too late for a successful harvest *this* season or not, only time will tell.

Eight of Pentacles

In the Eight of Pentacles, unlike the stress and strife of the other three eights, we see a contented worker busy carving the pentagram into the disk, creating yet another pentacle. Five are suspended from the tree (of life?) in front of him.

This is a card of timing. The pentacle offered from the divine hand in the Ace might now be perceived as the one being created by the craftsperson. The Eight of Pentacles teaches us about planning, about planting for the future. Whereas the other eights depict the seeker being transformed and tempered by the experiences of life, in the Eight of Pentacles the seeker is using his skills to bring about a transformation of the future.

The less mature reaction to the abundance of completed pentacles would be to gather them up and hurry off to the nearby town. There the seeker's skilled work would bring a fast profit. But this card speaks to us of an even deeper level of skill than that of the Three of Pentacles. It is similar in its indication that one is likely to be rewarded for skill, but here we see the deeper mysteries which speak of creating for one's future.

This Eight speaks of patience. The Eight of Swords is the reaction to life-changing communication in which the seeker is either held in bondage by what has been earlier spoken or by which she may find liberation. The Eight of Rods is the deeper level of the wands' activities, in which life changes so quickly that one may feel out-of-control as events race past. The Eight of Cups teaches us what happens when we feel overwhelmed by our own emotions, so much that we may wish to leave behind our present circumstances. The Eight of Pentacles depicts an abundance of patience, of perseverance, of choosing to work toward the future, investing one's time and skill in order to develop a self-perpetuating cycle of success. Thus will the seeker be transformed.

When this card appears in a layout, the seeker is admonished by the Tarot to transcend his human tendencies. We are reminded that the apron, part of the ritual clothing within at least one major magickal tradition, becomes the clothing of a priest/ess of labor. This is a card which is not unlike Initiation, but it is a slow and careful journey. It is the virtuous worker, the one who is prudent and wise, who seeks long-term skills and the ability to create a foundation which cannot be shaken. This is a path upon which to build a life and a future.

The Eight of Pentacles is a most constructive card. She who follows its advice and avoids the temptation of immediate reward will learn about planning for one's retirement and will joyfully hone the skills which allow one to create the pentacles to be hung from the Tree of Life.

reversed

The qualities of the figure in the card, when reversed, are in opposition to the above-mentioned virtues and, should this card appear reversed in a reading, I urge you to make major changes at once.

Although Pentacles teach us about taking our time and working diligently, the symptoms of this card reversed require immediate action. There is nothing flattering about the reversed Eight of Pentacles. Continuing to misuse one's talents will soon be costly for the seeker. The nature of the number eight continues to indicate transcendence, but in this case one must transcend whatever fears may be holding the self back. Perhaps the seeker is afraid to take the risk necessary to achieve career success. Or, perhaps, he is unwilling to make a commitment to learning what skills must be perfected.

And perhaps the seeker must recreate her character. The reversed Eight of Pentacles may also speak of a poor and wrongful attitude toward money and goods. An excess attachment to material things can hold one back from success in the future. Laziness becomes a path to failure. Debts, if not dealt with methodically and maturely, could ultimately lead to the Devil Card.

The reversed Eight of Pentacles cautions that it is time to embrace transformation. Simply wishing for success as one continues along a path to failure will likely lead to dire consequences, serious enough to impose moral change upon the seeker.

Nine of Pentacles

Our original pentacle in the Ace has borne fruit. The hedge in the background of the Ace is now at the foreground, the mountains of one's Highest Ideals remain in the distance. The image of the hedge has evolved into an arbor, laden with ripe bunches of grapes. The Nine of Pentacles is a card of abundance and fertility.

At center stage we see a Goddess type of figure, communicating with a bird. Her robes are flowing, embroidered with flowers. Her hand appears to be resting upon one of the pentacles, which are stacked upon either side of her.

She is balanced by two trees, easily interpreted as the two pillars seen earlier in the High Priestess. Off to the right is a fine chateau. And sitting upon her gloved hand, a bird. The bird represents timing, often a symbol for listening to the voice of one's intuition, of news found 'in the air.'

The Nine of Pentacles teaches the lessons needed in order to manifest one's resources as financial stability. This is a long-term fruitfulness. The grapes require annual tending, pruning and careful harvesting. Once again the suit of Pentacles teaches us the ethics of work and of patience. Where do we see patience? Take note of the snail slowly moving across the bottom of the card. But the rewards? This is a woman who enjoys comfort and security. She loves what she is doing and, as a consequence, manifests fruitfulness, fertility and enjoys abundance. She could well be Mother Nature incarnate, standing regally before us in her robes embroidered with flowers.

The seeker, having learned the lessons of this suit in the preceding cards, is now able to be calm in her beliefs, secure enough in her growing knowledge of pentacles that the bird is able perch without fear.

The Nine of Pentacles represents the abundance of the harvest and follows the eight lessons already presented in this suit which teach us of material gain. Now we can see what is needed in order to produce the harvest. While the Six, Seven and Eight of Pentacles gave us practical lessons the Nine presents the spiritual embodiment which is equally essential.

An abundant harvest is the product of foresight, discretion and wisdom. The seeker's personal interests thrive when nurtured. There is no public display and, despite the comfort already attained, there is an absence of ego. One may take pride from a mature understanding of the labor and commitment required but the honor is given to Nature, not perceived as a reflection of one's own merit.

The figure on this card represents what it takes to produce a harvest. Mother Nature is giving forth life, able to take care of things. She can meet her needs through providing a safe space for her creatures. And, although the vines are laden with ripe fruit, she knows that nurturing the smaller creatures may be even more important.

reversed

When reversed, this is not an enjoyable card. Now we address the loss of the security and comfort indicated by the Nine of Pentacles. One's life appears to be coming apart at the seams. The surety with which the figure enjoyed the harvest and the comfort of a secure home are no longer present. As life unravels, there are likely to be losses, financial losses, perhaps even the loss of one's home. One's ability to sustain the flow of resources has proven inadequate, the result of poorly-learned skills, of a lack of learning the Pentacles' lessons, or perhaps due to standards of ethical behavior which fall short of what the Universe deems necessary.

In some decks, the cards are designed to indicate the potential of losses arriving due to misplaced trust. Other decks describe this card to be indicative of losing what was being counted upon. And yet other decks say that it is not nearly so serious as one might expect. I recommend clarifying the meaning of this reversed card by studying the text which accompanied your deck. It is always desirable to work with the deck's interpretation in harmony with the intent of its design.

Ten of Pentacles

With this card are we able to see A. E. Waite's fascination with Kaballah. The original pentacle offered by the hand of Divinity has now manifested as ten, arranged in the pattern of the sephiroth upon the tree of life. Just as the Tree of Life represents the principles of manifestation, this card represents the stuff of which the suit of Pentacles is composed. This card teaches us how to bring the principles of manifestation into our lives.

Behind the diagram of the pentacles, we find an abundance of symbols. In the foreground an older man is seated, his hand reaching out to pat the head of one of the dogs. He wears a richly colored robe. Down below, at left, we see a mound of harvested grapes.

Just beyond is a large, masonry arch set with designs including ships, recurrent symbols of commerce throughout the Tarot. Above them is found a castle, representing success and social status. To the left is a panel which includes what appears to be a tower built upon a prominence. The arch itself brings back the theme of the two pillars. We see the one on the left.

Beneath the arch two figures are talking, a child by the woman reaching for one of the dogs. In the background are buildings which depict an urban setting. The placement of the windows provides perspective. The height of these structures indicates that this is far more than a simple village.

The Ten of Pentacles is teaching us about the far-reaching implications of accumulating substance with a view to that which extends beyond the self. This card represents more than one's personal budget. It speaks to the seeker of matters involving real estate, family wealth, long-term security and assets. The presence of three generations is a reminder that we cannot take it with us. What we have worked hard to accumulate may, if handled wisely, be left for the next generation and even the generation which follows that. Similarly, this card indicates the handling of matters of substance (money, possessions) which involve a number of individuals, usually related to each other - at least in spirit.

These dogs, unlike those which howled their fears and anxieties in The Moon card, are content and secure, affectionately petted by both the oldest and the youngest. There is comfort taken in knowing that the lessons of this suit have been implemented and that one's retirement is now comfortable and secure The work is now being done by the couple conversing with each other.

The elderly gentleman has done his part of the work. The fruits of his life-long labor and spiritually-balanced work ethic are represented by the grapes. Now he has time to sit back and enjoy the pleasures of his grandchildren and domestic pets. He knows he cannot take it with him. This is a card which juxtaposes procreation and the continuance of life with the realities of death's encroachment. It should be pointed out that the family name may also be considered an asset. The reputation of the oldest generation may well be of benefit to those which follow. It now becomes their role to sustain and improve the quality of the family estate.

The Ten of Pentacles is not so much a card depicting an outcome as it is one which represents issues which most of us will face. Even the young must often come to terms with the process of sorting through family possessions, deciding to whom which heirlooms will be passed.

The deeper levels of wisdom represented by this card are variations of the Hermetic Principle (as above, so below) and of the Kaballah (which may, in a metaphysical manner, be perceived as the ultimate view of recycling at the level of the Divine). We see the flow from the mundane to the spiritual, a flow from the spiritual to the mundane. The Ten of Pentacles represents all of the lessons of this suit thus far presented.

reversed

When the Ten of Pentacles appears reversed in a layout, the seeker is likely to encounter (or be encountering) actual loss. At the least we know that losses are apt to happen. Whether this represents a loss caused by a corruption of the family values or by poor planning, the card alone cannot say.

Money or possessions may be lost due to squabbling within the family, arguments which are based upon ego and emotion. Better for the family were there negotiation, leading to an amicable settlement. This card has been known to appear when one member of the family has gambled to excess, affecting others in the family.

Perhaps financial matters were placed unwisely in the hands of someone who was not worthy, resulting in a large tax burden which could otherwise have been avoided.

These reversals of fortune may imply far more than mere tangible goods, for it may refer to serious damage to the family name and reputation.

Should this card be reversed, take great caution in any financial dealings. It does not assign fault but implies that there were lessons unlearned or knowledge which has not been utilized. It becomes important to take immediate responsibility for your own role in your financial future. Changes can and must be made. Even though money lost may not be quickly recovered, all can be restored by embracing the wisdom of the suit.

Page of Pentacles

Of all the Pages, the Page of Pentacles seems to have a subtle relationship with the Ace of its suit. This can be found in the hand position of both cards. Although the scenic view is filled with potential, ranging from the spiritual heights of the mountain to the fruitful grove of trees and the well-plowed fields, the Page is not seeking answers in the surrounding reality. Her eyes are turned toward the pentacle which she holds as if it is lighter than air, barely touching the tips of her fingers and thumbs. Although you may see this as a great feat of balance, we would do well to use this card as a role model for learning.

The Page stands at the foreground. It is an interesting turn of perspective, for the artist's view is as one seated upon the earth, that element which is corresponded with the suit of Pentacles. By comparison, the Page seems much larger than the trees or even the mountain, as if to call attention to the action she is depicting.

Along with the other three, Pages represent the gathering and bringing of news, typically of a project or event. This Page in her wisdom, however, is not looking to the fruitfulness of the earth for her answers. Rather, she is contemplating the lessons of this suit. She does not grasp at the pentacle nor hold it too tightly. It sits there poised, in perfect balance.

We are taught by the suit of Pentacles to be realistic. Pentacles teach us that which we must learn in order to provide not only for our present needs but for those dependent upon us as well as for future needs.

Unlike his brother and sister Pages, the Page of Pentacles is not one to go rushing forward into this new direction. First he will give careful thought to all facets of this new idea. Even though being offered a new idea or direction, the seeker is asked to consider all of the 'if' qualities to determine mature plans. We can imagine the Page studying each of the five points in the pentagram (which represent air, fire, water, earth and spirit) to determine whether or not this idea is truly workable.

Pentacles teach commitment. Before the Page is able to make a commitment of time and energy to this project, he chooses to contemplate whether he has the resources, the skills and the time. You might think of this as a form of 'research and development' for it is anything but daydreaming (you can study the Knight of Cups for daydreaming skills!). The Page wants to be certain that he has enough desire to follow the path all the way to the mountain top. And if he has all he needs, then what?

The Ace of Wands presents us with a new beginning, one which is likely to be life-changing. Although not as comprehensive as the new start of the Aces, the Page's new beginning is significant. Sometimes this card reminds me of the Two of Wands, in which the figure is holding the whole world in his hands. Here the Page is examining all aspects of his work ethic.

This card represents a situation which can bear fruit. With enough thought and preparation, the results will manifest in tangible ways. The Page is not hasty. If representing a person in the seeker's life (or qualities the seeker must embody) this is an individual who is thoughtful and focused, someone who can study the facts and figures and use them as a foundation for the future.

It is only when the Page feels assured that enough resources, including time and money, that the project will be initiated. When that happens we are assured of success, for the Page is a hard worker.

reversed

The reversed Page of Pentacles depicts someone for whom hard work and responsibility have been set aside for the pursuit of pleasure. His life is out of balance. The news this Page brings the seeker is likely to be unwanted. His feet no longer on the ground, he chooses to ignore the necessary lessons of this suit. Perhaps it is illogical thinking or perhaps a desire to take get-rich-quick

KNIGHT of PENTACLES

shortcuts, but the earth which should be a solid foundation is now shaky. Without immediate action and responsibility, without putting one's ear to the ground (and getting to serious work), things are likely to become much worse.

Knight of Pentacles

Like the 'salt of the earth,' this hard working Knight is reflecting upon the values of his work ethic. The pentacle of the Ace is now a manageable size, reflecting real-life values brought down to daily living. It is held in the Knight's hand, easily balanced, for he understands the nature of labor, the value of tools, the fulfillment of manifesting a good work ethic. The pentacle is held in balance and harmony.

The horse stands upon a small hill of greenery in the foreground. Stretching out behind horse and rider is a gently undulating, fertile expanse of plowed field. At the horizon on a hill are two trees, symbols of knowledge and fruition. And in the distance we see the mountains, representing the achievement of one's goals, the attainment of wisdom.

Between the knight and the distant mountains waits the soil. The Knight of Pentacles has a strong bond with the soil. He is hard-working, industrious, and he is patient. The wisdom of this card shows us that good labor and methodical work will lead to success. Crops will not emerge from a poorly-plowed field. Time and effort will be wasted if the furrows are not laid down in an orderly and careful manner. Preparing a well-plowed field means removing the rocks, tending to the remnants of the previous year's growth, and spending many long hours working back and forth until the soil has been readied for the planting of seed.

The Knight has spent much time in motion. We cannot tell whether she has already planted the seed or is waiting the best weather conditions in order to plant the seed. Although she has toiled many long hours, she also knows when to wait and observe, for there is a natural cycle within which seeds sprout and plants grow. Patience and a connection with the natural cycles are the only path to a successful harvest.

The Knight of Pentacles is a mature, responsible individual. Like all Knights, we must assume that he has seen much of the world. By definition a knight is experienced but now is the time to reflect on life's wonders. Dependable, methodical and capable, the Knight is willing to spend time studying that which lies before. The production of a successful harvest is the goal and this card appears when the Tarot indicates the seeker is encountering a situation requiring methodical action and patience. Remember, you cannot make the crops grow any faster than is their nature.

The honor of a Knight is also essential to the values of this card. This includes truthfulness to oneself and to others. The Knight has taken vows embracing a willingness to serve others, indicated in this card by the field, which is far larger than what would feed one person, even one family. The ethics of the suit include being responsible and gaining the realization that ultimate success means it is now time to slow down and develop the above mentioned qualities. It is time for putting down one's roots even as do the seedlings.

reversed

The reversed Knight of Pentacles may indicate either a presence of 'too much' earth or an absence of the Knight's honor.

If the former, the card represents one who is slowed down, possibly even caught in a rut of his own making. This knight may be lazy and subject to lethargy. Relying upon past laurels will not bring success. A lack of motivation to do the work will lead to a crop failure.

If the card speaks of an absence of values, then she may be careless, lazy, unwilling to represent a generosity of the spirit and an ability to share. This is someone who may be selfish and small-minded. The wrong motivation can also be very damaging to the crop.

In either scenario, the reverse knight portends the likelihood of failure, for a fertile future is lost without restoring the higher values of the Knight of Pentacles.

Queen of Pentacles

The pentacle began this suit with the Ace, extended from the divine and loving hand. It has now manifested itself in the hands of the queen, a woman embodied as the fruits of one's labor and the fertility of life provided by a wise work ethic. She is a warm and giving woman, one who works well in partnership with the King of Pentacles.

The Queen sits upon her throne, surrounded by lush vegetation, gazing upon the mysteries taught by this suit. She sees great wisdom reflected to her from the pentacle. Her throne, upon which are carved fruits and creatures as symbols of a full harvest, represents her status within the community. She is much-loved by those of her realm. Although her life is one of plenty and her coffers are filled, she is not taken by the superficial values of money and, remembering the wisdom of the Six of Pentacles, understands that goods and wealth allow her to protect the people of her realm against hunger and poverty. She not only gives to them what is needed for a good life, she shows them how to cultivate their own food and how to have a successful harvest. She teaches them the ways of commerce and trade so that they can support themselves.

She is a loving, protective and nurturing Queen. She does not bear the weapons of aggression as do the Queens of Swords and Rods, but uses the pentacle as a shield of protection. In many ways, the Queen of Pentacles may be the most content of the four Queens.

The Queen of Pentacles represents the best qualities of nobility and teaches us that there is nothing wrong with having nice things. She exemplifies a knowledge of the spiritual essence found within all material and physical things. She does not see her things as *possessions* but as tools which lead to a greater fulfillment in life.

With the mountains of wisdom and spiritual attainment clearly visible behind her, she represents the best of both worlds. The card is abundant in symbols of the physical, manifest world, including the fertility of the bunny to the right of her feet. We can well imagine her days when young, quite

possibly studying as a fellow student with the High Priestess. Although the High Priestess was on a path which led to the temple, the Queen's path led to the throne. Yet the Queen quite likely has the training which allows her to cross the abyss and enter the familiar spiritual heights of those mountaintops. The wealth and comfort of her life have not separated her from her Highest Ideals.

Described as a warmhearted woman, providing strength for those in need, she is often described as the ideal wife and mother. She is a woman to whom you could turn in order to learn an understanding of life. She is a good manager, understanding how to sustain her family and her community. Never wasteful, she is intelligent yet conservative with her energy, appreciating the joy of having fine things yet generous and warm. It is no wonder that she is frequently a woman happily married.

reversed

The reversed image of the Queen of Pentacles is one in which you can imagine the pentacle becoming her foundation, the weight of the throne now borne by the Queen's ego. This scenario now depicts one who is attracted to wealth for what it can do for her, personally. Someone who marries for financial security rather than love and affection might represent this value (which is not inherently negative). But one who compensates for her own insecurities and inadequacies by surrounding herself with fine things, one who cannot control her shopping, might be the more negative value of this reversed card.

With money as the measurement of one's status, we see a woman prone to doubts and suspicions who is living a life of anxieties. Her moods are determined by the acquisition of new finery or the amount of money at her fingertips. Unable to understand the true meaning of life, she does not value herself. As a consequence, she is unlikely to value others. She is burdened by the superficial qualities of a value system based upon material things.

When describing a more serious turn of events, this card may indicate someone who has lost a sense of ethics and morality, who is willing to juggle the books or manipulate others in order to sustain her desire for an image of success, even as her spiritual health is failing.

King of Pentacles

The King of Pentacles brings to fruition the suit of Pentacles. The disk of manifestation we saw extended in the Ace now rests upon the King's knee. Many of the symbols we have come to know throughout the four

KING of PENTACLES.

suits can be found. The king, wearing his crown, carrying the orbed wand, sits upon the throne which indicates his station in life. The visible foot shows us that, despite his agrarian setting - surrounded by the fruits of the earth - he is prepared to join the Knight, if necessary, to keep his people protected. We see the masonry wall behind him, the urban towers on one side, and the mountains of wisdom at the other. No doubt, there must be an abyss to cross as well.

What a fine gentleman is the King. Often described as the 'salt of the earth' (appropriate for the gentleman of this earth-related suit) he is considerate, mature and faithful, and genuinely a kind and nice person. He is humbled by his position. The King exemplifies the best qualities of a man who has achieved the throne.

With the Taurean bulls upon his throne, this is a man who represents the sometimes unmovable quality of earth. He has strong beliefs and manifests unshakable confidence. The conviction he holds in his beliefs provides strength for those who follow him. Those symbols of Taurus also symbolize his loving character. Few men are so devoted to their wives.

The King of Pentacles understands the Mysteries of Fertility. Surrounded by many flowering and fruiting species, he wears his robe embroidered with the fruitfulness of grapes. The King's fruitfulness is not limited to the fields and orchards, as we see by the towers of commerce representing the world of business.

The King brings his strength of character to all his work. He is practical and takes his time, making decisions based upon experience and knowledge. He represents the best work ethic, doing good, methodical work - yet never delaying the harvest. In addition to this, he has a great love for the work he does. The King is able to delegate work when appropriate, but is also able to step in and do the work himself. Although he holds great power, it is always used with utmost care.

Knowing whether the King represents qualities which the seeker should be embracing, or whether the King represents someone to whom the seeker should turn for counsel, should be apparent from considering the adjacent cards in the layout.

reversed

When the King of Pentacles is reversed, the grapes are more likely to be indicative of someone who becomes intoxicated with power. The grapes are now going to his head! No longer a man of honor, he is prone to bull headed behavior, demanding that his way always prevail. His abuse of power leads to corruption and a perverse way of shifting his interpretation of reality and facts in order to maintain his hold on the throne.

Believing that everything is his domain, the reversed King can be so materialistic that you are cautioned to protect your own possessions. Despite this negative view of the reversed King, he remains handsome and charming, exuding appeal, even more reason for caution.

Having come to the end of the Minor Arcana, we can only hope this card advises the seeker to be wary of this reversed individual. If it is describing the seeker, then counsel must be taken, for this is an unhealthy and dangerous situation should it continue. Although difficult and temporarily discomforting to one's ego, it is far better to emulate the King of Pentacles in his loving position upon the throne.

The Numerology of Tarot

The following pages will introduce you to the principles and qualities of the individual numbered and court cards of the Minor Arcana. The more understanding you can develop of the nature of a number 'three,' for example, the better you will comprehend what each of the four threes might mean. An excellent exercise is to place all four suits of the same Minor card together. What do the Fives have in common? How are the Tens similar? The better you are able to grasp the esoteric meaning of the number the deeper your understanding.

This study of the meaning of numbers looks at the basic meaning of each number. It is a different approach to numerology than what is often referred to as a 'birth number,' calculated by one's name, birth information, and the like. To better understand the intrinsic energy of our numbers, begin to look about you. Listen to the conversations of those around you. Folk sayings often reflect popular understanding of the meanings of numbers. Some events are believed to 'happen in threes.' The more you understand the patterns of the numbers one through ten, the better you will be able to interpret the numbered Minor Arcana when they visit you in a layout.

1 - The Aces

Each Ace is the beginning of its suit. In esoteric numerology, the number one is an initiating force. Each Ace puts that suit into motion or into manifestation, as the case may be. While not royalty as are the four court cards (the Page, Knight, Queen and King), there is a noble and divine quality about the Aces. Each Ace is depicted emerging from a heavenly cloud, as if extended by the Hand of the Divine. The energy of this card may be thought of as emerging from the top of the Tree of Life and having a driving impulse behind it. A Deity represents the Highest Ideals which are manifest through self-awareness. It is Ego at its most supreme and thus, able to bring ideals into manifestation. The Ace becomes a role model by which the seeker might elevate her own ego but in a positive way. In this sense, the pursuit of wisdom is far more important than is the way in which success reflects upon the self.

The hand is holding the tool of that suit as a gift, able to establish life changing potential. If embraced and manifested in accord with the ethics and wisdom of that suit, the path will ultimately lead to the mastery depicted by that suit's Queen and King. Later in the suit, should one of the cards appear in a layout to indicate that something is lacking in the behavior or attitudes of the seeker, one may return to the Ace. It is the primary card of the suit. Its symbols contain the lessons one needs at the beginning of the endeavor. It teaches you about the knowledge one would hold when having evolved the wisdom and ethics of that suit.

The Ace is the primary lesson which introduces a suit. The cards which follow indicate skills and attitudes needed in order to achieve that mastery. Aces represent self-mastery, the ability to manifest those ideals in harmony with the gifts of creativity being offered. While representing an ideal, an Ace is not unrealistic. It represents great potential. It is not a 'law.'

Despite the joy we feel upon seeing an Ace in a reading (for they are 'good news'), to use an Ace successfully means developing the work ethic and discipline embodied by that suit. There may be the need for some level of sacrifice. The Ace may call for a willingness to set aside some of what we might otherwise have, in order to pursue the goal with success. When an Ace appears, it is important for the individual to contemplate what that 'something new' might be. It is that which the Ace wants the seeker to establish.

The Aces represent, in numerology, the energy of a number one. This is *the* primary number, one which represents change which simply is. It may also be perceived as change which may bring enlightenment and achievement or, if repressed, might implode or collapse under its own energy. Although some describe the energy of an Ace as being solar, I tend toward believing that an Ace's energy is determined by the elemental energy of each tool. Thus the Ace of Swords' energy is that of air, the Ace of Cups' Magick is feminine and of water, and so forth. Yet it can be stated that all four Aces represent the Yang, or positive masculine, force which is a healthy power and wise ambition directed toward creation. Both ambergris and lady's mantle have been corresponded with the four Aces.

2 - The Twos

The number two, in esoteric numerology, conveys the energy of the difference between two differing entities or that of two differing parts of a whole. What originally emerged as a single entity, as a unity, now moves into the polarities in order to become creative. Often indicative of entering a partnership, there are times when the process by which one questions the direction of her life may also be represented by a number two. Twos may indicate the need for adjustment, for compromise, and sometimes caution us to lighten up and take life less seriously.

In the practical sense this means that the numerical two is a number which may indicate choice, although it may not be the life-altering fork in the road as we see with The Lovers card. The type of choice suggested by a two is not so dramatic. Unlike the completeness and brimming potential of the number one, twos address matters of division and separation, but whether or not this sense of division or separation becomes a divisive factor - or whether it allows for a creative union - is the issue discussed within the individual suits.

There are many aspects of a working partnership which, by the very nature of two people learning how to work together to achieve common goals, brings forth the nature of this number. A number two may also indicate circumstances which head to hesitation, uncertainty and internal conflict within the individual. Twos may arise in a reading to discuss activity within a partnership or within an individual. Within a relationship, twos explore various levels of comfort and may indicate hesitation or uncertainty by the couple. A two of a suit may caution the seeker to set aside his ego. When a partnership is composed of two very different persons they may be like the polarities of the two pillars, learning to find that central energy which allows them to function as individuals yet combine their differences and compatibilities to create a third, more central energy. A working partnership requires cooperation, patience and, sometimes, forgiveness.

While it is possible to view numbers as they progress in size, growing larger, we may also see progress as we view them from the larger to the smallest. The lessons we see in the Twos of the Tarot provide us with guidelines so that a potentially divisive difficulty in a relationship may be maturely addressed. In this manner does a partnership become a working whole. The same movement toward unity indicated by a number two may apply to an individual.

The Two of Swords is a card which indicates that the two individuals have taken more space and that their discord is temporarily settled. Although addressing the process of thinking and communication, both functions of the intellect, the Moon is up above the water, although whether rising or setting we do not know. Not only is there separation between individuals but the number two recommends separation between facts and emotions.

The Two of Wands more clearly examines the fork in the road. Which path should the seeker take? The two staves are at differing heights and there are likely to be two opinions, neither of which may be the better.

Traditionally, the Two of Cups is a card which shows how two individuals, each unique and different, are able to bring their differences into a creative whole. Emotional balance and cooperation has been brought into play and the results are most positive.

The ability to ride the ups and downs, of juggling two realities which are not always in harmony, is depicted in the Two of Pentacles. It shows that we can maintain balance over physical reality but that it takes poise and adjustment.

Although I have seen a minority of authors indicate that the quality of a number two is lunar by nature, I am personally not so certain. What allows me to consider a lunar quality is that the energy of a two is not necessarily comfortable. It may also be posited that the duality of a number two may manifest as a form of hermetic energy, being above and below, being within and without. A two may be before and after. There is that quality of balance which is important if one is to bring the two parts together. In this hermetic sense a number two may also be thought of as mercurial.

Although I no longer recall where, I have seen the scent of musk corresponded with the number two. I do not have any personal experience in using herbes or scents with the numbers but have, rather, had a more passive and objective approach, observing the patterns of the numbers as they manifeste in life.

3 - Threes

Although I doubt it was considered *numerology*, the earliest lesson I learned was that 'things happen in threes.' It was a common folk saying in the 1950s when I was young. A 'three' is a number of manifestation and is typically a change which brings itself to one's awareness but one which does not bring undue difficulty. Unfortunately for my youthful understanding, the phrase most often seemed applied to deaths.

The Tarot takes a more complex view of this number. The four threes in the Tarot all indicate changes which are, metaphorically, three-part. The Threes provide us with information about our goals and how we might better attain them. The lessons each of these cards brings to us offer the potential for making this process more accessible and easier to manage. Although not always simple and without pain, the changes associated with the number three can definitely be manageable.

In religious metaphysics, a three is a number of manifestation. It is, after all, the number of a trinity. Many major religions portray their deity as manifesting through some version of a trinity. The Threes in the Tarot show us that, at some level, we must begin to acknowledge the presence of the divine within ourselves. In religious mythology a trinity is often that point which creates the bond between divine and human existence. Within the Minor Arcana the Threes are not nearly so dramatic but do represent how we might work through a balanced combination of 'two and one' within the daily progress of our own lives.

In general, threes represent the world of manifestation. In Chinese numerology, threes represent an aspect of perfection. Within nature we perceive three primary colors and many species of flowers display themselves in units of three: three petals, three sepals, a three-lobed seed, etc. In the earliest times of human intelligence the awareness of two parents creating a third human through procreation may have been the foundation for many beliefs about the number three.

The Threes of the Minor Arcana teach us about change as a creative, natural transition. Two of the cards (the Three of Swords and the Three of Wands) question one's path. The Three of Cups and the Three of Pentacles offer us a view of the potential of our goals, once attained. Structural engineers know that a triangle is a highly stable foundation. The next time you see a bridge supported by a framework of iron, note the use of the triangle as a means of distributing weight and adding stability.

The Three of Swords depicts what can happen when one moves endlessly around the triangle (the symbol for a number three), making no progress as the mind and heart become lost in thinking the change negative. The Three of Wands shows that we can achieve certain goals, but we must not hold the only Wand. We will fare better relying upon the support and stability of others. Handled well, the Three of Cups lets us know we will have cause for celebration. The Three of Pentacles is the completion of lessons: having learned so well that others now come to us for our skills.

When one of the Threes appears, it may answer the question of what your path is holding for you. It reminds you that you have talent and adequate creativity to bring this change into a positive manifestation, but success must come through wisdom and learning what the Tarot offers. It is good to be mindful that the triangle, a symbol of the number three, is not only representative of the most joyful creation but may also be a symbol of a wedge. The Three of Swords shows us this lesson clearly and painfully.

Decades ago I added a note to the book I compiled as my teaching guide. An author, one whom I unfortunately no longer can identify, had placed a correspondence with myrrh. In reflecting upon this I wonder whether there might have been any thought of the 'three' Magi, who brought not only myrrh, but frankincense and gold with them as symbolic gifts.

Although I do not personally relate to any table of correspondences which would align the numbers with astrology, I have seen Jupiter and, less frequently, Mercury both listed as having an association with the Threes of Tarot.

4 - Fours

My understanding of the number four has grown over the decades, perhaps through my increased use of atlases. I turn to them as I look for coordinates of latitude and longitude in order to calculate natal charts or to find the epicenters of earthquakes. Combined with my three decades' relationship of relating to the four directions ritually, eventually our Earth began to help me better comprehend the reality of the number four.

From what I've learned through studies of astronomy, it would seem reasonable to assume that the planetary shape throughout our Universe would typically be spherical. From this I would also presume that the way to indicate location, mark distances or provide any knowledge of topography or geography by any other sentient species would require a comparable method. The intelligent species of another system would relate the coordinates from the four directions, by whatever name. The plotting of those directions would be based upon that planet's rotational axis.

With this in mind, when I think of a number four representing a foundation, it is that number upon which one's future might be constructed. The four speaks to me with logic. A four teaches us how to work with the building blocks of reality. The Fours address physical, tangible things of the real world.

The history of a number four's numerical meaning includes being the number representing the principle of our planet Earth. Not only the planet, but the number four carries with it the potential with which to achieve perfection upon earth. The mystery of a number four is that which allows us to learn those lessons which help bring our creative work in the manifest world closer to our Highest Ideals.

And what might those lessons address? We are taught to be patient, conservative with our energy and resources. We are asked to be steady in our path, developing a strong work ethic. The Four of Pentacles is a clear example of what can happen when the glitter of the reward overtakes the joy of creation. The Four of Cups cautions us to hold to our goal, to avoid wallowing in superficial discouragement.

A four can be tricky. Not unlike a folding table, it may be rickety at the onset but the wisdom of the Four leads to stability. In addition to hard work, steadiness and avoiding waste, the Four leads to something which can be a joyful completion. Through order, through putting one foot carefully before the other and avoiding the pitfalls of emotional reactions (as in the Four of Cups), we have in this number the key to magickal doors, one which can lead us to the celebration depicted by the Four of Wands. This expansive quality has led some to consider the Fours to be Jovian, or corresponded with Jupiter. One working with magick might do well to use cedar as an herbe.

There may be found a deeper level of arcane wisdom within the number four and, for that reason, we should never be complacent about this positive number. Rather we ought be alert and introspective, just as the knight in the Four of Swords, who remains grounded in his spiritual path. A pyramid has four sides, constructed upon a square base and yet, combined with the four triangular faces, it ascends up toward the heavens. When the manifest realm of existence is balanced with spiritual wisdom and disciplines, the number four allows us to manifest our internal divinity.

5 - Fives

What is it about the Fives of Tarot? The four suits depict the Fives in the most unsettling of ways. Fives are challenging with quick-moving energy and events, sometimes described as mercurial.

The energy of a number five may move you beyond your comfort zone. A five is strong energy and intense. Fives clearly bring change. The average person does not like change. Most resist change, holding tight to what is familiar. I believe this explains why a number five represents discomfort and anxiety among the general public. Interestingly, it is the clover I once saw as the herb corresponded with the Fives. I would think it should be a five-leaved clover as the focus for our search, although practical matters lead us to the basic, good quality clover, *Trifolium pratense*.

Those who resist change encounter stress and pain, but learning how to make changes teaches us that we must let go and endure any pain. If we trust where the change will lead us, if we have faith in the Universe, then we will end up just fine.

Just as the five-pointed star, or pentagram, represents the natural forces of Nature (the four elements plus the fifth point for spirit), that symbol, the pentagram, is often misunderstood and regarded by many with fear and apprehension. When all four elements are in perfect balance we have the principle of manifestation or spirit. The energy of a five, however, indicates what may occur when all four elements are in the flux of manifestation. Into this is given additional energy by the presence of spirit! This is a quick lesson in magick, and fives are sometimes thought of as a trial by fire - although not as life-shaking as the Tower Card. No wonder it is said Pythagoras required his students to maintain a period of five years of silence to understand this number.

The energy or magick of a five is like stirring the cauldron and invoking change. The average person finds someone has set things in motion. Perhaps it is the powers of the Universe which are stirring the cauldron. Those who pursue the study of magick, systems of making change, or methods of connecting the self with the great forces of Nature will, at times, make a conscious choice to work with this energy. A five is more intense energy. It is, at times, a raw natural force and, if one is not able to handle it, will feel like chaos. While it may not have the depth of an eight, a five is also an initiatory number. These events are likely to leave you feeling changed. Perhaps this is why Christian numerology associated the number five with the rebirth of the Christ.

The Five of Swords depicts the result of words and communication being thrown about without regard for the pain of others. In the Five of Wands we see a struggle to see who will come out victorious, emerging from an ordeal. One's emotions are the overwhelming natural force in the Five of Cups and in the Five of Pentacles, the natural forces have affected one's ability to provide one's needed material resources.

Working with the energy of a five requires an inner faith. It is essential that you be not caught up in the drama (for these fives do seem to be more dramatic) but hold to your Highest Ideals and trust in the Universe. The experience of pain, of emotions, of loss and conflict will otherwise become the determining factor in your behavior. Having faith in the Universe and faith in your self provides you with control. When you feel out of control, panic and anxiety can set in. Out of desperation we cling to the past even when it leads to our unhappiness, and things will take a turn for the worse.

If you are able, and if a Tarot layout alerts you to a coming situation represented by one of the Fives, attempt to engage a sense of adventure. Be flexible and versatile. Be ready to trust your instinct but be certain it is well grounded in intelligence and factual knowledge. To have faith in one's self you must also know yourself and understand the foundation of your motivation. Approach change as a challenge, one which will better you. Working these changes at the expense of others could lead to an unhappy outcome.

I personally love the energy of the Five and think of it as a very positive card. It can be for you as well.

6 - Sixes

Most people think it a good thing that the energy of a six and the nature of its changes are not nearly as *exciting* as that of the number five. A six is much easier to handle than is a five. The life events are paced slower, more able to be understood and one has more ability to think and maintain emotional calm.

Sixes are easier if one has her life in balance. They are easier to embrace if one understands how life manifests itself. One of the recurrent symbols corresponded with a six is the six-pointed star. In magickal work, that star is formed by four triangles superimposed over each other, representing the four elements. In ceremonial symbolism, each of the four elements has a variation of a triangle with or without an additional line parallel to the horizon. The six-pointed star, sometimes referred to in magickal studies as Solomon's Seal, represents the nature of being in communion with the Divine, of having the four elemental forces in one's life in balance. To those who study numerology, a six may be thought of as 'two threes.'

Sixes represent change which is more transitional, which makes it easier to maintain a perspective of where the changes are moving you. The Six of Swords, for example, exemplifies being moved from one state of knowledge to another. It shows what must be done when another is in charge of that transition. The figures in the boat are not trying to give direction, but are shown calm and in a state of acceptance. The Sixes all depict one's interaction with others and with one's community. These four cards characterize the perspective of the self as it undergoes change while interacting with others.

Some who study the esoteric nature of numbers consider the six to be masculine, indicating the need for the individual to maintain an active control.

Others, by comparison, correspond it with Venus - which would be a feminine approach, one in which the individual is not trying to affect the outcome and is, rather, working to derive pleasure from the events of life. I have seen frankincense listed as an herb associated with the four Sixes.

A six brings things together in your life, and, when everything comes together one will generally find that change is taking place. At the least, this would be a change in one's outlook on life. The Six of Pentacles shows someone who is learning that one of the ways to continue to have resources manifesting in one's life is to be generous of spirit and to give to those less fortunate. This card shows us how one may choose to work with a six. Doing so would help invoke manageable changes within the real world which stimulate changes within one's spiritual awareness as well.

A six may represent that which you are seeking. Understanding how the Sixes are illustrated in the four suits offers you the knowledge of how to manifest your own ideals. Sometimes suggested to be the symbol of the magician, the six-pointed star indicates that ideal in which one lives life in union with the ideals of one's religion or spiritual beliefs and, in so doing, leads a fruitful, generous and balanced life. Such a person knows when to take steps and when to allow the Universe, itself, to be in control. Sixes teach us about faith and trust and, perhaps for that reason, I have seen the number associated with the concept of miracles. But what seems like magick or a miracle is only that perception to the outsider. To those who are wise, it is merely the nature of the Universe unfolding to those who live in harmonious balance.

7 - Sevens

Most of us have heard the phrase, 'lucky seven.' As do the other numbers, a seven also represents change, but one which is more comfortable. A seven does not leave a person feeling rushed. In the magick of numbers, sevens are pleasing numbers, likable and nice. Often considered feminine, they allow us to reach up to the spiritual.

Some consider a seven to be a 'lunar' number. The herbe benzoin has been associated with this number. I have seen the rose corresponded herbally for the Seven of Cups.

The process of a seven should lead us to further wisdom, to an awareness of the underlying spiritual nature of reality. The changes associated with a seven lead to introspection and may stimulate our intuitive functions.

But if a seven is such a good thing, why are the suits not all in agreement? The Seven of Swords, for example, is a lesson in the *lack* of trust. Unable to trust that the goal will be achieved, the figure on the card chooses to grab what he can and avoid being seen, indicative of someone whose intuition is cautioning him that this is not in anyone's best interest. This card shows us what happens when we do *not* trust the wisdom of the Seven. The Seven of Wands does not look like fun, either, but it addresses a situation in which adversity will show you how strong you are, admonishing the seeker to trust her own strength and to hold her will strong.

When we confuse our fantasies with the potential of the future, we escape reality by imagining all manner of possible rewards. The Seven of Cups reminds us that holding to our Highest Ideal will lead to the joy of one's success. It is with the Pentacles that we are reminded to allow the manifestation of a seven to occur in its own time - to be patient.

A seven shows us how to open our selves to the natural and fertile flow of energy found in nature. In numerical wisdom, a seven is sometimes taught as a union of the divine manifestation of a three with the manifest realm of a four. What this means as we study the Tarot is that the four suits bring us lessons regarding the nature of life and the essence of being.

We are taught to trust, to trust our intuition and to trust in the gifts of the spirit and Universe which are unfolding before us. There are Mysteries associated with the study of numbers. The teachings of Pythagorus were the foundation for his mystery school which taught his students how to use the study of numbers as keys which opened for them the mysteries of the Universe. A seven is often considered one of the numbers which can lead to the Divine Feminine. As such, it represents learning to be able to be receptive to one's intuition, to the spiritual essence in life, balancing your daily needs as you come to face the material world.

8 - Eights

There is a Saturnian quality to eights. They are often perceived as second only to the numerical fives when it comes to the intensity of their changes and difficulties. The number eight, in myth and esoteric legend, is a powerful number. The Mayan culture believed that the soul remained with the body for eight days following death. Only then would it be released. Some believe that the number eight is associated with the rituals of circumcision and naming in the Hebrew religion. Eight is considered an initiatory number and many believe it reaches further into the Mysteries of Death than do other numbers.

The eight is considered to be very potent, a number which has great power with it. The events of an eight can move swiftly, trying all of one's weaknesses. We see this in the Eight of Wands. Understanding the energy of the eight is important in learning the Tarot. Two herbes have been corresponded with this card, should someone wish to use them to further their understanding. They are elecampagne (or elfwort) and storax.

The nature of change indicated by the Eights is that of two forces which are not concentric. In esoteric numerology this may be seen as a combination of two fours, of two non-concentric sources of energy trying to manifest toward goals which may not be compatible. The resulting situation suggests conflict and, perhaps, loss. With two sources of energy moving in directions which may oppose each other, these forces may not always be external. A card may suggest one's desire to have and to not have. The Eight of Swords shows someone who is left completely dysfunctional by conflict. Certainly the mystery of an eight is one in which we must nearly always let go in order to make changes. Perhaps that is what the figure in the Eight of Cups is doing?

The eight also teaches us of matters of survival, of what is needed in order to sustain our lives. The work ethic depicted in the Eight of Pentacles shows that the craftsperson has set aside the potential for wealth and recognition. She has removed herself from friends and community in order to perfect the skills of her craft.

The changes associated with the numerical eight are those which represent significant turning points in one's life. There are no halfway measures with these cards. They reach into your very soul and are considered primeval in that basic sense. An eight may feel like death but it is important to remember that this card is still part of the Minor Arcana. It is not a Major Arcana card.

Although an Eight may indicate that it is time to face the music and learn important lessons, these cards also bring great insight into sustaining our manifest life. Eights also address planning for the future. They teach us about promises and growth but, if we cannot embrace change, they may suggest a level of destruction and fear. In this sense they are procreative.

9 - Nines

The Nines in the Tarot have, generally, a good reputation, although there seem to be two views of the nine. One perspective considers the nine a number of very active and possibly complex change. This view believes a nine has a martial quality to it. We see this possibility in the Nine of Swords and the Nine of Wands.

But, to other authors, a nine is considered a feminine number, one with an intricate form of changes which evolve and emerge. This is the manner in which we see the Nine of Cups and the Nine of Pentacles.

All four suits address internalized issues. The Swords examine what takes place when one gets caught by the inability to move forward. Self doubt and mental anguish get in the way of reality. These nine wands provide a lesson which shows how to face external adversity by transforming one's inner self.

When one's manifest life is full and one has many rewards, the Nine of Cups reminds us that we must continue to move forward, to seek the Mysteries. The nine is often described as a number which has an initiatory quality. It may be thought of as three threes. In this context not all is apparent to the seeker.

This is true in both Swords and Wands and in the suit of Cups a curtain conceals much from the seeker.

But what a beautiful card is the Nine of Pentacles! In this card the issues of morality inherent in the number nine have been brought to their Highest Ideals. The seeker is at one with her world, fully in harmony with life and with the earth. The Nine of Pentacles brings to us all the potential of this number.

To manifest a nine we must remain focused. We must continue to move forward. The changes we embrace and manifest are primarily internal, not overt. A nine will only work for the seeker if she is ethical at all levels of reality: the reality of human incarnation, the reality of nature, itself; and the psychic reality. Although we may not understand the laws of nature nor fully grasp the astral reality, a nine will move us forward. It is a number which is connected with the Divine. We may attain success when we seek to have our spiritual selves grow toward wisdom. Two herbes have been found in correspondence with the Nines. They are broom (as in Scotch broom) and catnip.

Within the world, nines are sometimes considered numbers of 'rulership.' If we understand the mysteries of this number, we may move toward success. This is a number which addresses matters of one's belief system, of religion and spirituality. A nine is a good number. Although there may be some challenges and even some pain, I encourage you to always greet a nine in a reading as welcome.

10 - Tens

To understand the nature of a ten one must consider a five. A ten may be thought of as two fives. A five indicates times that are likely to be difficult and challenging. But the situation represented by a ten is that, unlike the five, one is now not alone. In fact, there may be times when one person in a partnership is undergoing the intense and difficult changes characterized by a five and the other person might learn of that difficulty when a ten appears in a layout.

The Tens in the Minor Arcana may be seen as different than a ten in traditional numerology. The traditional, esoteric study would consider a ten as a one plus a zero, in the context that adding zeros to a number adds degrees of power and depth. In that context the addition of one (or more) zeros elevates the number in its cosmic intensity.

Carrying with it some aspects of what we call 'karma,' my Tarot teacher referred to a ten as the 'hand of God.' A ten may be that point at which one moves into the realm of magick, of manifestation. They sometimes may represent a point of departure for the individual.

In this sense the ten may indicate a period in one's life which has been cyclical, when that cycle has reached a level of completion. Now one must either return to the recreation of a new beginning (e.g. an Ace) or step into the court cards with a new position among one's peers.

A ten calls for activity. The Ten of Swords, for example, indicates what may happen when one avoids activity and wallows in a mental quagmire. The alternative to forward progress, the inability to recognize that one has reached the end of a cycle and needs to move into a new level of reality, is likely to create stagnation. In the Ten of Wands, the old ways of accomplishing one's tasks keep one from completing that cycle. This leads to one's projects losing joy and life becoming burdensome. Both of these suits can be remedied when one realizes that the Ten is a card of activation, one which calls for recognition that these external events are an alert. It is time to take an active role, to recognize that our interaction with others is a source of strength. Life as it was will be no more.

Should you wish to turn to an herbal source to better understand the Ten, older correspondences suggest dittany of Crete. There are two species of plant known by this common name. Which is the better? Sometimes it is simply a matter of which is available, for neither is always found with ease.

It is as strength we might think of the Ten of Cups. What a joyful card! Here we see how the completion of a period of time in one's life, when working with others cooperatively, brings vitality and strength into existence. There is a quality of faith needed to best manifest a ten and the Ten of Cups is an excellent role model.

The Ten of Pentacles looks even further toward the completion of cycles. We see different generations with different levels of achievement and goals. Because a ten might indicate the end of perfection within a cycle, the Ten of Pentacles is a fitting card with which to bring to a close this discussion of Tarot numerology.

The Court Cards

In similar manner to a regular playing deck, once we leave behind the cards Ace through Ten, we meet figures historically found in a Medieval or Renaissance Court. In regular playing cards these cards (the Jack, Queen and King) are very much like the eleven, twelve and thirteen. Perhaps it is the general public's nervousness with things numbered '13' which has kept playing cards from being so numbered. (In psychology the fear of the number thirteen is *triskaidekaphobia*.)

A 'court' implies the residence and surrounding buildings which encompass the life of the sovereign. It will often include those who live within those surroundings. The figures which ended up being claimed for the Tarot include the Page, Knight, Queen and King. Although archaic in modern democracies, it is important to remember that these are *archetypes*, and very relevant in today's world.

The Page may offer the easiest transition for our awareness, for you may be paged in a hotel or, when young and if fortunate, have a summer job as a page in Congress.

The Knight has been relegated to that of a romantic figure. Originally a mounted, armed man who served a local sovereign, his position was that of defence and, as time passed, implied issues of morality. Knights became figures who were inducted through rituals. There were virtues associated with knighthood but they were also known to wear shining armor and figure in the seduction of winsome lasses.

There are not many Queens and Kings in today's world but even in the business realm we see many figures who would, in older times with far smaller populations, easily have held that title. In its oldest meaning, a queen was a the female chieftain of her people. In the courts she would hold the highest position available to a woman and many historical queens held a more prominent role than any man.

As a King or Queen one may be loved, ethical and benevolent. Just as we see in modern society a person who has been elevated in stature, who occupies a social 'throne,' may also be a despot.

Spending some time and thinking about these four roles before you, then as they appear in the individual suits, will further your understanding.

The Pages of Tarot

These are the first of the court cards. Historically, Pages were hopeful that some day they might complete their training and become knights. A Page was a boy who had entered the first levels of his training. Fortunately, the Pages in the Tarot are not so gender specific. Usually depicted as androgynous, they could be a lass or a lad. Part of the training involved service, usually that of running errands, fetching things, carrying messages and other deliveries of import. Pages had access to many areas of the castle, and were expected to know their way around. Pages served as guides to visitors or guests to the castle. We also find the potential for a ritual or religious overtone when reading *Webster's* definition, "a youth in ceremonial attendance or employment at court." Even today the description of page can be applied to the young person who carries the bride's train in a wedding as she walks down the aisle.

The page is found in today's society as well. As mentioned, they are paired with flower girls and flower boys in weddings. And pages are found in Congress where they serve the same functions as their historical prototypes.

A Page provides the seeker with assistance, often representing the arrival of some message or news. Each of the four Pages suggests a different aspect of the Page's duties. Although not fully trained in the Mysteries, a Page has been taught that there is more to reality than the what can be touched. The appearance of a Page in a reading ought remind the seeker of this variation of the Hermetic Principle: keep your ear to the ground and your mind open.

The Page of Swords stands upon a rise, able to readily sense which way the wind blows, looking off to the horizon. Keen of mind, this Page represents a situation which requires having one's mental abilities in fine working order. This Page is telling the seeker, "Be observant. Be watchful." The Page of Wands brings news of the need for taking action. She is examining the staff, noting that it is strong yet fertile. It will be necessary to have one's strength and stamina in good working order for there is much which must be done.

Holding a chalice from which a fish emerges, the Page of Cups is looking internally whereas the preceding two Pages were checking their environments. A sense of rejuvenation of one's creative spirit is at hand. This news is of some creative or spiritual growth. The Page of Pentacles stands in a field of flowers, the tool lightly balanced upon her fingertips. The news coming forth is that which will bear fruit if you remember the lessons of the pentacles and have your work ethic in good working order.

Unless reversed, the Pages represent news which provides you with opportunities to make something important and beneficial happen in your life. These events are not those removed from your real life. They do not ask you to remove yourself from daily living such as the Hermit or High Priestess or even the Four of Swords. Pages move freely within all levels of society. When one appears in a reading it would be worth your while to reflect upon all of the cards of that suit. Each of them offers certain lessons which, when learned, allow you to bring the new project or direction into manifestation. Do this well and your next reading will present you with some wonderful cards!

Knights

The presence of a Knight in a layout may indicate that there are intermediary forces moving one's life along. The Knight is not always an end unto itself. They have goals to accomplish. Highly active by nature (although the Tarot appropriately shows *inaction* as well) the Knight shows us what manner of motion, what type momentum will be needed to accomplish the task at hand.

And Knights love tasks. They love the Quest and their lives are measured by seeking grails, saving maidens, slaying dragons and having adventures. Each of the four Knights indicates that there is a goal to accomplish. It is important when interpreting a card layout to take time to understand the nature of the goal, of what the 'quest' might be for the seeker.

The adventures of a Knight might well lead him (or her!) into battle. They are depicted wearing armor, an indication of the vulnerability of the human body. The Knights have horses as well. The Knight of Swords is charging forward, cape streaming behind. The horse is at full charge as well.

These are active cards and, in that sense, represent masculine, outgoing energy. The Knight of Wands is fiery, action-loving and impetuous, indicative of someone who needs to be always on the go. This Knight may be unable to curb his momentum. Curiously, the only herbe I have seen associated with this card is tobacco.

Although the Knight has this martial, challenging and masculine energy there is the presence of the feminine. Epona is a Celtic goddess associated with horses. Originally a fertility goddess, her worship spread even into Gaul and Rome and she became known as protectress of horses. Her image was found in stables and was associated with cavalries. The sensual aspects of the horse are seen by some as a counterpart to the sometimes brash and aggressive haste of the Knight.

Time is a luxury for the Knight. His horse is a mode of transportation which can take him to battle when he is needed, carry him away from danger yet the suits also show us what manifests when the Knight is unable to balance time in his life. The Knight of Cups is a dreamer, unable to transform his fantasies into action, even though the horse appears to be ready for motion. Once again it is the suit of Pentacles which brings forth balance. This Knight has come to understand the passage of time. The fields are tilled and waiting.

A Knight arrives at this station in life often through an initiatory process. There is a ceremony, often a religious one. A Knight in waiting may have to spend a wakeful night in prayer, solitude and contemplation, undergoing trials and tests before receiving this honor. There is no 'in between' with a Knight. Whether one of King Arthur's legendary Knights or Joan of Arc - truly an archetype of woman-as-Knight - knighthood is a path for the chosen, not for everyone. When a Knight appears in a layout, the seeker's motto becomes 'be prepared.'

Kings and Queens

It is difficult to describe the Queen without describing her partner, the King. These two indicate a partnership of two individuals who work together toward the common goals of the people whom they represent. I shall introduce them together.

From one perspective they represent the archetype of the two pillars in the Tarot. The Queens represent the ability to manifest mercy and compassion. They may also indicate the difficulties in meeting that expectation. This is balanced with the Kings, who could be perceived as the need, when appropriate, for severity.

Both the Queens and the Kings are shown with thrones. They occupy an elevated status. Their people look up to them. They respect their judgements and accept them as authorities. One who seeks their favor may supplicate them, asking humbly. Their elevated status grants them great power and yet, history shows us they might be deposed or, even worse, assassinated. When either a King or Queen appears in a layout it generally indicates turning to someone in one's community who holds an elevated position, who is a respected authority.

Elevation to the throne will often be done in a splendid ritual or ceremony, often a lavish event, one which indicates the relationship between the throne and the religion(s) of the land. Kings and Queens may be respectful of religion. Many of them were well-trained in a religion and its Mysteries but we also know there may be a ruler who considers the throne of greater value than any religion. And, although they may be placed upon a throne in a grand ceremony, Kings and Queens may, should their realm not be harmonious and loved, be subject to removal.

At the same time they must learn to live in a public manner. Nearly everything they do, whether they quarrel or bear children, whether they embody fidelity and love and show how well they represent the Highest Ideals of ethics, is done before the public. Despite their roles of power they are humbled and recognize that, in many ways, they are there for the people (not the other way around).

In the Tarot we consider the Queens and Kings as pairs within their suit. Even if only one of the couple appears in a layout thought is given to the partner as well. And yet, they are not shown as a couple. Each has her or his own card.

Queens

The Queen represents the feminine aspect of the power of the throne, of the leadership of the people. She is loved by her people for her ability to be nurturing. She is accessible and would open her arms to them much as would a mother.

The Queen represents that power which is a role model for those who are mothers. She is grounded and settled. Whereas her partner must be ready to travel great distances to protect the people and guard the borders, her role includes protecting her people's future by bringing forth the heir, the child who will be the successor to the throne. She has stature and is kept upon her throne through the love of the people. She represents the the ideal partner for the situation being described in the layout of cards.

Although she has been schooled in the Mysteries and understands the spiritual implication of the Divine Marriage in which she represents aspects of the Goddess just as the King is the God, she has also been trained in skills of defense.

When the King is away she must be able to rule. The Queens are depicted with the weaponry of their suit: the wand, the staff. The cup (which is a weapon when poison is given to one's enemy) and the pentacle which, within the court, may be depicted as a shield. In addition, while she may leave such matters in the hands of the King, a Queen best serves her people when she is knowledgeable in trade and business and understands how her realm's economy is best served by the ways it conducts its affairs with others.

She is never unaware of the King, even when they are separated by great distance and by time, just as he is always aware of her. His physical strength in battle is balanced by her courage at facing the pains of birth at a time when pregnancy could well be a life-threatening event for a woman. An herbe I have seen corresponded with the Queen is myrrh.

Kings

The King represents the masculine aspect of the power of the throne, of the leadership of the people. Although this is the masculine aspect of strength, do not trip yourself up with stereotypes and believe this card must indicate a man. When one of the Kings turns up in a layout, it could indicate a woman.

The Kings are shown removed from the domestic and social comforts of the castle. It is their role to be able to travel, to defend the far, isolated reaches of the realm. The Kings of Swords and Wands appear to be far removed from their people. The King of Cups has but a sailing vessel in sight and even that is behind his throne. It is the fertile nature of the King of Pentacles, closely connected with the land, that shows the turrets of the castle in the background. Yet his throne is not within the walls. Indeed, there is a wall separating him from the people.

How does one become King? Perhaps through marriage, although marrying a woman who is the stronger presence of the throne would indicate his role to be that of consort, more spouse than leader. Whether he is at home or whether at the distant borders, the King is an ideal partner, valuing the Queen and knowing that he would not hold his throne without her.

As a youth the King was trained in the skills of battle. He studied history, learning how things have come to be, understanding the various layers of politics both within the peoples of his realm and also those which determine the relationships between his realm and other kingdoms. His was an education beyond that of the average person and his coronation was likely to have been a great event, both religious and ceremonial.

The King must hold his throne by being smarter and wiser, by being stronger and more astute and by having forged relationships with those who will keep him in power. He must be a good man lest his people revolt and depose him.

The character of the King is described as someone who is professional, who carries the skills of social responsibility. He is respected and his decisions accepted. The King has the ability to inspire, to be a leader whose troops would readily follow him into battle should the realm need defending. He must be capable of representing the discipline essential for surviving the rigors of war and of patrolling the furthest reaches of one's kingdom.

The King is protector and defender but this role leaves him less accessible to the people. He is more effective when slightly removed and his work keeps him away from home for periods of time. While he is human and may be seen as human, he must also be symbolic of that which holds the kingdom together.

Herbes and scents reputed to assist the student in working with the nature of the Kings are hyssop and musk.

Bibliography

Beyerl, Paul - *A Compendium of Herbal Magick*, Phoenix Publishing, © 1998

Beyerl, Paul - *Gem and Mineral Lore*, The Hermit's Grove, © 2005

Beyerl, Paul - *Painless Astrology*, [revised edition], The Hermit's Grove, © 1996

Beyerl, Paul - *The Master Book of Herbalism*, Phoenix Publishing, © 1984

Greer, John Michael, The New Encyclopedia of the Occult, Llewellyn Publications, St. Paul MN © 2004

Guiley, Rosemary Ellen, Harper's Encyclopedia of Mystical and Paranormal Experience, Castle Books, Edison NJ © 1991

Heline, Corinne, Sacred Science of Numbers, New Age Press, Inc., Los Angeles CA, fourth edition 1977

Kaplan, Stuart R., [Instruction booklet for the] *Giant Rider-Waite Tarot Deck*, U.S. Games systems, Inc., Stamford, CT 06902 © 1992

Kozminsky, Isidore, *Numbers: Their Meaning and Magic*, Samuel Weiser, New York, 1972 edition

Pollack, Rachel, *Seventy-Eight Degrees of Wisdom: A Book of Tarot*, Part 1: The Major Arcana, The Aquarian Press, Northamptonshire, England © 1980

Pollack, Rachel, *Seventy-Eight Degrees of Wisdom: A Book of Tarot*, Part 2: The Minor Arcana and Readings, The Aquarian Press, Northamptonshire, England © 1983

Waite, Arthur Edward, *The Pictorial Key to the Tarot*, Samuel Weiser, Inc., York Beach ME, originallyi published 1910, American edition ©1984

Revised Standard Version of the Holy Bible, pub. Collins World © 1971

Information on the "History of Egyptian Tarot Decks" may be found at: http://www.meta religion.com/Esoterism/Tarot/ a_history_of_egyptian_tarot_deck.htm

"The First Specifically Esoteric Tarot Deck" may be found at http:// www.villarevak.org/bio/etteilla_2.html

Additional information on the two pillars was found on the internet at:

Lord's Temple, Sacred Architecture, and Sacred Sex, by Jay http:// prophecymysteries.com/links/S6ARCHITECTURESACREDSEX.htm

What Church Members Should Know About Masonry, Jack R. Elliott © 1961 by Radio Church of God, http://www.destiny worldwide.net/rcg/masonfnp.htm

about the author:

Well-known throughout the neo-pagan and Wiccan world, Beyerl's columns and articles have appeared in many publications beginning in the 1970s. *The Master Book of Herbalism,* first published in 1984, remains popular today. Beyerl has been teaching workshops and courses since 1976.

Beyerl is the founder of The Rowan Tree, a Wiccan Church, which obtained legal recognition in 1980. He is the creator of The Tradition of Lothloriën. *A Wiccan Bardo, Revisited* describes this Tradition and Beyerl's view of ritual theology. Within the Rowan Tree, The Mystery School is the educational forum for its inner teaching, combining The Tradition of Lothloriën with a broad-based metaphysical curriculum, including the Tarot. Originally centered in Minneapolis, The Rowan Tree Church moved west with Beyerl.

In addition to his work as herbalist and astrologer, Beyerl is known for his presentations on aspects of ritual, death and dying, ethics, alchemy, initiation, meditation and visualization techniques, and for his performances of ritual which incorporate skills of theatre and music. Beyerl's work has reached a vast number of students over the past thirty years. Many of his former students have moved on to become reputable teachers.

In 1989 Beyerl moved to Dallas and began a circuitous journey which would return him to a northern climate. His work completed in Texas, he moved to Los Angeles to teach for three years. It was while there that he and gerry became partners. In 1994 the Beyerls returned to their roots, opening their herbal gardens. Their home became a religious and educational center known as The Hermit's Grove in Kirkland (a Seattle suburb). The gardens and land were a project begun over twenty years ago by gerry on land known for its stone circle and herbal dreams. Today, Beyerl teaches courses in herbal medicine, horticulture and other studies at two Community Colleges and is the administrator of a Master Herbalist Program.

For further information:
paul@thehermitsgrove.org

The Hermit's Grove
P.O. Box 0691, Kirkland, WA 98033-0691
www.thehermitsgrove.org

The Hermit's Grove is a non-profit organization dedicated to the healing of body, soul and planet. Founded by Rev. Paul and gerry Beyerl in 1994, our educational programs include many related fields, ranging from herbal medicine to herbal magick and many other disciplines. We teach the traditional sciences used by healers, including astrology and spiritual wisdom. The Hermit's Grove offers workshops and classes, over an acre of gardens with hundreds of species and other resources. Its publishing program makes the books of Paul Beyerl available to you, as well as offering a monthly journal.

Through the Hermit's Grove you may study by correspondence, or purchase dried herbs and botanicals (nearly two hundred are offered). The Hermit's Grove is centered in the Beyerls' private home. To protect the gardens and sacred spaces and to respect the needs of our students, we are open by appointment only.

The Memorial Grove: A small woodland at the east end of our gardens is the Memorial Grove. A path through the sacred woodland brings you to a small, stone circle, a safe, private place for meditation and prayer. The Circle has stones from many sacred sites all about our planet. Bells hang from the trees, their sound ringing out in memory of those passed into the Otherworld. Sitting around on the stones is a small herd of Unicorns... If you wish to have a bell hung or a unicorn placed in our garden in memory of a loved one, please contact The Hermit's Grove to make arrangements. Weatherproof unicorns are always welcome!

Do you want a magickal stone??? Magickal stones from our garden are available, tumbled and polished. Send one from your home garden or sacred space for our Stone Circle and we will send one to you. Because The Hermit's Grove is definitely non-profit (sometimes too non-profit for its own good) this project will welcome any donations. The cost of a stone (including postage, mailer, and the tumbling grits and polishes) runs one or two dollars for stones sent within North America and more when the stones are honored by becoming foreign travellers.

The Hermit's Lantern A monthly publication for those concerned with wellness of body and of spirit. Features include our garden journal and an 'herb of the month. More reading includes herbal lore, tarot, gem and mineral lore, an astrological guide for ritual work during the coming month and more.

For a current price list, catalog and a sample issue of *The Hermit's Lantern*, send $5.00 to The Hermit's Grove.